Direct Selling
From door to door to network marketing

About the author

Richard Berry was educated at Malvern College and Bristol University, where he graduated in Engineering. After National Service, and a period spent in the TA with a Royal Engineers Parachute Squadron, he joined Tube Investments as a graduate trainee. After a number of production and sales management appointments he became a management consultant with AIC-Inbucon. His first involvement with direct selling was with Kleeneze, an AIC client, in 1969. Later, as Kleeneze's managing director, he transformed the direct selling operation into the UK's first substantial network marketing business and the first to be accepted into the Direct Selling Association. He is a former chairman of the DSA and, since retiring from Kleeneze in 1985, has been the Association's director. In 1996, for his services to the direct selling industry, he was installed as only the third member of the DSA's Hall of Fame.

Richard Berry, who is married with three children, is the current chairman of the Sales Qualifications Board, serves on the advisory group of The Marketing Council and is a non-executive director of the electrical equipment manufacturer Arcontrol.

Direct Selling
From door to door to network marketing

Richard Berry

Butterworth-Heinemann
Linacre House, Jordan Hill, Oxford OX2 8DP
A division of Reed Educational and Professional Publishing Ltd

A member of the Reed Elsevier plc group

OXFORD   BOSTON   JOHANNESBURG
MELBOURNE   NEW DELHI   SINGAPORE

First published 1997

British Library Cataloguing in Publication Data
Berry, Richard
   Direct selling: from door to door to network marketing
   1. Direct selling   2. Marketing
   I. Title
   658.8'4

ISBN 0 7506 2235 0

Composition by Genesis Typesetting, Rochester, Kent
Printed in Great Britain by Biddles Ltd, Guildford and King's Lynn

Contents

For my wife, Aurea

Forewords

Foreword by Ric Hobby

Direct selling is a dynamic, vibrant channel of retail distribution. Although still relatively small, it is expanding rapidly and is singularly well positioned to become increasingly profitable for those who wish to invest in it. This book is a definitive, yet easily read, guide for all those who wish to understand more about this 'people business' – as the author so aptly describes it.

For those already involved in direct selling, little introduction is required to explain how compelling that involvement can become. In over twenty years in direct selling, I have observed the power of this form of direct marketing. Yet it is enigmatic. Giants, both corporate and individual, have tried and failed to grasp success. Yet individuals, often with little experience or resource, but with a burning passion, have used the simplicity of its business principles to forge huge successes, both privately and in business terms. So how does one unlock the key to the treasure to be found within?

Interestingly, over the past few years, there have been more books written than ever before, by self-styled 'gurus' rushing to explain the phenomenal successes that have been achieved. I have read many of them. Yet almost all are centred around the same common theme of today's business, management and success stories – the personality ethic, or how to rapidly enrich personal profit. A dearth has existed in books that explain, accurately and objectively, what direct selling is all about.

Richard Berry is uniquely positioned to provide the explanation that follows. He describes the experiences of his own story, weaving it like a thread through the pages. He has been the chief executive of a major direct selling business, but in the last decade has been the guiding influence for good in promoting ethical standards in direct selling, as Director of the Direct Selling Association. His advice is regularly sought from UK and international companies, both within and outside the direct

selling sector. He advises government agencies (both local and international), the media and business school academics, as well as scores of
private individuals seeking a knowledgeable yet unbiased source of
reliable information.

In a logical and cogent style this book explains why direct selling exists,
its roots, its power as a distribution channel, its international perspective
and its future. In clear and concise terms, whole chapters focus on the key
elements for success in any direct selling business. What is particularly
useful is the author's account of the rise of network marketing and the
way he covers the key criteria for managing this type of business. It is
essential reading for a full understanding of the key reference points of
law and governance. At the same time the book is filled with examples of
individual and corporate success stories and revealing personal anec-
dotes and illustrations.

Richard Berry's book will become a reference text on direct selling.
Read it and enjoy the magic of this prodigious people-powered and
ultimate customer-focused business.

Ric Hobby
Managing Director
Herbalife Europe Limited

Foreword by James R. Threlfall

I was delighted to be asked to write a foreword to this book, particularly as it is the first of its kind, in that it covers virtually every aspect of the direct selling channel of distribution. Richard Berry has combined a clear analytical approach with his enthusiasm for and fascination with direct selling – both of which are continually apparent throughout his book. It is a book he is well qualified to write. He has the advantage of first-hand experience as chief executive of a major direct selling business and the many years he has spent advising numerous other businesses as Director of the Direct Selling Association.

He gets down to the 'nuts and bolts' of direct selling in what is a really practical book. It is a splendid guide to both the novice and seasoned professional and to any business seeking an alternative, or additional, marketing outlet to its existing distribution channel.

The publication of *Direct Selling* is most appropriate at a time when interest in the industry is rapidly increasing and when more and more businesses are thinking about diversification. Business schools and academics, too, are now showing a great interest in direct selling and including the subject in their curricula – particularly in the United States. *Direct Selling: From door to door to network marketing* will be a valuable addition to their libraries.

James R. Threlfall
Immediate Past Chairman
World Federation of Direct Selling Associations

Preface

It is now twenty-five years since I first became involved in the direct selling industry. It happened more or less by accident. At the time I was working for a major firm of management consultants. We were called in to advise the directors of a publicly quoted and diversified group of companies which produced domestic and industrial brushes, industrial seals, plastic components and household chemicals. I was asked to examine what they thought were manufacturing management problems. Certainly there were productivity gains to be made and we put that problem right fairly quickly.

However, from the outset what really intrigued me about my client was the original direct selling division of their business. It had survived, but had hardly changed since it was founded fifty years earlier. The company was Kleeneze Holdings which had developed from a business formed in 1923 by Harry Crook, an out-of-work Bristol man who, a few years earlier, had set off to make his fortune in America. He quickly found work with the Fuller Brush Company and did well enough to be convinced that the simple idea of selling a novel range of brushes, door to door, would work equally well in Britain. He was right. Within a few years the Kleeneze Brush Company was a huge success and Harry Crook became a very wealthy man. The business continued to thrive throughout the Depression as he was able to offer one of the few job opportunities to the millions of unemployed – many of them professional people desperate for work. However, by the late 1960s the Kleeneze brush man was still a household name but the business had run out of steam. It had a good brand name but was in need of a bit of fresh thinking.

At the time my particular interest was aroused by a letter we received from a US shareholder who was unhappy with his investment. With his letter he enclosed a press clipping from *The Cape Cod Times* describing a new US business which was doing rather well by direct selling household cleaning products in a completely different way. That business was Amway, which had yet to expand into Europe.

All this was back in 1970. Seeing the business as an interesting management challenge, I accepted an offer to join the board of Kleeneze, and decided to go and see for myself how direct selling had evolved in the United States. I came back with a firm conviction that, with some changes, the business had enormous potential in the UK. The fundamental simplicity of the direct selling approach generated an enthusiasm for this way of doing business which has stayed with me ever since. It is that enthusiasm which is the source of inspiration for this book. In what I shall set out to explain I shall draw on some of my early experiences in changing Kleeneze's method of direct sales and on later experience both as Chairman of the Direct Selling Association (DSA) and more recently as Director of the DSA. Over the past few years the direct selling industry has developed strongly and I have seen many new businesses start up in the UK. On numerous occasions my advice has been sought as to whether or not plans for direct selling business were viable. Quite often I felt that they were not – for reasons which had not been properly considered. The direct selling option is not suited to the marketing of all consumer goods. For many, however, it is. Providing some advice on how to make this assessment is the purpose of this book.

It is a truism to say that direct selling is a 'people business'. That is its great strength. In today's business environment, where efficiency and productivity are so often associated with investments in technology and in reducing labour costs, direct selling businesses are, by contrast, unashamedly labour intensive. What I hope to show is that, when it comes to competing for a share of consumer demand, there is, at the point of sale, no better substitute for human contact, good service, enthusiasm and personal endorsement. That is what good direct selling businesses are all about. In addition, they have an ability to bring out the best in people in dealing fairly with others, in encouraging enterprise and leadership, and in motivating and helping others. Another reason for the wider public recognition of direct selling is the opportunity such businesses provide for flexible, self-employed earnings opportunities, not just for married women wishing to return to work, but as a valued alternative to conventional employment for both men and women.

Despite the long history of direct selling and its recent growth, it is still underrecognized for what it is today, as a strong and significant sector of retail trade. Although still small, it is growing faster than conventional retailing. With manufacturers looking for ways to expand their channels of distribution, with worldwide competition for space in the existing promotional media and with the growing demand for part-time earnings opportunities, direct selling deserves more attention. This is also what this book sets out to do. It is designed to interest those involved in the manufacture and distribution of fast-moving consumer goods (FMCG), entrepreneurs, business school academics and those students who are increasingly looking at this growing industry as the basis for research projects.

I hope that this book will also be of interest to those direct sellers who are now earning their livelihood from direct sales and wish to have a greater understanding of the industry as a whole. For those in network marketing businesses, and in whom are entrusted responsibilities for recruitment, training, motivation and recognition, I hope that the sections dealing with the managing of a salesforce will be of particular interest.

Definitions

A list of specialist terms and acronyms used in this book

big ticket a direct sold consumer transaction for a single item in excess of £75.

frontline those direct sellers directly sponsored by another direct seller.

low ticket a direct sold consumer transaction for a single item less than £75.

party plan a selling method in which goods are sold to a group of customers.

payline those direct sellers on whose sales, bonuses are paid.

royalty bonus the profit earned on one or more groups of direct sellers each of whom is entitled to the maximum wholesale volume profit.

sales plan a direct selling reward system for the payment of commissions, bonuses and royalties.

sponsor to introduce and subsequently assist another direct seller.

wholesale volume profit the profit earned on the sales of a group excluding royalty bonuses.

BV	Business Volume – a notional value of sales volume used in a sales plan
CEO	chief executive officer
CTP	Cosmetics, Toiletries & Perfume – industry classification
DSA	Direct Selling Association
DSO	direct selling organization – i.e. a direct selling business
DTI	Department of Trade and Industry
FEDSA	Federation of European Direct Selling Associations
FMCG	fast-moving consumer goods – industry classification
IT	information technology
MLM	multi-level marketing, otherwise known as network marketing

NM	network marketing
NM DSO	direct selling organization based on network marketing.
PGV	Personal Group Volume – a volume of sales achieved by a group of direct sellers, used in a sales plan, on which an individual obtains a wholesale volume profit
PV	Points Value – a notional value of sales volume used in a sales plan
SLM	single-level marketing – i.e. a conventional sales management structure
SQB	Sales Qualifications Board
WFDSA	World Federation of Direct Selling Associations

Acknowledgements

Ever since I first became involved in direct selling there is one special feature of the most successful businesses that I have always found most appealing. It is a readiness to exchange, between companies, ideas, experience and information on the best way to develop the direct selling channel. It is an openness that is, sadly, rarely found in any other industry. It is an attitude that is born of the view that direct selling businesses can best grow not so much in competition with one another but in effective competition with other channels of retail distribution. This characteristic of the best direct selling businesses is illustrated by the following, frequently heard, comment of chief executives: 'I am quite happy to tell you exactly what we did yesterday and, indeed, what we are doing today – and why. Naturally, all that I am sure you would expect us to hold back on are our precise plans for tomorrow!' Retail distribution, through every channel, is a dynamic industry which is evolving rapidly to meet the ever-changing demands of the public and to make the best use of current and future technological developments. Direct selling is no exception. Without this openness it would have been impossible for me to write this book.

My first acknowledgement is, therefore, to all my past and present colleagues in the Direct Selling Association. In particular, I want to thank my old friend and original mentor, Jim Threlfall, a former chairman of the World Federation of Direct Selling Associations and a man whose personal vision of a strong European direct selling industry, bound by common high standards in doing business, led to the creation of the Federation of European Direct Selling Associations.

I also owe much to my longstanding contacts with direct selling businesses around the world, particularly in the United States. For many years I have been made warmly welcome at meetings of the US Direct Selling Association. To past and present directors of the US DSA I owe a great debt of gratitude. In particular, I want to give my thanks to Neil Offen, the longstanding and internationally acclaimed president of the US DSA.

For their kindness in checking the first drafts of this book, and for their most valuable suggestions as to how various points could be made more easily understood, I want to thank Tom Davies, Bill Thomas, Kent Grayson, Stewart Brodie and Julie Donabie.

Finally, going back to the 1970s, I want to record my thanks to the management team and to all those independent distributors and agents in Kleeneze, Britain's oldest direct selling company, who were in the business at that time. It was their hard work and enthusiasm in putting into effect some major changes to the way the company was run, that laid the ground for the successful business it is today. As it is with so many good direct selling businesses, it is a tribute to their enterprise, and a source of great satisfaction to me, that many of those distributors are today, over twenty years later, still with the business.

Richard Berry
London, 1997

Introduction

Let me start with a definition. Direct selling, as a description of a channel of distribution and which I shall be examining and explaining in this book, means:

> The obtaining of orders and the supply of consumer goods to private individuals away from normal retail premises, usually in their homes or places of work, in transactions initiated and concluded by a salesperson.

There is nothing new about the concept of direct selling; the supply of goods from a manufacturer directly to the users of those goods. It is the way in which most raw material, components, equipment, goods and services are supplied to industry and commerce. However, when it comes to consumer goods, we have all got rather too accustomed to other channels of distribution.

There can be few chief executives of a direct selling business who have not been asked, at some time or another, why, if their products are so good, they do not sell them in the normal way. They mean, of course, through retail stores. It is a fair question, and one that this book aims to answer, but to start with, it is equally fair to ask why it is that we still accept retail stores as being the normal method of distributing consumer goods. To begin with, let us consider briefly the history of retailing.

From the Middle Ages onwards, as small communities grew into towns and cities, street markets gradually developed into retailing from fixed locations. Quite sophisticated retailing developed much earlier in Europe. As early as the thirteenth century, the Thibauts, in the French province of Champagne, exercised considerable political and commercial power through well-organized fairs, at specific times and places throughout the year, that sold a wide range of locally produced and imported goods. By the sixteenth century, in The Hague, in Holland, retailing had reached the point where certain streets were designated for the retailing of specific products and where retailers competed vigorously with one another.

In Britain these developments arrived much later. The first British retailers were in competition with itinerant pedlars – the first direct sellers. These 'chapmen', as they were called, many of whom regularly travelled from Scotland down into northern England with a wide range of household products, were resented by the growing retail community. The results, in the seventeenth century, were that some of the earliest local bylaws were introduced, not for consumer protection reasons but to protect local tax-paying retailers from what they considered to be unfair competition. Later, in the United States, the Yankee pedlar, the first American direct seller, provided a greatly valued service to isolated communities and they were able to go on doing so until the end of the nineteenth century.

By the mid-nineteenth century most of the goods that we find in today's superstores were supplied by craftsmen or local manufacturers who dealt directly with their customers. In Victorian Britain virtually every town was self-sufficient in the supply of household products – from chemists who bottled their own potions to the ironmongers who made and sold household utensils. As manufacturing methods improved and as the road and rail transport network extended, there developed specialist manufacturers who needed retail stores to sell their goods. Many created demand for their products by national advertising. However, dealing with a growing number of small retail outlets was burdensome and so there also developed a network of wholesalers who specialized in certain products and who were able to satisfy the demands of the small retailers. This was a system of distribution that continued largely unchanged until the 1960s.

The next big revolution in retailing was the emergence of the retail chains and later the superstores who were large enough to deal directly with the manufacturers. A good example of the effect of this retailing revolution is in the hardware industry. In 1970 there were over 100 hardware wholesalers who accounted for 70 per cent of the trade. By 1995 the number had dropped to 30 and their share of the £6 billion trade in hardware and DIY products was no more than 13 per cent. At the same time the number of manufacturers has halved and the number of product lines on offer to the public is a third of what it was twenty-five years ago.

One result of this change is that, today, any small manufacturer or supplier, with an alternative brand or even a new product, faces a huge problem in getting it to market. The major retailers are constantly striving to improve their stock turns and reduce the number of product lines they carry. The result is that multiple retail stores are getting more and more restrictive in the number of suppliers with whom they are prepared to do business. Unless a supplier can guarantee an annual sales volume of at least £250 000 for any one product, and unless they are prepared to support the product with national advertising, then their chances of getting it onto the shelves of a major superstore are slim. This is just one trend that has given a new impetus to direct selling.

As the retail industry has developed over the past twenty-five years, there is another weakness in their system that has been readily exploited by direct selling organizations (DSOs). (Incidentally, DSO is an acronym that I have borrowed from Dick Bartlett, the Vice Chairman of Mary Kay Cosmetics Inc. and the author of an excellent book on direct selling – *The Direct Option* (Bartlett, 1994) and which I shall use hereafter.) This weakness is their inability to maintain close contact with their customers and to respond quickly to any changes in demand. Any manufacturer would like, if it were possible, to deal directly with their ultimate consumers. For most FMCG manufacturers it is, until recently, simply impractical for them to do so. The result is that they are forced to trade off logistical and account management benefits against the problems of being insulated from the consumer by a powerful and independent distribution network. DSOs, by comparison, know within a matter of days which of their products are selling best and in what volume. Manufacturers with their own retail store chains, and those who supply the major food retailers, get an equally prompt feedback, but for others, particularly those marketing seasonal lines, responding to changes in demand can be a major problem. Some resort to ingenious solutions. Black & Decker is a good example.

> Black & Decker found, some years ago, that an analysis of the guarantee cards they had received each week from retail customers gave a good picture of the mix and change in volume of products sold in the high street a few days earlier. Although only a small proportion of customers fill in guarantee cards, it was statistically useful information in planning production programmes. The point is that it was received earlier than the reorder schedules that came, in due course, from their retail customers and wholesalers.

The information a DSO receives, from the orders of its salespeople, is based not on sales expectations but on current sales demand. It is invaluable in forecasting and maintaining efficient inventory levels.

Direct selling is not the only distribution channel through which a manufacturer or supplier deals directly with its customers. Mail order and direct marketing achieve the same result – with many of the same benefits. Direct selling is, however, growing faster. In the future there may

Table I.1   Home shopping channels in the UK

Channel	Sales (£m)	5-year growth (%)	Home shopping market share (%)
Agency mail order	4300		58.9
Other mail order catalogues	998		13.7
All mail order catalogues	5298	24.7	72.5
Direct response, mail shots and ads	950	13.2	13.1
TV and electronic	42		0.6
Direct selling	967	54.1	13.2
Total	7257		100.0

Source: Verdict Home Shopping

be another serious contender and that is TV home shopping and the Internet. However, at present, the business achieved by QVC and others and through electronic sales is still quite small. Early indications are that the available market may be restricted to a narrow section of the consuming public but this is a matter of debate.

Table I.1 is a comparison for 1995 of the way in which the £7.3 billion, home shopping market was divided between the five prominent channels.

Direct response home shopping is, in some respects, similar to direct selling and the next chapter compares these two channels in more detail. There is, however, another technological development that has given a strong impetus to the growth of all direct distribution channels; this is the information technology (IT) revolution which DSOs have adopted with enthusiasm. The growth of information technology and relatively inexpensive computerized data management systems now make it possible for a business to administer economically small accounts in a way which was previously impractical. And it is not just the ease with which even a small DSO can now store, retrieve and reproduce information on each one of thousands of predominantly part-time independent salespeople. The revolution in banking and payment systems and the growing use of credit cards both by consumers and by direct sellers in settling their own accounts with a DSO again provides the opportunity for DSOs to deal efficiently with a multitude of small accounts. Quite apart from other changes in patterns of employment and in the sociological, demographic structure of society, which I shall be

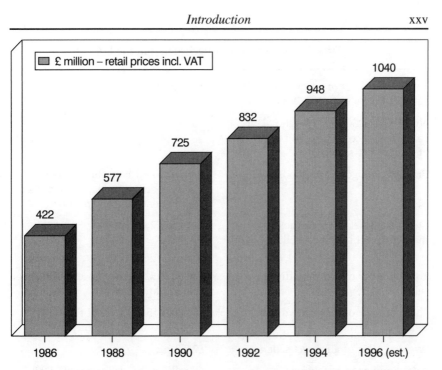

Figure I.1 *Direct sales of consumer goods (UK). (Source: Direct Selling Association)*

dealing with later, it is these technological developments that have a major contributory factor in the challenge now presented by DSOs to conventional retail stores. Figure I.1 shows the growth in the direct selling of consumer goods over the past ten years in the UK.

Table I.2 gives a more detailed picture of the shape of the direct selling channel of distribution in the UK in 1995.

Providing some explanations for each one of these statistics is the purpose of this book.

Let me return for a moment to the question frequently asked of executives who manage DSOs, that I referred to at the beginning of this introduction. It is a question that illustrates a widespread ignorance not only of the size of the direct selling industry, but also of its recent growth. One of the reasons for this ignorance in Britain is that there are very few major UK-owned DSOs – and even fewer publicly quoted DSOs that are in a position to receive any degree of informed comment in the financial press. The worldwide market for direct selling exceeded $72 billion in 1995 and, with the exception of Japan, the channel is dominated by US multinational corporations. Even in Japan, US corporations have a major

Table I.2   Overview of direct selling in the UK

Total direct sales of consumer goods at retail prices including VAT	£967 million
Number of DSOs in UK who collectively account for 90 per cent of total direct sales	101
Principal categories of goods sold	Personal and household goods, frozen foods, diet plans, nutritional supplements, books and toys
Overall market share of those markets in which direct sellers compete	Between 2% and 3%
Total number of full-time direct sellers	16 000 (0.5% of all those in full-time self-employment)
Total number of part-time direct sellers	403 000 (15–20% of all those in part-time self-employment)
Average sales of all direct sellers	£2400 p.a.
Total number of consumer transactions	67 million (average value £13.90)
Methods of direct selling	Party plan – 18% of sales volume and 19% of DSOs Person to person – 82% of sales
Methods of organizing a DSO	Network marketing – 28% of sales and 55% of DSOs Single-level structure – 72% of sales

Source: Direct Selling Association's Annual Survey – *Direct Selling of Consumer Goods in the UK, 1996*

presence. For operational reasons, these DSOs rarely disclose their sales in overseas markets, although cumulative data are provided to the WFDSA.

Despite this low profile, direct selling is now, throughout the world, a major channel of retail distribution. Table I.3 is an analysis, for 1995, of worldwide direct selling volumes of retail sales and numbers of direct sellers.

There is, however, another, and more significant, reason for this self-imposed low profile of direct selling. It is that DSOs rarely advertise their

Table I.3   Direct selling activity in worldwide markets

Region	Countries	Retail sales ($US million)	Number of direct sellers	Average sales per direct seller ($US p.a.)
North America	United States	17 940	7 200 000	2 491
	Canada	844	600 000	1 407
	Mexico	1 200	1 000 000	1 200
South America	Argentina, Brazil, Chile, Peru and Uruguay	4 216	1 392 000	3 209
Europe	European Union (UK, included in EU)	9 792 (1 498)	1 621 000 (450 000)	6 041 (3 189)
	Czech Republic, Hungary, Norway, Poland, Slovenia, Switzerland and Turkey	590	443 000	1 332
Africa and Middle East	South Africa and Israel	345	108 000	3 194
South-East Asia	Hong Kong, Indonesia, South Korea, Malaysia, Philippines, Singapore, Taiwan and Thailand	5 208	4,937 000	1 055
Pacific	Australia and New Zealand	1 732	683 000	2 536
	Japan	30 400	2 000 000	15 200

Note: In some countries, including certain EU member states, these data understate the true size of the direct selling channel as the statistics only refer to DSOs affiliated to WFDSA. Some markets are excluded for lack of any data – even though substantial direct selling businesses are now known to be operating. These include Russia, India and China. In China the Ministry of Internal Trade reported 500 000 direct salespeople in 1995.

Source: WFDSA

brand names. They do not do so for good reasons, which are explained in Chapter 6. However, the effect is that many DSOs are familiar only to those who are either participants or regular customers. Even in the latter case, the customer's image of a DSO is bound to be heavily influenced by the image put across by part-time independent direct sellers. In practice it is difficult for them to do any DSO full justice in projecting to consumers the size and commercial strength of the business. Just compare this with the public awareness of the brand names of other consumer goods.

Every day we are all confronted with ads on TV, street posters and other media for a vast array of products and services. A few of these ads are able to influence a future purchasing decision of everyone who sees them – but not many. Most are targeted at specific sectors of the consuming public in the certain knowledge that they are lost on the majority of those on whom the ad makes an impact. Conventional brand advertising, while effective, is demonstrably wasteful. Direct sellers, on the other hand, are able to give clearly focused 'live commercials'. While this, as I will show, can be highly efficient, it does tend to disguise the true strength of direct selling. This is one of the biggest promotional challenges that confronts every DSO.

1

Direct selling versus direct marketing

Selling 'off the page'

Direct selling is itself a form of direct marketing in that an approach is made directly to the consumer, inviting them to make a purchasing decision. The essential difference between direct selling and what is generally referred to as direct marketing, is that while the latter's message also goes directly to a potential customer, it relies solely on the media of print or audio vision to impart the selling message. Direct selling, on the other hand, relies heavily on the presence of a salesperson to communicate the message and to influence an early buying decision. Direct sellers may well use catalogues and other sales aids, but it is the effect of that physical involvement of the salesperson that makes it such a powerful technique. Direct sellers also provide consumers with an opportunity to interact with the manufacturers or suppliers of the goods on offer. DSOs are able, through their salesforce, to personalize their approach in a way which is almost impossible with other direct marketing methods.

Some DSOs, and some products, do require salespeople who are well trained in presenting the benefits and special features of the products they have on offer. In effect they are giving 'live commercials'; but this is not always either necessary or indeed the best way of involving the direct seller in the process of making a sale. For many low-cost consumer goods, a catalogue presented or shown by a direct seller to a prospective customer can still be relied upon to do the greater part of 'talking'. To illustrate this point let us examine the conventional process of making a sale.

Most sales trainers deal with the selling process as a series of logical steps. It is an approach which is equally familiar to those creating any direct marketing campaign. The following is a typical way of describing this approach.

The first step in the process is to gain the *attention* of the prospect and the second is to convert that attention into an initial *interest* in the product on offer. It is relatively easy to gain anyone's attention but that attention may be momentary. To convert it into interest in what is on offer requires skill.

The next step is similarly to convert that interest into a *conviction* that what is being said, or claimed about the product or service on offer, is actually true and believable.

The fourth step is to build up that conviction into a *desire* for ownership. A prospective customer may well be totally convinced that what is being claimed is true but, at the same time, still not feel a pressing need or desire on their part to make a purchase.

The final step in the process is to *close* the sale; to make it as easy as possible for the prospect to fulfil their desire for ownership. The closing of a sale should be the natural outcome of the preceding steps in the process.

The very best direct mailing pieces aim to achieve, in design, copy writing and print, all five steps in the selling process. Just let us look at how they do it.

An attractive overall presentation of a single mailing piece or a catalogue attracts attention and goes on to create interest with a bold and well-written opening message. When it comes to the third step, product claims backed up by testimonials from a recognized authority or from previous customers provide conviction that what is claimed is true. In the next step good direct mailing pieces create desire in a number of ways. It could be through examples of the financial, health or other benefits that ownership could bring. It could also be through powerful visual association; an attractive model, a beautiful home or another visual image that is subconsciously associated with ownership. The fifth and final step of closing the sale is achieved by making it easy for a purchasing decision to be made. Direct mailing pieces do this by offering a range of alternative decisions – all of them positive. It could be the number of items you may order, colour and size options or whether you wish to pay by cheque or one of several credit card options.

The power of a personal sales presentation

A really good salesperson can master all five stages of the selling process, with the minimum of sales aids, just by creating verbal images. However, it is not easy; it needs training and that is why DSOs are keen to make available as many sales aids as they can, to help de-skill the selling process. No DSO should ever imply that achieving a sale is the automatic outcome of making a product available to a prospective customer – no matter how attractive and well priced it may be. In this context, de-skilling means providing those tools and well-tested advice that have been proved to simplify greatly the selling process. This is particularly important where a DSO relies on part-time salespeople, where a high turnover of those salespeople is inevitable and where time and cost restraints mean that the opportunities for comprehensive training in personal selling skills are limited.

As we shall see in the next chapter, with some products the opportunity to gain conviction by demonstrating the product on offer, or simply giving a personal testimonial, is the key to making a sale. It is rarely done in conventional retail outlets and impossible in direct mail. However, with many low-cost products, demonstration is not necessary, so where is the edge that a DSO has over direct marketing? The answer, very often, is in the very first step in the selling process – gaining attention. The reason is simple. A friendly salesperson offering a catalogue to a friend or neighbour, with an invitation to read it at their leisure, is more likely to find that it is studied than a mailing piece delivered by post – particularly if the direct seller says that he or she will be calling back to collect the catalogue. In practice, for this method to be effective it does not even require that the direct seller should speak to the prospective customer at the time they leave a catalogue. Some DSOs find that a more effective technique is to leave the catalogue, possibly opened at a page of likely interest. Attached would be a handwritten note from the direct seller, saying that he or she will be calling back on a specific day – usually in one or two days time.

The competitive edge of direct selling

There are also strong economic advantages that favour a DSO marketing low-cost consumer goods, as against the same products marketed through direct mail. To illustrate this point let us consider two marketing campaigns designed to create a market and obtain orders for a new household product, with an RRP of £20 using a four-colour leaflet to describe the product.

First let us consider a mail order campaign. Assume that the company decided to mail the leaflet with an order form to 50 000 likely prospects using a rented list of demographically likely prospects with whom they had not previously done any business. If the response rate was 2 per cent, that would be considered to have been a successful campaign. In the direct marketing industry a 1 per cent response is nearer the average. The cost build-up of delivering the mailing piece might be as follows:

Print – origination costs, leaflet, order form and envelopes	20p
List rental @ £60 per thousand names	6p
Envelope 'stuffing' and mailing administration	4p
Postage – including prepaid response with Mailsort discounts	30p
Total	60p

If the response rate were 2 per cent then it would require 50 mailing pieces to result in one order. This would be a cost of 50 times 60p – and a marketing cost per order of £30. This is greater than the sales revenue and is clearly uneconomic. It is therefore difficult to justify direct mail as a way of marketing low-value products. The only exception is if the item is one of a range of lines, in a catalogue, offered to a 'house list' of regular mail order customers. In this case response rates could be as high as 20 per cent. At that response rate the resulting cost per order would be reduced to a much more reasonable figure of £3.

As a general rule, a successful direct marketing campaign requires a mark-up, from cost price to RRP less VAT, of at least three times. This means that it would be difficult to justify direct mail as a way of making any sale with an order value of less than £50. For a small-time mail order trader there is also a substantial fixed-cost commitment to the campaign. Allowing for the non-use of reply paid envelopes, the fixed cost of a 50 000 mail shot, based on the above costs, would be £30 000. This is a substantial and risky investment for a small trader or even a small business.

Direct selling, on the other hand, offers a much less risky and very often a more effective way of introducing low-ticket products to new customers. Assuming the same new household product, priced at £20, with a potential demand in every home, and using a catalogue with the same message as a direct mail shot. Assume also that the catalogue is presented by someone who is unknown to the prospective customer, but who appears to represent a credible business. In these circumstances the order rate can easily be between 9 per cent and 10 per cent. For lower-ticket lines it can be as much 20–25 per cent. The reason for the dramatic increase in response is just that the personalized presentation demands more attention, particularly if the direct seller explains that they would like to leave the catalogue and to call again to collect it, a day or so later.

In organizing a direct selling business a DSO has to operate on a multiplier from cost price to RRP that is similar to, if not slightly higher than, successful mail order businesses. This will be explained in more detail in Chapter 6. The big difference, however, is that the bulk of the cost of making a sale is a variable cost. Those DSOs that use catalogues have much the same print costs, but the majority use self-employed salespeople who are rewarded on results. While almost 90 per cent of the cost of a direct mail campaign is a fixed cost, with a DSO the fixed cost element can be as low as 10 per cent. The key to the system working is the higher response rate. In theory, a DSO could operate profitably on a response rate of 2 per cent. In practice it would not work. The reason, quite simply, is that few direct sellers, working on commission, would find it in their interests to make sales of £20 to only one in 50 of their catalogue placements. Low response rates can be made to work effectively in direct selling, but only where target order values are around £1000 or more and where a full sales presentation is involved. This type of business will, again, be dealt with later. Direct selling can offer mail order businesses a highly effective way of building a strong house list of regular repeat customers. One British DSO that has pioneered this approach is The Children's Warehouse which, in 1996, won the DSA's New Business Award.

> The Children's Warehouse was founded in 1995, by Bernard Bunting, to market children's designer clothes through a mail order catalogue. This DSO's innovative approach was to offer customers an incentive to promote the catalogue to their friends, with rewards based on the volume of business achieved through a network of personal contacts – like themselves, mothers with young children. These agents are not involved in product sales and distribution, as the resulting orders are fulfilled on a normal mail order basis. In this DSO the agents are rewarded for their selling skills in promoting the catalogue and giving personal endorsements for quality and style of the merchandise.

In summary, the principal window of opportunity for DSOs is in the marketing of low-cost consumer goods in competition with conventional retailers and with mail order traders using established catalogues with strong house lists. Table 1.1 shows the average value of direct sold consumer goods transactions over the past six years.

The year-on-year variation is accounted for by inflation, changes in product mix and the changing fortunes of DSOs marketing big-ticket products. The main point I am making is that average transaction values, achieved through direct sales, is low – under £20.

Table 1.1   Average value, direct sold transactions in the UK

Year	Total direct sales (£ million)	Average transaction value (£)
1989	636	10.25
1990	725	8.08
1991	796	11.36
1992	832	12.45
1993	913	10.47
1994	948	12.96
1995	967	13.90

Source: Direct Selling Association

Integrated marketing

DSOs do not tend to find themselves in competition with individual product-based direct mail campaigns; usually because they are sensibly geared towards higher transaction values. This does not mean that direct marketing skills are not of interest to DSOs. Many of today's best-run DSOs use retail customer databases, provided by their salespeople, for several very good reasons. The first is to enable the DSO to maintain contact with 'stranded customers', those who have lost contact with a direct seller, and to reallocate them to another direct seller. Another purpose is to provide a direct marketing service to the existing customers of their salespeople with a degree of professionalism, and at a lower cost, than would be possible were direct sellers to try to provide this support themselves. This technique is particularly effective in encouraging consumers, who have an immediate demand for a replacement product to make contact with a direct seller prior to their next call, or to make them aware of new market offers. The use of direct marketing techniques by a DSO is now generally known as integrated marketing and is not limited to direct mail.

The techniques of supporting direct sellers with a comprehensive integrated marketing programme, including inbound and outbound telemarketing, have been pioneered in the United States by Mary Kay Cosmetics Inc.

> Mary Kay encourages their consultants to provide to the company details of their own retail customers. For a modest cost, of around 60 cents a letter which is charged to the consultant, the company will

produce personalized, laser-written letters and send them directly to the customers in a form which is perceived as coming directly from their local direct selling consultant. This is, in effect, an excellent 'house list' from which a good response can be expected – with orders phoned or posted directly to the consultant.

This combination of direct selling and direct marketing techniques provides those DSOs offering repeat purchase consumer goods with a good way in which they can re-cement a relationship between a former customer and a direct seller.

Direct sellers can and should ensure that their customers have a telephone number or at least an address as a point of contact for future orders. Some provide this resource through *Yellow Pages* but no system that requires a customer to go to that level of trouble, let alone requiring them to locate a past order form, is conducive to good service. Integrated marketing campaigns are one solution.

Direct marketing campaigns by a DSO also serve to motivate direct sellers and help in the retention of their salespeople. Self-employed direct sellers can be easily discouraged by a period of difficulty in obtaining orders. A call from a past customer requesting a product gives a small but important psychological boost. To someone who had been thinking of quitting just such a call could easily result in a decision to stick with their part-time business. For any DSO an integrated marketing programme can also help to forestall one of the few inherent weaknesses of direct selling; the practical difficulty in responding to unsolicited or potential demand from a former customer, when the direct seller who established that customer has left the business. However, setting up these programmes demands that a DSO carries with them the confidence and support of their sales force. It is not unreasonable for a direct seller to suspect that providing consumer data to their DSO is a prelude to the DSO becoming a direct marketing business and perhaps denying them a future livelihood. For this reason, even if the programme includes outbound telesales, it is sensible to allocate commissions to the salesforce.

Amway is another multinational direct selling business that uses direct mail to keep in touch both with existing retail customers and with former direct sellers. In the UK, Amway mail out a regular magazine *Connexions* with reminders and updates on Amway's product range and details of special offers on other products and services which are available to *Connexions* Club members. Orders are supplied directly to the customer, with a commission going to the Amway distributor who introduced them to the business –

provided they are still with the business. This continuing relationship with the DSO also serves to remind former distributors of the advantages of re-establishing their direct selling activities.

Yet another emerging direct marketing channel, TV home shopping, can be melded into the marketing strategy of a DSO. This approach has been used to good effect recently by a US DSO, Multiples at Home.

> Multiples at Home is a ladies' fashionwear company whose principal sales method is home demonstration to a group of prospective customers. This company also sells certain lines on HSN, the US TV home shopping network. At first sight it might appear that such an approach would alienate the DSO's direct sellers. In fact, research showed that the HSN audience were not those likely to be contacted by direct sellers and direct response TV sales would not deprive them of business. The company therefore advises all its direct sellers of the date and time of forthcoming TV demonstrations. This gives direct sellers the opportunity to arrange home demonstrations to coincide with the TV transmissions. The direct sellers benefit from a highly professional demonstration and, for a given period, are able to offer their customers the demonstrated lines at the same discounted price that is offered to the TV home shopper. For the DSO, the extra discount is more than covered by the revenue from TV sales.

In the United States some DSOs use low-cost, off-peak, TV infomercials in the same way.

The continuing development of IT, particularly database management and electronic payment systems, offers DSOs a wealth of future possibilities in melding direct selling techniques with those of other direct marketers. The great strength of direct selling is the ability to capitalize on the availability of data by creating and retaining the loyalty of customers from the data provided. Direct mail is becoming ever more personalized but there is still no better substitute for the personal human touch in converting interest into a decision to purchase.

For years most DSOs have considered it to be a logistic necessity for direct sellers to be involved in the distribution of products to their retail customers. Current distribution patterns, employed by DSOs, are considered in Chapter 6 but it is sensible to review the case for this involvement continually. The physical nature of the product is one reason for involving the direct seller. Heavy, fragile or bulky products may be too costly to distribute in any other way. Follow-up contact with a customer, at the point at which products are delivered, may also lead to further orders or referrals. However, the most common reason for direct sellers being responsible for delivery is that it has been the point at which the customer normally pays for the goods. This is not, of course, the way in which mail order or direct marketing works – these home shopping channels require payment with order. To provide consumer confidence that this prepayment is safe, many direct marketers are members of the Mail Order Protection Service (MOPS). Those customers that buy from a DSO, which is a member of the DSA, are offered consumer protection under the DSA code. They also, in some circumstances, have the benefit of statutory regulations. While there is a continuing case for direct sellers delivering products and collecting payment, it can be an unpopular and largely unproductive use of their time.

With the rapidly increasing use of credit cards and other electronic payment systems within all socio-economic groups it is now quite feasible for DSOs, marketing certain goods, to receive payments from and to deliver those goods directly to retail consumers – in response to orders obtained by a direct seller. Using the full spectrum of facilities offered by integrated marketing, it is possible for direct sellers, through personal contact, to create a high-quality database, to obtain orders from those on the database and, by maintaining personal contact, to extend the database and the opportunities for further orders. Furthermore, these activities, which make the best use of a direct seller's skills, can be supplemented and enhanced by direct communication between the DSO and the retail consumer.

This scenario, while possible, can be difficult to implement. The remaining chapters in this book attempt to explain why. However, the potential opportunities and benefits presented by integrated marketing should be borne in mind by every DSO.

Key points

- As a marketing channel the great strength of direct selling compared with direct marketing is its cost-effectiveness in the first two stages of the normal selling process – gaining the initial interest and attention of a prospective customer.
- Direct selling is particularly effective in the marketing of low-cost consumer goods – where the RRP of a typical product is under £20.
- Direct marketing skills and database management can be used to great effect in direct selling, not so much to sell products but to support and motivate direct sellers.

What products can be direct sold?

The basic criteria

It is safe to say that, with the exception of some fresh foods and those personal items where mail order gives the purchaser a desired degree of anonymity, virtually anything that can be conventionally retailed can also be direct sold. In Japan just about every category of consumer goods is both direct sold and conventionally retailed – from cosmetics to sewing machines, furniture and tatami floor mats. In 1995 total direct sales of consumer goods in Japan exceeded $30 billion. This makes Japan not only the largest worldwide market for direct selling businesses but a market that is almost twice the size of that in the United States. One possible reason for the size of the Japanese direct sales market is the nature of Japan's retail distribution structure – although this is changing with a recent growth in multiple retailers. At present, not only do wholesalers still dominate Japanese retail distribution but they are also maintained in a multiple-layered wholesale structure of extraordinary complexity. This structure has the effect of increasing overall retail distribution margins and so gives a direct seller an opportunity to compete in product markets that in Europe would be difficult.

Table 2.1 compares the volume of direct sold consumer goods in several developed markets. Although retail market conditions in mainland Europe are similar to those in Britain, the reason for the current higher per capita direct sales in France and Germany has more to do with the higher proportion of full-time direct sellers in those countries.

In the UK and in Europe, what a DSO should look for are those products where it is economically practical for a direct seller to gain a competitive edge over retail competition. Over the past twenty-five years DSOs in Europe and North America have found that if a product is to be

Table 2.1   Annual direct sales of consumer goods, international comparisons

Country	Total sales (£ billion)	Sales per head (£)	Sales per home (£)
UK	0.97	17	42
France	2.56	44	107
Germany	5.03	62	147
USA	11.50	46	123
Japan	19.49	157	480

Note: Figures are at current exchange rates, October 1996
Source: Direct Selling Association

successfully direct sold, then it should meet at least one of the following key criteria. These are that the product should be novel, that it should have mass market appeal, that it should be easily demonstrable and finally that it should offer repeat purchase potential. Very few products can meet all these criteria. Some do, but almost certainly, as I shall illustrate later, it will be a product that later invites retail competition and therefore removes the competitive advantage of novelty and, in time, reduces the necessity of demonstration.

Table 2.2 shows the breakdown of direct sold consumer goods in the UK.

Let us look now at each of the key criteria in more detail.

Novelty

It was, I recall, either the advertising guru David Ogilvy or another great advertising man, John Caples, who first said that the word 'new' is the most powerful word in the lexicon of any copywriter. Anyway, it still is. John Geeson, a former managing director of Tupperware's UK business, had an equally succinct dictum for the guidance of all those writing company literature and sales force communications. It was that every piece should use as many as possible of the following words – 'new', 'now', 'free' and 'fresh'. For direct sellers, whether they rely on catalogues or whether they create 'live advertisements', these words are all-powerful in attracting attention and creating interest in what they have to offer. For a brief period it suspends any consideration of price and is a natural introduction to the process of gaining conviction. Novelty, in one form or

Table 2.2   Range and value of direct sold consumer goods in the UK, in 1995

Product	Value of direct sales	
	£ million	%
Cosmetics	59.2	6.1
Fragrances	62.4	6.4
Skincare	54.3	5.6
Jewellery	56.0	5.8
Fashion accessories	15.3	1.6
Women's and children's clothes	108.1	11.2
Other personal products	26.3	2.7
All personal products	**381.8**	**39.5**
Frozen foods	37.0	3.8
Nutritional supplements	33.9	3.5
Diet plans	9.3	1.0
All food products	**80.2**	**8.3**
Security, water treatment and energy saving products	14.4	1.5
Electrical goods	46.2	4.8
Home decorative items	25.3	2.6
Household furnishings	43.2	4.5
Cookware and tableware	18.4	1.9
Kitchenwares and housewares	77.5	8.0
Home and car cleaning products	53.1	5.5
Other household products	16.1	1.7
All household goods	**294.2**	**30.4**
Books	60.2	6.2
Toys and games	34.7	3.6
Audio and video	20.2	2.1
Financial services	32.8	3.4
Other products	28.5	2.9
All family products	**176.0**	**18.2**
Business aids	**35.0**	**3.6**
Total direct sales	**967.2**	**100.0**

Source: Direct Selling Association Annual Survey, 1996

another, is the essential ingredient for any new direct selling business and it is instructive to look briefly at the history of Britain's first substantial direct selling company.

In the Preface to this book I referred to the formation of Britain's longest-established DSO – the Kleeneze Brush Company. At the time the business was started there was nothing new about such a basic household item as a brush; everybody used them. What was novel was the idea of selling them door to door and the way in which they were made, a simple twisted-in-wire design that Harry Crook brought back from the United States. The new design gave the salespeople some-thing to talk about and to demonstrate. Today this business is still going strong with annual sales approaching £40 million. Although there have been substantial changes, both to the selling methods and in the way the sales operation is structured, the continued success of Kleeneze is based on continuing to offer novel product lines and other household products that are not readily available in multiple retail stores. This has been achieved despite strong competition in recent years from Betterware plc – a company that was originally founded in the late 1920s by some former Kleeneze salesmen. Although structured in a slightly different way, Betterware has been even more successful in the past few years by exploiting the same gap in the retail market for novel household products by achieving sales in 1995 of over £50 million.

Along with quality and style, a novel product concept can be conveyed to a prospective customer through media advertisements, but it is not always possible. Skincare is a good example.

> In the 1960s Oriflame pioneered the market for skincare products by setting up a direct selling organization, based on the party plan concept where a trained consultant demonstrated the product to small groups of customers in their homes. At that time there was no equivalent range of products available in retail stores. Over a period of ten years Oriflame created a new sector of the cosmetics, toiletries and perfume (CTP) market with a steady demand for repeat purchases. The inevitable result was that what had originally been a novel idea became an established and significant product line where Boots and other major retailers were able to capture repeat purchase demand. This is an accepted challenge faced by all DSOs who pioneer and create new markets. In the case of Oriflame, the company reacted by widening its product range and abandoning its reliance on demonstration in favour of a catalogue, which was better able to cater for repeat business.

Novelty is rewarded with consumer demand, as much by the way a product is sold, as the product itself.

> Eismann is a German company specializing in up-market frozen foods and which started trading in the UK in 1990. Salespeople, who operate on a full-time, self-employed franchise basis, start their business by distributing catalogues in an allocated territory and collecting orders. Subsequently, a telesales team telephone past customers and collect repeat orders, which are later delivered, at an agreed time, by the franchisee in a freezer van provided by Eismann under the franchise agreement. Certainly the products on offer are distinctively different from the mass market brands available in food stores, but it is the novel approach to distribution that has accounted for the success of the business.

Recently a number of other direct selling food companies have adopted the same approach. Even the major multiple grocery retailers are now testing direct sales as a way of extending their market offer. In a collaborative venture with Sainsbury's, Flanagans offer customers in the London area the opportunity for home delivery of a range of top-selling grocery lines with a telesales ordering system.

The opportunity to sell novel products is an important factor in another respect, that is, in motivating salespeople. Inexperienced direct sellers, when they approach a past customer for a repeat order, are always a little nervous that they will face rejection. For those DSOs that have an extensive product range it is, in theory at least, an illogical fear; it is almost certain that the business has something else on offer that is of interest to the customer. That additional item was not purchased on the first occasion for reasons that will be explained later in this chapter, but it is difficult to explain those reasons to every direct seller. An easier solution is to make frequent additions of new lines to the range on offer. Doing so encourages direct sellers, gives them something to talk about and serves to attract the attention of a customer.

Another useful technique, available to DSOs, is to give a novel product a 'rest' and to reintroduce it at a later date. The inherent turnover rate of salespeople is such that, after a year or so, a reintroduced product will once again be novel to a large proportion of the salesforce and to their customers.

Mass market appeal

The success of virtually every long-established DSO is based on marketing products that have a potential use in every home. Generally, direct selling is not a good way of introducing specialized products to niche markets. Specialist retail stores or selective direct marketing campaigns using selected mailing lists is a better method of distribution. Let me illustrate this point.

> A few years ago I was approached by the owners of a new small business that had developed a range of equine health products; a line of nutritional products for horses that was neither quite appropriate for prescription by vets nor one that those shops that sell riding gear were able to demonstrate or sell effectively. It was explained to me that in the UK there were over 550 000 horses and over 200 000 private owners of horses with an interest in keeping them healthy and that their product range had a potential UK sales market of at least £10 million. The owners had developed a multi-level marketing plan and wanted me to check it out in terms of its compliance with the law. In that respect there was no problem. However, what I was able to explain was the unlikelihood of the market potential being met through any type of DSO – whether it be multi-level or single-level.

Virtually all the sales of any type of DSO are achieved by the part-time sales activities of self-employed direct sellers. The appeal of the business is that even with a small commitment in time it is possible to achieve sales through neighbourhood or other contacts. An Avon representative or a Betterware distributor is given a geographic territory in which to distribute their catalogues on the clear understanding that every home represents a potential market for at least some items in the catalogue. They may not make a sale in every home, or on every occasion they call, but the potential is there. In a multi-level sales organization direct sellers do not have territories; they rely instead on a mixture of neighbourhood, social, workplace and other contacts. Again, if the products on offer have a mass market appeal they will know that if they talk to everyone they meet in the course of their daily life, about their business and its products, then they are talking to potential customers. Limiting any sales presentation to those who share any special interest or hobby with a direct seller is too restrictive for a part-time direct selling business to work profitably.

> Going back to the case of the horse-care products, riding enthusiasts do not live in close-knit communities; they are spread around the country, many in widespread rural areas. Two hundred thousand horse-owning families, while significant, represent only a mere 1

per cent of UK homes. Anyone trying to build a business, just contacting those other horse owners they know, would find it enormously time consuming not just in prospecting for business but in the subsequent distribution of orders and collection of payment. In this particular case the business would be much more successful using direct mail targeted at horse owners or distribution through livery stables.

Selling similar products to families owning dogs or cats is, in comparison, quite another matter. In 1993, 25.9 per cent of UK homes owned dogs and 24.6 per cent owned cats (source: British Market Research Bureau) and over £1 billion was spent on pet foods. Despite the strong customer loyalty to the conventionally retailed brands of pet foods, some DSOs have successfully marketed special concentrated pet food products, although usually as part of a wider product range.

Even a large consumer product market such as dog food, which at first sight might seem attractive to a DSO as a single-product line, illustrates the problem of not having a product with universal appeal. Response rates to various methods of direct sales presentation will be dealt with in a later chapter, but a fair average response rate to a personal presentation of a fairly priced, good-quality product to a potential customer is one sale in five presentations. In the case of a DSO selling only dog food, where the direct seller does not know whether the prospect is a dog owner, then the chances of them making a sale can be no better than one sale in twenty presentations; for the simple reason that only one home in four has any possible use for the product. For part-time direct sellers, any reduction in the statistical chances of their making a sale is a serious disincentive to continue with the business.

By contrast, the direct selling of utility services in a newly privatized market does represent a realistic opportunity for competing suppliers to gain new customers. Virtually every home in the UK uses water and either gas, electricity or both. In the UK in 1995, following privatization of all these services, a number of regional supply companies in gas and electricity set up DSOs to win customers from the former monopoly supplier. In these cases the DSOs had a specific short-term objective; to gain, as quickly as possible, a customer base for a new business. Direct selling proved much more effective than any method of direct marketing. These DSOs were not created as long-term businesses but as organizations that could be gradually wound down when the principal objective had been achieved.

The power of demonstration

For many novel products, the opportunity to demonstrate is the only effective way of convincing a prospect that what is claimed is true. Consider domestic vacuum cleaners.

In 1932 the Hoover Company opened up its UK business to market a type of household cleaning appliance that, at the time, was completely unknown. As they had done in America, they recruited a direct salesforce who took the machines to private homes and encouraged house-proud women to try out the machine and to demonstrate to themselves the huge labour-saving potential of this new invention. Even if TV advertising had been available in those days, it is doubtful if it would have been anything like as effective as a demonstration in the place where it was intended to be used – the home. It is this ability to demonstrate products in a home environment that still gives DSOs the edge over in-store demonstrations. Hoover created the market for domestic vacuum cleaners and, for over thirty years, despite the inevitable direct sales and later retail competition, dominated the vacuum cleaner market. In 1968 with over 60 per cent of the UK market and still operating a direct salesforce, which by that time had a similar pioneering job in introducing washing machines to British homes, the company decided to abandon direct sales in favour of retail distribution.

The rationale for Hoover abandoning direct sales was the growing involvement of retailers in servicing washing machines. It was felt at the time that with what was now no longer a novel product retailers could do an equally good job in selling new machines. The subsequent trading results of Hoover showed just how wrong they were. In 1996 Hoover's share of the UK vacuum cleaner market of over one million machines a year is barely 15 per cent. Hoover today is now just one of a dozen brands competing for retail store space, supported only by corporate advertising and promotional campaigns.

In Europe, the vacuum cleaner market was also pioneered by direct sellers, notably the Swedish-owned business Electrolux and Vorwerk in Germany. Unlike Hoover, both these companies have continued as DSOs, despite retail competition. They have been able to do so by focusing their attention on the top end of the market where demonstration of special features and superior performance can still influence consumer choice away from cheaper competitors. Commercially that decision has paid off.

In sales revenue terms, Lux, Electrolux's direct selling brand, does more business in Scandinavia than any of its competitors. Similarly, Vorwerk's direct selling business is today the major supplier of vacuum cleaners in the German market, as it is in several other markets around the world. Even in the United States, where Hoover also abandoned direct sales, other long-established DSOs marketing vacuum cleaners, such as Kirby, still have a major share of the market. They have all retained their market positions for exactly the same reason – the ability to demonstrate quality and performance.

However, just because a domestic appliance is novel does not mean that prospective customers will respond well to demonstration. An example is seen in the fortunes of the Fountain House Corporation.

Fountain House was set up in the UK to market a novel carbonated drinks dispenser, a machine which would from concentrated syrups and a small carbon dioxide cylinder produce a range of carbonated soft drinks at costs much less than those of proprietary brands. The appearance, performance and convenience of the machine in use represented a great advance on the carbonated drinks dispensers that had been available for many years. Initially, the machine was made available through electrical retailers, but with disappointing results. The founders felt that advertising was not the answer to the problem and what was needed was in-home demonstration. They therefore set up a DSO in 1990 to market the product at a RRP of just under £100.

The problem the founders faced was that, outside the limited AB market, a non-essential, non-labour-saving domestic appliance selling for £100 is not an impulse purchase, it required a convincing demonstration of both convenience and cost benefits. In the majority of UK homes the latter was not easy to justify. This would not have been such a problem if the direct sellers' demonstrations had been more interesting and varied. They were not. The demonstration was convincing enough but it was just too simple and not sufficiently entertaining for it to form the basis of either a party plan or a single-product personal sales approach. Worse still, prior to the launch of the business, the management had not tested, proved and refined a demonstration technique that could be guaranteed to result in an order – if carried out correctly. It was an excellent domestic appliance and the management simply assumed that with its inherent benefits the appliance would sell itself. The result, sadly, was that Fountain House's direct selling business had to be abandoned.

This example of an unsuccessful DSO illustrates another important ingredient for the success of any DSO. It is a grassroots 'feel' for what is happening at the point of sale. Many of those who today run substantial DSOs either started the business by direct selling the product themselves, or worked their way up through the sales organization. Either way, they consider it essential to maintain close contact and constantly to renew their personal experience of direct selling and the reaction of their customers to sales presentations. Senior executives of most successful high street retailers do much the same thing by spending several days a month out in their stores judging customer reactions and constantly looking for ways of improving their standards of service and customer satisfaction.

The opportunity for interesting, varied and entertaining demonstrations of low-ticket products was the secret of success for Tupperware. The story of the creation of this great multinational DSO, based on Earl Tupper's invention, has been well documented, but it is another example of a novel product that at first failed to gain the interest of the public through retail distribution, but which, through party plan sales, achieved worldwide recognition.

Although novelty is a justification for demonstration, DSOs that are based on demonstration do not necessarily require novel product lines. To illustrate this point it is instructive to look at some recently successful businesses and their products. Clothes parties are a good example.

> Pippa Dee was in 1965 the first British-owned DSO to adapt the Tupperware party plan concept to the selling of lingerie and subsequently a wide range of ladies' fashion wear. The opportunity to try out garments and to get the reassuring opinions of a group of friends and neighbours at a sales party has proved to be the basis of business. Today, the Dee Group has annual sales in excess of £40 million and is a leading supplier in the large but highly fragmented market for ladies' fashion wear.
>
> Ann Summers has done exactly the same at the more raunchy end of the lingerie market with a jolly 'hen party' atmosphere that provides a buying experience that would be impossible to achieve in a conventional retail store.

The competitive edge that both of these DSOs have in competing with conventional retailers is not so much the products on offer but the ability to offer consumers a distinctly different, enjoyable and convenient buying environment. Another fashion business that has made good use of the power of demonstration is a Canadian-owned multinational DSO, organized on a network marketing basis.

Weekenders Ladieswear started trading in the UK in 1992. Again there is nothing really novel about their product range. It consists of a number of simple knitwear lines which, in different combinations, can be made to produce quite different effects suited to a range of social occasions. In the late 1980s Laura Ashley experimented with this approach with a small number of retail stores, trading under the name Units. It was not a success as they could find no way of doing justice to the concept through static store displays. Shop-window dummies could not demonstrate adaptability and the items could only be stocked, within the store, in somewhat unappealing pigeon holes. What Weekenders have achieved, through well-trained direct sellers, in demonstrating the versatility of the garments, was to put on fashion shows to groups of friends and social contacts. In short, they have used the power of demonstration to build a multi-million-pound business in a fiercely competitive sector of retail trade.

Demonstration can also be used to bring back interest and to create demand for traditional products that manufacturers and retailers rarely consider to be worth supporting through advertising and sales promotion. Another British party plan company, Princess House, shows how well this can be done.

Princess House was founded in Britain as Fiesta Parties and was later bought out by Princess House Inc., a division of the US multinational Colgate Palmolive. In 1994 Janet Hewitt and Colin Malia, who were directors of the UK business, bought the DSO from the US parent company and revitalized it with a wide range of home decorative lines from ceramic figurines to crystal, porcelain, tableware and pictures; the sort of items you would expect to find in a good department store. The big difference is that, whereas in department stores the items are simply displayed on shelves, a demonstration in the private home of a party hostess enables them to be displayed in the environment for which they are intended. The demonstrator also has the opportunity to talk about how they are made, the craftsmen who created them and to point out particular quality and traditional features.

The group demonstration technique applied to traditional products can create surprisingly large businesses. An American DSO, the Longaberger Company, is a good example.

Longaberger is an old-established business founded by immigrants from Germany who settled in Dresden, Ohio. For generations, using local maple wood, this family-owned business made baskets for both industrial and domestic use. In the 1980s a bright new generation of the family realized that there was scope for widening the range of domestic baskets and promoting them as items of home decoration. By 1996, using a hybrid network marketing structure and a party sales technique, this DSO had created a business in North America with annual sales in excess of $500 million and, at the same time, providing work for the greater part of the local population of Dresden. Under its current president, Tami Long-aberger, this DSO's sales have been boosted by a skilful product diversification into other home decoration lines, such as fabrics and pottery – all with the same high-quality and traditional hand-crafted appeal that can be well demonstrated at sales parties.

In summary, the opportunity to demonstrate a product, while it is not vital to the success of every DSO, is clearly a great advantage where a product is novel or of high value or where it is not effectively promoted through conventional retail outlets.

Repeat business potential

The importance to many DSOs of marketing products with the potential for repeat business has more to do with motivating direct sellers than satisfying consumer demand. In this sense, a DSO is quite different from a conventional retail business. The two factors that determine the growth of any DSO are the ability to increase the number of direct sellers in the business, the 'retail outlets' of the DSO, and to maintain at a reasonable level the average number of sales presentations that those direct sellers make each day. With the possible exception of a large and mature DSO, these are more important considerations than attempting to increase the number of lines on offer, or even attempting to increase the personal sales volume of each direct seller.

Each new direct seller joining a DSO, marketing low-ticket consumer goods, wants to feel that having made one sale to a new customer, then there is a good chance of getting a repeat order. The quite natural feeling is that having achieved a repeat order, then there is a better chance of adding to that order with sales of other lines. In other words, the repeat order opens the door to further business.

An equally effective product policy is to offer product lines with the opportunity of collectability. This is a technique used by Princess House,

Tupperware, Dorling Kindersley Family Library and many others. A guest at a sales party may well decide to buy an item which is just one of a range of products. At the time, each one of the products may have a strong appeal, but the customer may feel that they cannot afford to buy them all on the first occasion. An invitation to attend a future party provides that future opportunity to add to their collection and, of course, motivates the direct seller.

Any DSO marketing fashion goods such as clothes and jewellery has a readily understood reason for re-establishing contact with past customers and offering them an invitation to see the latest fashion collection.

The opportunity for repeat business is rather more difficult for those DSOs selling big-ticket lines, but not impossible. Every direct sold vacuum cleaner has a future demand for dust bags and the occasional drive belts. Encyclopaedia Britannica and World Book International, the UK's largest direct sellers of reference books, bring out supplementary annual volumes. They may not offer the direct seller the same commission prospects, but they do give a valuable opportunity for re-establishing contact with past customers and to gain referrals to new customers.

The possibilities of repeat business are clearly a bonus for DSOs and their direct sellers. However, even where it does not exist, all is not lost. The fear felt by a direct seller of running out of potential customers is natural but is in reality unfounded. One way in which DSOs explain this in their training programmes is to illustrate how their market of home owners is constantly 'on the move'. In 1991 there were 350 000 marriages in the UK (source: *OPCS Monitor*) and virtually the same number of new homes being set up, a number that has changed little over the past thirty years. For most DSOs, with an already small market penetration, those new opportunities that become available every year are usually enough to allay any fears of market saturation.

Niche markets

Having emphasized the importance of a mass market to a successful DSO, particularly to one marketing low-ticket lines, does not necessarily mean that a product with a niche market appeal cannot be direct sold. If a product has limited appeal, then it is unlikely to achieve good retail distribution for reasons that I have explained earlier. This increasing trend among multiple retailers is to the advantage of a DSO. Furthermore, if a large enough collection of specialist products can be put together in one catalogue, where each product has an appeal to a different niche market, then the result is an offer with mass market appeal. This is exactly what is done by Innovations and other specialist direct mail catalogues. Using a similar catalogue is the way that DSOs such as Kleeneze and Betterware have created mass markets for low-ticket lines.

The party plan business, Ann Summers, is now a major supplier of lingerie in the UK. It has done so by expanding the market in line with a gradual change in the public's libido. This DSO has been able to exploit a market opportunity the size of which other high street retailers were slower to appreciate. Ann Summers has also had great success recently in the niche market represented by larger women. It has not concentrated on that market but just extended its range to accommodate it.

Size of product range

Although an extended product range is one way in which a DSO can market niche products, there are other reasons why any DSO, particularly those relying on part-time salespeople, has to have a carefully considered range policy. It is a policy which is closely linked with that of pricing (see Chapter 6). They are both quite different from those of a conventional retailer.

Unlike retail stores, where customers go with the deliberate intention of shopping, direct sales are very largely an impulse purchase. To be more precise, the initial purchase made by a consumer from a direct seller and a DSO with which the consumer is unfamiliar, is likely to be an impulse buy. The National Lottery proved this point.

> When the National Lottery was launched in November 1994 it had for a short period a small adverse effect on the average customer order values of a number of DSOs marketing low-ticket lines. However, after a few weeks and when research indicated that the weekly purchase of a lottery ticket had become part of the weekly household budget, the DSOs' average order values were restored to their previous levels. It was clear that during that period the sale of lottery tickets was competing for the amount of money that many households subconsciously allocate for impulse purchases.

Of course, the objective of any DSO is to build up repeat business from regular customers, but a high proportion of sales will be to new customers. It is for this reason that average transaction values are low, as are the number of product units bought on any one occasion. This is the nature of the business and the reason why for the management of a DSO, growth in the size of a salesforce is a more important priority than attempting to influence average order values. The variables, of order

Table 2.3   Purchasing patterns in direct sales

Type of DSO	Average order value (£)	Average number of product lines purchased
Big ticket – person to person	629.00	1.00
Low ticket – person to person	7.71	2.82
– network marketing	22.17	2.74
– party plan	21.82	2.19

Source: Direct Selling Association

value and transaction value, depend on the type of DSO. Table 2.3, based on UK direct sales in 1995, in which 'big ticket' means a transaction in excess of £75, illustrates this point.

Apart from big-ticket direct sales such as vacuum cleaners, where DSOs tend to use well-trained, full-time direct sellers, most DSOs rely on those for whom direct selling is a part-time occupation. For many, fear of rejection when they call on a customer for a second time is a common concern. Bearing in mind that on the first occasion a customer may only have purchased two items out of a range of 200, the fear is illogical, but it is there nonetheless. It is possible to train a direct seller to overcome this objection, but an easier solution is to make regular introductions of new lines as a way of providing them with a method of re-establishing the interest of a customer.

For a DSO wishing to expand and to motivate its direct sellers, a radical extension of the product range into a totally new product area is sometimes justifiable. This could be the result of an existing product being subject to legislation, severe price reductions by retailers or a major change in consumer demand. As DSOs collectively account for a very small share of individual product markets this is rarely a logical justification for a major change in a DSO's product range. More often, radical diversification is a sign of weakness and can easily be interpreted by direct sellers as being a lack of confidence by the DSO in the sales potential of the original product specialization. This is borne out by an analysis of those DSOs that have failed within a year or so of starting up. In many cases, particularly in the early 1990s, these failures were preceded by a major departure from the original product range. The golden rule for radical product diversification, rather than product line extension, is to choose a product that responds to precisely the same proven method by which the existing direct sellers are making sales. For example, for a DSO to introduce products that require demonstration to direct sellers who were previously successful through allowing customers to select items from a catalogue would be a very risky strategy.

For those DSOs selling fashion lines such as clothes and jewellery new product ranges are, by definition, part of the marketing approach. These DSOs have to offer a reasonable range which has to be changed two or three times a year to meet seasonal and fashion demand. In this way a DSO has a built-in method of dealing with the problem of the repeat order.

For DSOs marketing household or personal goods with a catalogue, which is simply distributed by the direct seller and where there is no demonstration or explanation, determining the size of the catalogue and the number of lines on offer follows much the same rules as those that apply to mail order traders. Extending the range by 50 per cent will not necessarily increase the size of a customer order. What it will do is command more attention. Used by a direct seller, the 'bulk' of an A5 catalogue with 60 pages is much more likely to encourage a potential customer to sit down and read it, than one with only 30 pages which might command only superficial attention. The cost of producing such a catalogue and the cost of the logistic support means that it is a direct selling technique which can only be used by a large DSO. Building up a new business on these lines with modest capital resources would be very difficult.

Product market shares in the UK

Every new direct seller joining a DSO with the expectation that it will be a good earnings opportunity, needs to be assured that there is a good strong market for what they have to offer. Conventional retailers do not have this concern as they react to demand created by manufacturers and location of a retail site can almost guarantee the 'footfall'. The easiest way of providing this assurance is constantly to remind direct sellers of the total size of the retail product markets in which they are competing. Very few DSOs in the UK have a market share in excess of 10 per cent.

Table 2.4 shows the market shares held by DSOs for a range of some of the more significant markets for consumer goods in the UK in 1995.

Excluding household services, food, drink, tobacco and costs related to motoring, the total annual expenditure in the UK on consumer goods was £70.6 billion in 1995. In the UK, DSOs do not compete in all these market sectors – in particular, white goods, carpets and furniture. They do, however, compete in a total annual market worth £34 billion. In 1995,

Table 2.4   Principal categories of direct sold consumer goods

Product group	Total consumer expenditure (£m)	Direct sales (£m)	Market share %
Women's and children's clothes*	10 192	108	1.1
Vacuum cleaners	299	24	8.0
Household textiles, curtains and blinds	1 404	43	3.1
Household cleaning products	3 778	53	1.4
Hardback books	954	60	6.3
Jewellery	2 294	56	2.4
Toys, games and hobbies	2 008	35	1.7
Toiletries and cosmetics	2 594	122	4.7
Skincare	548	54	9.8
Nutritional supplements	560	34	6.1

Sources: Direct Selling Association, NTC & *The TMS Partnership Ltd

total direct sales were £967 million. This indicates that direct selling currently accounts for just 2.8 per cent of that market. In the United States direct sellers currently account for double that proportion, which is a measure of the growth potential available to DSOs.

As I have explained earlier in this chapter, what some DSOs have been able to do is not only create markets for novel products but also expand the markets for others. Two good examples are Cabouchon Ltd and the direct selling division of the publishers, Dorling Kindersley plc.

Cabouchon is a costume jewellery DSO, founded in 1990 in London by a newly qualified MBA graduate Petra Döring. In 1994 this DSO achieved European sales of £140 million and the distinction of becoming, through direct sales, Europe's largest brand of costume jewellery. The business was focused on up-market costume jewellery of a design normally only available in exclusive London shops. There is evidence that this DSO's sales were not at the expense of retail business but were achieved by encouraging more women to wear high-class costume jewellery.

Dorling Kindersley Family Library is another network marketing DSO set up on the initiative of Peter Kindersley, the founder of the business, as a solution to a problem that besets the book trade: the fact that 60 per cent of the UK's adult population never regularly visit bookshops. A DSO, as he saw it, represented a way of taking a 'bookshop' to the public. Over the past four years the business has grown strongly and proved his point. At the same time, the business has built up an organization of several thousand direct sellers who are enthusiastic admirers and collectors of the company's distinctively illustrated books.

Can branded products be both retailed and direct sold?

In taking up a business opportunity with a DSO, direct sellers commit themselves to the selling of one or more brands of merchandise – the brand-name ownerships of which are the intellectual property of the DSO. In return the direct sellers are offered either the exclusive right to sell those branded goods to potential customers in a defined territory or, more commonly, the non-exclusive rights to any potential customer of their choice. To this extent, direct selling is similar to a franchise – although most product-based franchises are based on territories. To justify this commitment to a brand, the direct seller is entitled to expect the DSO to protect the integrity of the brand and, to some extent, their recommended retail prices. For the following reasons it is normally extremely dangerous for a DSO to permit the retail distribution of their branded products other than through the direct selling organization – although there are a few exceptions to this rule which I shall examine later.

If direct sellers were to see on the shelves of a retail store the same products that they were offering, then many would feel demotivated. They would feel that they were being denied the benefits of exclusive novelty, that consumer demand was already being satisfied and that even if they succeeded in generating demand, then the customer may choose to buy elsewhere. Furthermore, they may feel that if they had succeeded in making sales of a consumable product, then future demand would be satisfied by a purchase from a retail store. Amstrad experienced this problem in 1994.

> Electronic Innovations was a direct selling subsidiary of Amstrad, using integrated marketing techniques, set up to sell some novel electronic consumer goods – the first of which was an index phone. Alan Sugar, quite rightly, judged that it was a product that really required demonstration and one that would never be done justice by the passive displays of the product in retail stores. The problem was that by the time the business was launched, there were still products available in some retail stores and in specialized mail

order catalogues. The effect on the direct salesforce of this potential competition was one of the reasons why the business never developed.

Even more of a problem is that of retail pricing and the high street retailer's freedom to offer discounts. In the UK the supply of most categories of consumer goods is free of retail price maintenance agreements. This applies to direct selling just as it does to conventional retailing. If a direct seller chooses to offer a discount to a customer then he or she is free to do so. In practice, DSOs discourage the offering of discounts, even for large orders, on the grounds that it is rarely necessary as a means of achieving an order. High street discounting is usually adopted as a means whereby one retailer can compete with another in the sale of a similar brand of goods. This does not apply in practice in direct selling. The other reason why DSOs should discourage the offering of discounts is that few direct sellers are able to appreciate the true effect on their income of offering even a modest discount. For example, just consider the effect on the earnings of a direct seller, whose retail commission is 20 per cent of the VAT exclusive price. Were he to offer a 10 per cent discount on the full retail price, including 17.5 per cent VAT, then his effective commission would be more than halved. It would drop from 20 per cent to 8.25 per cent. To restore his earnings level he would have to more than double his volume of sales. While that may be possible for a retail store, a small discount offered by a direct seller would have little, if any, effect on his sales volume.

However, the major problem for any DSO, if its products were offered at a discount in even one retail store outlet, would be the demotivating effect on the salesforce as a whole. To begin with, the news would travel fast throughout the salesforce. They would all assume that the discounting was in connivance with the DSO and that it was going on all over the country. Not knowing the volume of sales being achieved by retailers offering a discount, they would imagine that these retail competitors would capture the major demand for the products they were having to sell at a higher price. They would question the fairness of their own commission structure and the integrity of the DSO. In short, it would cause a problem out of all proportion to any marginal increase in sales for the DSO.

Avoiding the opportunity for direct sold goods to be sold at a discount requires a DSO to be extra vigilant when it has any of its products manufactured by a third party. I experienced this problem many years ago with Kleeneze.

At that time our range of household products included aerosols which we had manufactured for us by a specialist aerosol filler. Then it was not unusual, in the subcontract manufacture of aerosols, for the supplier to produce more than the quantity specified in order to allow for a proportion of the cans to fail the on-line pressure test. If, however, the failure rate was lower than anticipated then it was accepted practice for any excess production, for any of their trade customers, to be sold off to 'remainder men'. These branded goods, sold at a 'knock-down' price, are the source of supply for many street traders. This is exactly what happened on this occasion. It led to one direct sales agent, who saw the aerosols for sale at a fraction of their RRP, communicating to many more that Kleeneze was supplying goods to street traders. Needless to say, we had to tighten up on our supplier contracts. While this would not be such a problem for other retail brands, it represents a much bigger threat to the integrity of a DSO.

Having said that it is dangerous for a DSO to become involved in retail distribution there are exceptions. One of them is where there are statutory agreements in controlling retail prices. Until 1994 this was the case in the book trade. Furthermore, there still are, in the book trade, other factors which enable direct selling to survive in brand competition with book retailers. One of them is the small proportion of the population who ever visit a bookshop.

> It was this analysis of the book-buying habits of the British public that led Peter Kindersley to create a new direct selling division of his international publishing business. It is Dorling Kindersley Family Library. Through direct selling, this DSO, first in the UK and later in the United States, takes a 'bookshop' to the public and has succeeded in expanding the demand for its uniquely illustrated books.
>
> Usborne Books at Home is another DSO that has succeeded in melding direct sales with conventional book retailing. This direct selling business was founded with the simple objective of introducing its children's educational books to a wider market in the hope that this would stimulate demand from bookshops. In the event, the direct selling business has proved to be a remarkably successful business in its own right and is also now trading in the United States.

There are two other scenarios in which the conventional retailing of consumer goods may co-exist with direct selling. The first is where there is common management of the product brand in both channels of distribution. An example of this is The Body Shop, whose retail outlets are mainly franchised.

In 1995 The Body Shop started testing a new direct selling business, Body Shop Direct. This is a party plan operation in which franchisees are encouraged to participate in the management and administration of party selling activities within their franchise territory. Orders received at parties are fulfilled by supplies from the franchised shop. The franchisee has the benefit of first-class direct selling training programmes developed by the company, there is no problem of price competition and they are not threatened by losing retail sales. The principal aim of the direct sales operation is to build up a growing clientele of committed future customers from former party guests. These new customers will have had the opportunity of attending a comprehensive demonstration and explanation of product benefits that is difficult to present in a retail shop environment.

In 1986 DMC, the French-owned manufacturer of sewing threads and needlepoint accessories, launched a similar party plan business in the UK, Creative World. The company supplied it products, in competition with others, to many small independent craft shops. At the time, these small shops were facing a downturn in sales. Research showed that one possible cause for the declining sales of needlepoint kits was that needlework was no longer being taught in schools. It was felt that if the appeal of the pastime could be resuscitated through training and demonstration at home parties, then demand would be stimulated. To some extent the plan succeeded. However, Creative World did not develop a national coverage. There were several reasons for this. The first was the problem faced by management of enforcing the necessary direct selling disciplines in a fragmented, independent network of small retail shops – many of which sold competitive products. The second reason was that while some shops-owners were keen on the idea of either personally organizing sales parties or recruiting local organizers, too many others were not.

The other way in which direct selling can co-exist with other retailers in selling the same branded goods is where those goods are clearly seen as not being part of the DSO's core product range and where the DSO is large enough to buy competitively. This is the case with Amway. The Amway Corporation has a worldwide sales organization of over one million distributors. That is in itself a sizeable market and one which enables the DSO to negotiate excellent buying terms for a wide range of other brands of goods and services. This range of products is available both to distributors and their customers at competitive market prices. As these goods are not part of the DSO's core product range the profit margins on the sale are, quite reasonably, lower than for Amway products. Their availability, however, serves to enhance the overall market offer to customers and the appeal of being part of the distributor network.

Key points

- Criteria for successful direct selling products or services: mass market appeal; novelty; benefit from demonstration; offer repeat business potential.
- Direct sellers seek customers. It is the reverse of conventional retail practice. Mass market appeal, the opportunity for a direct seller to make a sale in every home, is the most important criterion for success.
- Novelty in distribution methods can be as appealing as product novelty.
- The ability to create a convenient and enjoyable shopping environment is more important for most direct sellers than personal selling skills.
- The first purchase made by a consumer from a direct seller is likely to be an impulse purchase – of, at most, two or three items.
- The main justification for a direct selling business to change its product range, or to add to it, is to motivate direct sellers and not to satisfy customer demand.
- A direct selling opportunity is a 'franchise' to market a brand of product. Only in the most exceptional circumstances is it practical to permit that brand to be sold through other distribution channels.

3

Choice of direct selling method

Public attitudes towards selling

Before describing which direct selling methods are most appropriate for particular types of product, it is worth considering public attitudes towards selling in general and direct selling in particular.

In 1996 Wirthlin Worldwide, the market research organization, conducted a public attitude survey for the US that DSA designed to test attitudes both towards buying from a DSO and becoming a direct seller. Although no such recent survey has been carried out in the UK and although the volume of direct sales per home in the United States is twice that in the UK, the profile of the industry is similar and it is reasonable to assume that US attitudes may anticipate future attitudes in the UK. Of particular interest is the change in attitude towards 'doing business in the home' both as a buyer and as a seller. Professor Kent Grayson (Grayson, 1996) has examined the origins of these attitudes. He reminds us that in pre-Industrial Revolution Britain it was common, apart from the small aristocracy, for artisans and the majority of the population to allocate a part of their homes to their trade or occupation. This practice changed markedly with the emergence in Victorian times of factories and large office workplaces. Grayson explains that in the late nineteenth century the privacy of private homes began to be jealously guarded. Possibly as a reaction against tough working conditions, they clearly wanted their private lives to be segregated from work. What we are seeing today, with increasing reports of how IT will enable more corporate staff to work from home for at least part of their working week, is simply a reversion to old-established practices.

The Wirthlin study showed that 42 per cent of the US public have a positive attitude towards buying from a DSO and that half of those who

did so, bought from a direct seller who was previously known to them –
as a relation, friend or acquaintance. Those who have negative views,
mainly those without experience of buying from a direct seller, expressed
some concern about feeling under pressure to buy.

In the United States direct selling is a rather more established channel
of distribution. This is shown in Table 3.1. The study also showed that 78
per cent of the US population have at some time been contacted by a
direct seller with a view to making a sale and that 64 per cent had at some
time attended a home sales party. Perhaps the most encouraging statistic
is that while 30 per cent of the public purchased from a direct seller in the
past 12 months, 37 per cent expressed an interest in making a future
purchase. One overall conclusion is that the positive benefits of direct
selling exceed expectations. The challenge for DSOs is to devise a
marketing strategy which improves those expectations.

While most people enjoy buying things, very few of us like to feel that
we have been 'sold' something. One of the few exceptions are other
professional salespeople who are inclined to admire a good presentation
and have a natural inclination to reward a good salesperson with an
order. However, this general antipathy to the word 'selling' is a particular
problem for most DSOs whose success is based on their ability to attract
and recruit a non-professional part-time direct salesforce. They need to
show that obtaining orders is not difficult. Too often this leads to a degree
of dishonesty. How often have we all seen job opportunity advertisements that say 'no selling required'. Some network marketing businesses
are particularly guilty of this deception when they claim that the earnings
opportunities on offer are based on networking and not direct selling. In
practice, of course, no one earns anything unless goods and services are

Table 3.1   Home shopping channels of distribution in the United States

Retail channel	Expression of interest (%)	Have ever purchased (%)	Have purchased in past 12 months
Retail store	96	97	95
Mail order	79	83	69
Direct selling	37	53	30
On-line computer	30	6	5
TV home shopping	25	21	11
TV infomercial	23	21	14

'sold' to end users. Selling is a vital commercial activity; unfortunately, it has an image problem.

As a vocational activity, selling, and sales training throughout industry and commerce, is normally associated with an individual making a personal presentation to an individual prospective customer. It is the way most business is done. The Sales Qualifications Board (SQB), which was established in the UK in 1989, to create the first nationally recognized vocational qualifications for salespeople, defines the key purpose of selling as 'to obtain, through personal contact, a decision from a customer, to purchase products and services which meet the needs of customers and the business objectives of individuals and organizations'. Direct sellers do this, in selling consumer goods to domestic consumers, in just the same way as industrial salespeople sell products and services to industry. Good personal sales practice can, in many ways, be likened to the skills used in court by an advocate, making a convincing case for his or her client in front of a jury. In selling, the salesperson presents, with as much evidence as he or she can make available, a convincing case for the product with the aim of obtaining a decision in favour of that product – a decision to purchase. Having provided the evidence, some of the best salespersons really do no more than help their potential customers to buy. Creating an agreeable atmosphere for a purchasing decision to be made is the essence of good direct selling. For this reason a good definition for direct selling might be 'creating an environment in which a decision to purchase, made by a prospective customer, is the natural outcome of a personal, face-to-face presentation of products or services'.

However, all too often good salespeople are seen as those who are able to persuade a customer to make a purchase against their better judgement. This problem leads many businesses to use euphemisms for salespeople such as consultants, financial advisors, agents or representatives. In attracting people into sales occupations this is a problem as much for industry as for DSOs. However, over the next decade this attitude could well change, to the great benefit of DSOs, from the work of the SQB.

> The SQB's objective in creating standards of competence and the first nationally recognized sales qualifications is to ensure that selling becomes recognized for what it is, a truly professional occupation. In the UK there are now over 700 000 people engaged in full-time sales occupations. It is incidentally one of the few occupational areas that it is certain to grow as industry and commerce become even more competitive. Those that are in employed occupations represent an annual cost to industry, in salaries and expenses, of over £12 billion – almost 4 per cent of gross

national product. For most businesses it is their biggest overhead expense and there is a clear need for this expense to be operated efficiently – with a means of judging that efficiency. This future growth in sales occupations and a change in public attitude towards selling is likely to result in a greater interest in the earnings opportunities and sales experience offered by DSOs and in a greater level of acceptance of the direct sales method by their customers.

DSOs such as Encyclopaedia Britannica and World Book International, who market high-ticket products, have for years offered some of the best sales training programmes in the country. This is borne out by the fact that many of the top salespeople in British industry gained their first experience of selling with a DSO. Although no DSO likes the idea of losing direct sellers to industry and commerce, it does have a positive effect; that is, to create influential ambassadors for the direct selling concept.

Most sales trainers now disagree with the old adage that 'good salespeople are born and not made'. Certainly some people are born with the aptitude, but virtually anyone with reasonable communication skills can be trained. Sales training can, however, be a time-consuming and costly activity and every business looks quite naturally for ways of simplifying the selling process. Some aim to eliminate it altogether. High street retailers, marketing low-ticket consumer goods, are a good example. This approach to training has been highlighted by the work of the SQB.

> Marks & Spencer, in their training of shopfloor staff, require that in effecting sales they shall not 'enter into conversation with a customer'. At first sight this might seem curious advice; but for M & S it is logical. The fine reputation of this multiple retailer is based on quality and good service. Most of those who enter the store do so knowing what it is they wish to purchase and therefore the merchandise is laid out in clearly identified displays. If a customer cannot locate the item they are looking for, or if they wish to seek advice, then staff are on hand to provide help. The sales training in M & S is therefore all about staff being readily available to 'react' helpfully to customer queries.

Making a direct approach to customers, as they enter a retail store, with the words 'Can I help you?' is rarely helpful and can all too easily create an oppressive environment. The problem faced by retailers is how to train shopfloor staff to use a more welcoming or more neutral form of approach. The best solution is perhaps to avoid saying anything more than 'Good morning'.

For most DSOs and their direct sellers this reactive approach to selling would be of little use. It is the task of a direct seller to create a buying environment and this requires verbal communication. Training in how to make an approach to a prospective customer is an essential part of all direct sales training programmes. It also dictates the choice of sales method.

Let us now look at the principal methods used in the direct selling of consumer goods.

'Low ticket': person to person

As the majority of direct sold consumer goods in the UK involve individual transactions of less than £20, this is the method used by most DSOs. It is a method that is dictated by the nature of the product, the limited opportunities available in a typical day for a direct seller to obtain business and the practicality of training predominantly part-time salespeople. To illustrate how a DSO should adapt its strategy to meet market conditions, let me describe in a little more detail the problem that confronted me at Kleeneze over 20 years ago. It may also be relevant to a business considering a change or diversification of its channel of distribution.

In 1970 Kleeneze was trading with a marketing plan that had not really changed since the business was founded in 1923. Full-time salespeople, mainly men, were still selling brushes and cleaning products, by demonstration on a person-to-person basis, using a case of samples. Each direct seller was allocated a territory and they each had a credit account with the company. Orders were sent in each week and the company delivered those orders to each salesperson approximately 10 days after receipt of their order. It was a system that continued to work well until the early 1960s. However, by 1970, the business was facing social and demographic problems represented by the growing proportion of homes where, during normal working hours, there was no one at home. Young married women were either going out to work or were simply not at home when a salesman called. Interestingly, in Germany and to an even greater extent in Switzerland this social trend is even today much less developed than in Britain. The result is that in these countries DSOs employing salespeople, on a full-time basis are still doing well. This is despite an additional growing demand for part-time occupations.

The effect of this earlier social change in Britain meant that, apart from some rural communities where it was still possible to find customers at home during the day, the opportunity for direct selling was being limited to a few hours in the late afternoon or early evening. For a direct seller marketing low-cost products this severely restricted the opportunity for a full-time earnings occupation. At the same time, however, there was a growing demand for part-time jobs and Kleeneze's business in 1970 was being sustained by part-time salespeople. A high proportion of the demand for part-time sales opportunities came from women, who did not want to carry about with them a suitcase full of brushes. They wanted, quite reasonably, a more socially acceptable selling method. This we eventually provided with a catalogue-based approach used to great effect by Avon Cosmetics. However, at the time, the business faced an even more serious problem. It was the logistical cost of dealing directly with a very large number of small sales accounts. Something had to be radically changed. Either we had to have new big-ticket products, which would enable a full-time direct seller to earn a living from making a limited number of presentations a day, or we had to change the sales structure to accommodate a part-time, mainly female salesforce.

In 1970 a consumer attitude survey of the business and its brand name indicated that both options were viable. The Kleeneze brand name had a very high awareness level, particularly in AB social groups. It was confirmed that the name was associated with high-quality relatively expensive brushes and cleaning products but, reassuringly, items that represented good value for money. The company's salespeople were also held in high regard in terms of integrity and selling methods. At the time, I seriously considered abandoning low-ticket housewares in favour of higher-ticket domestic appliances. This would have pleased many of the good full-time salespeople and increased our chances of recruiting those who could make a good living with big-ticket sales from a limited number of sales calls.

In fact, years later, in the mid-1980s, in a joint venture with Rotork plc, we did launch a new and quite separate direct selling business to market a cyclonic vacuum cleaner invented by James Dyson. It was a revolutionary concept, well suited to a direct sales demonstration. Although the business started off very well, we were soon faced with a rapidly increasing number of guarantee claims resulting from design weaknesses in the first model. Putting the problem right would have needed extensive retooling which we were unable to finance, and the business had to be abandoned after a year's trading. Later, as a more developed and refined machine, the Dyson vacuum cleaner went on to be a best-seller, marketed through both retail outlets and DSOs throughout the world.

At the time, in 1970, Kleeneze had substantial manufacturing assets in brush making and in polish and household chemicals production and packing. These would have been difficult to dispose of profitably and I decided that we had to stick to low-ticket household products. This meant a radical rethink of the way in which we deployed a predominantly part-time salesforce.

The sales structure we developed was to become what is now Britain's longest-established network marketing business. As an organization structure, the great advantage of network marketing is the flexibility it offers in accommodating those direct sellers whose personal commitment to the business ranged from just a few hours a week to a full-time occupation. At the time an even bigger attraction of this structure was that the task of administering the accounts of small part-time agents, and arranging for the distribution of small orders for products which were often bulky, difficult and costly to ship by other means, could be delegated to distributors. At a local level, they could do this much more effectively than the company. A few years later, Betterware, Kleeneze's longstanding competitor, tackled this problem in a slightly different way.

> Betterware plc, which is now a highly successful public company, having been restructured by Andrew Cohen and a new management team, tackled the logistics problem by using local distributors organized in a non-network marketing structure.
>
> While Kleeneze's networking concept still accommodates that minority of direct sellers who wish to gain a full-time income from their own selling efforts, without building and administering a team of others, Betterware's sales structure is clearly focused on part-time direct sellers. The Betterware structure is also subject to territorial control of their part-time, self-employed field salesforce. Like Avon Cosmetics, and unlike Kleeneze where the networking concept precludes sales territories, each part-time direct seller in Betterware has a geographic territory allocated to them. The difference between Avon and Betterware is that while Avon administers the accounts of all their representatives, the accounts of Betterware's salespeople and the distribution of the goods they have sold are handled by a local distributor. Cosmetics are easier and less costly to distribute than housewares and this illustrates the reason why a choice of distribution strategy should be dictated by the nature of the product.

In the 1990s any DSO planning to market low-ticket consumer products is going to have to rely on the activities of part-time direct salespeople.

Although a good marketable product range is important, it is the ability of a DSO to recruit, train, motivate and, as far as is possible, retain those direct sellers, that is the key ingredient for success. Good direct sellers need enthusiasm and commitment but, almost certainly, they are unlikely to have any previous sales experience. Also, most people looking for a way of supplementing their family's income are put off by the prospect of having to sell things. While some people are naturally good at selling, and enjoy the challenge, what most job seekers want is a good, reliable, well-proven system of enabling them simply to collect orders.

Using a catalogue is one of the best ways of de-skilling the selling process. This is the technique used by Kleeneze, Betterware and Avon. In these DSOs it has been proved that completely inexperienced direct sellers who place 100 catalogues can be quite confident that when they call back to collect them they will receive a minimum of 20 orders, total sales of at least £100 and a profit of £30. It is simply a matter of numbers. The more catalogues that are placed, the more they will earn. Provided the catalogue offers a wide range of several hundred lines, and provided it is updated regularly, direct sellers will have no difficulty in obtaining orders for, on average, two products, on each occasion the catalogue is placed. As a direct seller builds up a relationship with a customer the order value is likely to increase.

For the first few years after this system was introduced into Kleeneze, some of the long-established full-time salesmen thought that the catalogue approach was rather sissy; suitable for women but not for any self-respecting salesman. They still preferred the challenge of gaining an order in a doorstep presentation of sample products. However, when part-time saleswomen began to record similar sales volumes for the same hours worked they were at last persuaded to adopt the same system of leaving a catalogue and calling back the following day for an order. Interestingly, experienced direct sellers using what might seem to be a passive sales system were immediately more successful than new recruits. The reason was that a naturally good salesman was more successful in placing catalogues and persuading customers to read it. They were showing a mastery of the first step in the selling process – gaining the attention of the prospect. Today, an experienced direct seller with an established customer base expects to receive an order from 75 per cent of the catalogues they place. Also, the orders received from regular customers tend to be two or three times the value obtained by a new agent.

Clearly, using catalogues and distributing them in large numbers to potential customers is an effective way of de-skilling the selling process. However, for a new DSO the initial investment required to create a catalogue with sufficient 'bulk', that is, the fifty or more pages needed to distinguish it from a direct mailing piece, can be prohibitive. Even if direct sellers are required to pay for these catalogues, it is rarely possible to produce them economically with print runs of less than 250 000. This is a daunting investment, made worse by the need to update the catalogue at least twice a year.

In low-ticket direct sales there are, of course, other ways of de-skilling the 'attention-gaining' step in making a sale. Herbalife, the US multi-national DSO marketing diet plans, has from the day the business was founded in California by Mark Hughes used a very simple attention-grabbing technique. It is for every new direct seller to wear a badge saying 'Lose Weight Now? – Ask Me How'. It is brash but highly effective. It gives an instant source of conversation on what their business is all about.

If the product on offer is intrinsically attractive then the product itself can be a conversation opener. Cabouchon, the costume jewellery business, encourage all their salespeople to wear as much of the jewellery as they can, on every possible occasion when they might meet people. The inevitable result is that someone is going to remark on how good it looks and provide the perfect opening for a sales presentation. Generally speaking, in low-ticket direct sales, if a DSO can encourage new direct sellers to become personally committed to using or wearing the products they are selling, then at the outset of their involvement in a part-time business they will not need to be too worried about sales techniques. A good proportion of their business will come just from sharing their enthusiasm with others and receiving orders as a natural by-product of that enthusiasm. Direct sellers who are enthusiastic consumers are more likely to enjoy what they are doing and will stay longer with the business. The converse is equally true!

If attractive or interesting products cannot be worn or used in such a way that they gain the attention of potential customers, then there are others ways that a direct seller can put them on display. A home party demonstration is one method, as are product displays at places of work. The latter is a technique used most effectively by Colour Library Books, The Book People and a few other similar DSOs.

> Colour Library Books encourage their direct sellers to leave a selection of books at the reception desks of large offices, having previously offered the receptionist a small incentive to collect orders. They would also have previously gained an assurance from the management of the office that this would be acceptable. The books are not so much sold, as easily made available for employees

to browse through and to place orders for, as they pass in and out of the office building.

The direct selling of low-cost consumer goods at places of work, including product demonstrations held during lunch hours, is a growing sector of the industry and is largely welcomed by employers – particularly those whose business locations are some way from shopping centres and who are keen to improve the facilities available to their staff. This type of direct selling offers DSOs one of the few opportunities to recruit full-time direct sellers for the sale of low-ticket products as it provides an opportunity for doing business throughout a normal working day.

In summary, the key to the success of any DSO marketing low-ticket products through an organization composed of predominantly part-time direct sellers is to avoid the need for traditional selling skills in person-to-person presentations. Providing such sales training to a part-time salesforce with an inherently high turnover is expensive; but, more importantly, it is also a disincentive to would-be direct sellers who are looking for a simple and enjoyable way of supplementing their family income. This does not mean that any DSO can afford to ignore the method by which a sale is made. Successful DSOs are those who have found a way of de-skilling the selling process and are able to offer their direct sellers an easy way of helping their customers to buy from them. Any analysis of DSOs that have failed will invariably reveal either a disregard for the selling process or a misplaced belief by the management that direct sellers, offered an attractive and well-priced product, will simply find their own way of making sales.

As we have seen, the provision of attractive catalogues is one well-proven method but one which, for a new venture, represents a daunting financial commitment. The party sales technique is another. If neither of these is possible, then the best approach is for a DSO to devote resources to 'selling' the product range to their salespeople. By encouraging every direct seller to be totally committed to the products, and to use the products themselves, then they will make it that much easier for them to pass on their personal enthusiasm to others in the form of personal recommendations.

'Big ticket': person-to-person

It is generally considered that any single direct-sold consumer transaction over £75 is no longer an impulse purchase and becomes one that does require professional selling skills. Providing an adequate return on a

DSO's investment in training usually demands a full-time commitment on behalf of the direct seller. There are, of course, exceptions. World Book Childcraft International has built up in the UK a substantial business selling reference books, based on part-time direct sellers – many of whom were, or still are, school teachers.

The success of any DSO depends on the ability of the business to recruit, train, motivate and retain its salespeople. For big-ticket DSOs this is a major challenge. In industry and commerce, selling is one of the occupational areas that is least affected by recession. Recruiting good full-time direct sellers for a DSO which offers no fixed salary, no car or other benefits and an income based solely on commission is therefore difficult. Inevitably, the appeal of such an occupation will be to those who are inexperienced but who are, at the same time, attracted to the idea of selling and the opportunity of an unrestricted earnings opportunity. If a DSO is to be successful in marketing big-ticket lines, it has to offer a realistic earnings opportunity, a proven selling method and first-class sales training.

Let me consider first the earnings opportunity. An attractive full-time direct selling occupation in Britain today has to offer a realistic minimum earnings potential of at least £500 per week. If a DSO were to market a product with an RRP of, let us say, £100 and were to offer the direct seller a 20 per cent commission on each sale, then that direct seller would have to make 25 sales per week, or five a day, to earn £500. Now, a sale of £100 is just beyond the limit of an impulse purchase and, in a private home, would usually require the agreement of both the prospect and their partner. As with all direct sales, this would invariably require an evening presentation. With a realistic expectation of converting only one in three presentations into firm orders, this would mean that direct sellers in this DSO would have to make an average of fifteen evening presentations every day of the week – if they were to achieve a weekly income of £500. In most parts of Britain this would virtually be impossible. The purpose of this illustration is to show that there is a bracket of retail selling prices, above an impulse purchase, which is not, in practice, accessible by DSOs. As a general rule it is not practical to direct sell any goods or services, with full-time direct sellers, where the average selling price is less than £500.

Although in this book I am examining the direct sales of consumer goods, it is instructive to look for a moment at the way double-glazing, kitchens and other home improvements are direct sold. This is an industry with annual sales in excess of £1 billion and represents an area of self-employment for several thousand full-time direct sellers. The average contract value for the sale of a replacement window installation is £3000 and the commission available to the salesperson is commonly 15 per cent for a self-generated sale and 10 per cent if the lead were provided by the company. This means that only two sales a week would provide a reasonable earnings opportunity. This could realistically be achieved by making no more than two sales a week from eight presentations to prospective customers who had previously registered an interest in double-glazing. It is against this type of competition for the recruitment of direct sellers that any DSO, selling big-ticket products, has to prepare its marketing plan.

The selling of big-ticket products requires the direct seller to go through each stage of the selling process outlined in Chapter 1. Any help that can be provided by the DSO to simplify this process will serve to enhance the appeal of the job and so improve the chances of recruiting a good sales team. The first way in which this can be done is by attracting the attention of the prospect and creating interest in the product on offer and so providing the direct seller with a qualified lead. This is the way in which most home-improvement businesses operate. Many of these DSOs with products that are visually attractive on the printed page do this through media advertisements or direct mail, which encourage a prospect to complete an enquiry form requesting further information. However, today, as media-generated leads are becoming much more expensive, an increasing proportion of their leads are generated from telephone canvassing. If these leads are generated by the DSO, they can either be given free to the direct seller or charged at a nominal rate against the direct seller's commission account. The latter has the advantage of making sure that the direct seller makes full use of the leads they receive. However, providing leads from media advertising or from telephone canvassing is not always practical for those products which require either verbal explanation or practical demonstration.

As in low-ticket direct sales, a DSO which requires its direct sellers to gain an interest in the product on offer, has to develop a foolproof prospection system. The simplest but possibly the hardest system is to train direct sellers in how to start talking about their product to every person they meet in the course of a normal day. The idea is either to book an appointment for a subsequent sales presentation or to gain a personal referral to another likely prospect. If it can be proved that a certain proportion of all those personal contacts will lead to an appointment, and a similar proven proportion of all subsequent demonstrations will lead to an order, then the direct seller can be given the necessary confidence to take on the job. However, convincing a prospect for a full-time self-employed occupation in direct selling that this is true is not easy. It is for this reason that some DSOs show their faith in the statistical approach by offering new recruits a fixed cash sum for every presentation they make. Other DSOs, for the same reason, offer new recruits for an initial period a guaranteed basic weekly or monthly payment. They know that the unpaid commissions on every sale made will more than cover the costs of the demonstration fees or guaranteed basic payments. After a period of time the direct seller will then have the confidence to opt for the normal commission-based reward system. A DSO using this introductory system will, of course, have to employ a rigorous procedure for ensuring that full demonstrations have been made.

A rather simpler variation on this approach is to train new direct sellers, or a supporting team of canvassers, to call on every home in a given area with, once again, the objective of booking a demonstration. This can be done by offering an incentive, such as a prize draw or gift, to all those who are prepared to have a demonstration. This is the technique used by Vorwerk and Lux, in the direct sale of vacuum cleaners, in each one of its worldwide markets. The direct seller has the confidence of knowing that every home represents a potential customer and that, on average, vacuum cleaners are replaced every ten years or so. In their major markets Lux has shown that a well-trained canvasser can book one demonstration in every ten calls made by a canvasser and that one sale will be made from every three demonstrations. Experienced direct sellers obtain considerably better conversion rates. However, what is essential is to be able to prove to a new recruit that a realistic conversion rate is within their ability. It is just a matter of calling on enough homes.

This approach is used to very good effect in the United States by the Southwestern Company based in Nashville, Tennessee.

> Southwestern was founded in the nineteenth century to sell bibles in the southern states. Today this DSO markets a range of school revision manuals geared to the demands of the US academic curriculum. The salesforce is composed of university students who over the long summer vacation are trained to call on homes all over the United States. Not only are these students able to earn and contribute a substantial sum towards their own higher education, but the experience is seen as being valuable in its own right and one that is highly regarded by future employers. The value of this experience is now appreciated in the UK. Over the past few years over 500 British and French university students have been recruited to go over to the United States each summer to join the programme. The sales approach is very simple. Teams of students, each under the leadership of a student who has had previous experience of the programme, go to a designated territory and rigorously call on

every home. They are made to appreciate that they cannot expect to find a prospective customer in every home. However, if they are able to make thirty demonstrations a day, each taking no more than twenty minutes, then from the previous experience of others they can confidently expect to convert 15 per cent of those demonstrations into orders. With this particular DSO the average customer order value, at around $70, is on the borderline between an impulse purchase and a big-ticket sale. It is therefore quite practical to canvas for business throughout the working day.

The training psychology adopted by the Southwestern Company is also interesting and is borne out by one of the company sayings – 'Where else can you earn $10 000 in your summer vacation by being unsuccessful over 90 per cent of the time?' This approach deals effectively with a common criticism of many sales training programmes, which is that recruits are given an unrealistic expectation of success in the hope that this will serve to motivate them. Usually, it has just the opposite effect and, after the first few rebuttals, can easily lead to a feeling of failure and premature decision to quit.

In Britain and throughout Europe the growing numbers of students in higher-education programmes represent a potentially valuable source of good direct sellers. Even though their availability is limited to vacation periods, there are many opportunities for new DSOs to use students to market specialist products. A good example is Airpic.

Airpic is a business which was establised with the aim of selling aerial photographs to private home owners and which in 1995 achieved sales of over £1 million. The founder, Steve Cooke, was one of the first UK students to work for Southwestern in the United States and he used his experience to offer the same type of opportunity to students in the UK. The average selling price of a framed photograph of a private home is around £50 which, while not an impulse purchase or an item which needs to be professionally sold, does not require a joint husband and wife decision. In rural areas sales can be made throughout a normal working day. In fact many are purchased as gifts for a spouse. Although Airpic was founded in the UK, in 1994 the company opened up a subsidiary operation in the United States which, using US students, has proved to be equally successful.

The essential difference between big-ticket and low-ticket direct sales is the need for comprehensive sales training; in particular, training in how to gain conviction, how to create a desire and how to handle the most common objections as being merely requests for more information and reassurance. A product that the direct seller may not own themselves requires the essential skills needed by any good salesperson. As we have seen, with low-ticket direct sales this can be achieved by a strong personal endorsement by the direct seller when they are a user of the product themselves. For the big-ticket DSO this demands a strong commitment to sales training, particularly in how to use endorsements and referrals from existing customers. Referrals, both from customers and from prospective customers, are the lifeblood of every DSO.

Party plan selling

A well-proven method of direct selling which throughout Europe and North America currently accounts for over 20 per cent of total direct sales is the 'party plan' approach, in which a direct seller demonstrates products to a group of guests, invited by a hostess, in whose home the sales 'party' is held. Excluding the sales achieved by full-time direct sellers, DSOs using a conventional 'single-level' organization structure results in the highest sales productivity among part-time direct sellers. The data in Table 3.2 are from the 1996 UK DSA Annual Survey.

The party plan technique was pioneered in the United States by Stanley Home Products, another offshoot of the Fuller Brush Company which at the time marketed a similar range of home-care products. For the first few years after this business was founded by Stanley Beveridge in 1931 the demonstrators were men and it was some time before they realized that the direct selling opportunity on offer was ideally suited to women. Ironically, it was even longer before this business, later to be known as Stanhome, realized the potential of women as senior managers of the business. It was during this time that a number of outstanding women entrepreneurs left the company to start businesses of their own. Two of the most notable were Mary Crowley who founded Home Interiors &

Table 3.2   Sales productivity of part-time direct sellers

Type of DSO	*Average annual sales per direct seller (£)*
Party plan	4217
Low-ticket, person to person	1892
Network marketing, person to person	1623

Gifts and, of course, Mary Kay Ash who left Stanley to create Mary Kay Cosmetics – now the world's largest direct selling skincare business and an organization dedicated to giving women the chance of gaining financial independence. It is the huge worldwide demand by women for part-time earnings opportunities that continues to account for the success of party plan businesses.

However, the company that for almost fifty years has been synonymous with party plan direct sales, and which has continued to expand, achieving total worldwide sales in 1994 of $2 billion, is Tupperware. It was yet another Stanley Home Products manager, Brownie Wise, who in 1951 left that company to help set up the new Tupperware business based on demonstrating and selling plastic food containers. In doing so, they created a business that has served as a role model for virtually every other party plan company.

The party sales approach is not suitable for every DSO, but is applicable where the product on offer is low ticket, is demonstrable, is 'appealing' and is one for which there is a demand in every home. Although Tupperware created a business format that has been copied by others, party selling, in which the direct seller makes a demonstration to a group of prospects, is as a sales technique equally suited to other types of DSO. It is, for example, used by many network marketing businesses as a suggested alternative to a person-to-person presentation. Many of these DSOs use the sales party not so much as a business format, but as a means of introducing new customers to a range of repeat purchase lines that can thereafter be supplied on a person-to-person basis.

The great strength of the traditional party plan sales organization, as developed by Tupperware, is that it offers predictable business format and reassurance to the direct seller that if they follow the advice they are given they can expect a reasonable level of earnings for every party they arrange. A typical format is as follows.

If a demonstrator finds two hostesses who both agree to invite twenty guests to a party, then she can be confident that at least one party will eventually be held. Out of twenty invited guests, ten can be expected to attend. Of the ten guests who attend, at least nine will place an order and the average order will be for two or three items with an average order value per guest of £18. This will result in a party sales value of £162. Commissions can vary slightly but the average commission payable to the demonstrator is 20 per cent which will yield an income to the demonstrator of £32.40. If the reward to the hostess is the opportunity to receive goods to the value of 10 per cent of party sales, then she is also likely to feel well rewarded by receiving products worth £16.

The party plan approach gives a DSO the opportunity to offer direct sellers a well-proven method of achieving sales. There are, however, several key criteria that a DSO should consider if opting for this direct sales method.

The first concerns ticket prices. The most successful party plan businesses offer a range of products with selling prices ranging from £3 to around £50. Their aim is to achieve an average guest order value of under £20; with 90 per cent of those attending being happy to buy one or two items and leaving the party feeling that there are other items they might still like to buy on another occasion. Achieving a high percentage of purchasers is crucial to the success of the party plan system for one simple reason. It is this. If, at the end of the party, the demonstrator has not booked two other follow-on parties (booking two is necessary to ensure that at least one is held) then the business will have no momentum. The most obvious and most easily accessible source of new hostesses for follow-on parties are those who are at the party. If at a party too many of the guests feel restrained by high prices to place an order then they are unlikely to volunteer to be a hostess for another party for fear that their own guests will feel similarly restrained. This will be their reaction, regardless of the appeal of the product and the fact that in other circumstances they may well decide to make a purchase. It is for this reason that party plan is rarely suitable for a DSO marketing big-ticket lines. There are, of course, exceptions. One of these is the Swiss DSO, AMC, where well-trained direct sellers demonstrate top-quality cookware to a small group as a prelude to a later person-to-person presentation.

Ticket prices also influence the level of earnings that a demonstrator can expect to achieve from holding a party. If unit prices are too low then this can result in low party sales and a reduced commission to the demonstrator. Unless a sales party can generate a commission of at least £30 then recruiting good demonstrators is likely to be difficult.

The second criterion is the 'appeal' of the product range and the opportunity it presents for an interesting, informative and entertaining demonstration. The great strength of party plan is that, unlike a retail store, it provides an opportunity for products to be demonstrated and tried out in a friendly home environment where the positive opinions of other guests can be as influential as those of the demonstrator. For this reason it is a sales method that is rarely suited to the sale of 'serious' products such as health and nutrition, home-security systems, or even vacuum cleaners, where any demonstration or dialogue with guests might expose a need that a guest may not wish to discuss in the company of others.

Apart from products such as clothing, cosmetics and skin care which can be tried out by guests, the party plan approach is suited to products that benefit from an interesting and entertaining demonstration. This was the basis of Tupperware's early success. Well-informed demonstrators gave the sort of demonstration that is not possible to provide in a retail store. It is an approach that is applicable to a wide range of household goods, particularly home-decoration lines which can be well displayed in a home setting. It is also possible to give an interesting account of how goods are made and what constitutes good quality. Princess House demonstrators do just this when they talk about the company's range of crystal and porcelain figurines. They are even able to talk about the craftsmen who designed and made the items on display.

Giving guests an incentive to come to another party is the final criterion for the success of a party plan DSO. The most usual method is to make regular introductions of new lines, an approach which is easily achieved by those DSOs marketing fashion goods, such as clothes and jewellery. Another approach is to market 'collectibles', ranges of household goods or decorative products that offer the inducement of further sales. Offering guests the prospect of discounts based on the collective value of goods purchased over a period of time, is another powerful technique for encouraging attendance at future sales parties. Above all, the most effective way of encouraging guests to come to another sales party is to offer them the prospect of an enjoyable evening.

The fun element of a sales party was yet another of Tupperware's innovations. It is this particular appeal of the party plan concept that ten years ago prompted Jacqueline Gold to establish Ann Summers as a party plan business. Her business has been an extraordinary success with current annual sales of lingerie now exceeding £40 million. Hers is a good example of the effectiveness of a DSO based not just on products that are hard to find in a retail store but on offering ladies, in all-female company, a highly entertaining evening.

Peer-group relationships in direct selling

To conclude this chapter on selling methods I want to refer to one truism in selling that should be considered by every DSO. It is that salespeople are likely to be most effective when making a presentation to someone like themselves. In Chapter 1 I described the selling process that is most commonly used by sales trainers. The second step in that process is the one whereby the seller gains the conviction of a prospect that what is being claimed for a product or service is true. This can, as I described, be done with the support of printed sales material or by demonstration.

However, a personal endorsement by someone with whom a prospect can easily relate and who also likes and uses the product or service is even more effective. This is one of the reasons why DSOs are rarely able to offer even part-time earnings opportunities to the long-term unemployed. The brutal fact is that if such a direct seller were to attempt to sell products which they were through economic circumstances unable to afford themselves then they would be denied one of the opportunities to gain conviction for that product.

I first learned the lesson of peer-group relationships many years ago, when I set up a new business to sell DIY products to the independent hardware stores. Our customers were, in the main, the proprietors of their businesses, middle-aged men steeped in the traditional hardware trade. To liven up the field salesforce I thought it would be a good idea to recruit a few personable young women with good sales experience. The results were disappointing. Although professionally more competent, the women found it much more difficult to relate to their customers and were no more effective than the men.

By its very nature a DSO's recruitment strategy is self-selective. If the product on offer appeals to women, then it is that much more likely that the sales opportunity will appeal to women. It is this that gives direct selling its most powerful competitive edge over other methods of retailing. If, for example, a DSO wishes to market a range of personal care products designed to appeal to women in the age range of mid-twenties to late thirties, then the most effective salesperson is likely to be a woman within that same age band, who is totally committed to the products on offer. To a large extent this avoids the necessity of training part-time direct sellers in the full range of professional skills. This point is well made by Imelda Roche, a recent Chairman of the World Federation of Direct Selling Associations and who, with her husband Bill, has built up their Australian DSO, Nutri-Metics, to be the largest cosmetics company in Australia and also a major international business. Her approach has been not to teach selling skills to her salespeople but to 'encourage total belief in Nutri-Metics' products to the point where they will want to recommend them to others'. This is a strategy that is applicable to any DSO.

Key points

- Public attitudes towards doing business in the home, both as a buyer and as seller, are changing to the benefit of direct selling.
- Successful direct selling is 'creating an environment where a decision to purchase is the natural outcome of a personal, face-to-face, presentation'.

- Throughout the world, direct selling is now mainly a part-time occupation, which as it offers a flexible commitment in time has greatest appeal to women.
- Other than for repeat purchases of food it is impractical to direct sell low-ticket lines using a salesforce of full-time direct sellers.
- There is a product price window of between £75 and £500, between which it is very difficult to offer an attractive earnings opportunity for direct sellers.
- The essence of a successful party plan direct selling business has always been, and still is, ' to earn, learn and have fun'.
- Direct selling is likely to be most successful when a direct seller is marketing products of interest to consumers in their own peer group.

4

Network marketing

The basic concept

Network marketing, or multi-level marketing (MLM) as it was originally described when it was introduced into the UK in the mid-1960s, is not in the strict sense, a marketing method. It is simply a way of organizing the field sales operations of a DSO. It is an alternative to a conventional single-level (SLM) organization structure. Furthermore, it is not, as some believe, an alternative to direct selling. Products still have to be sold and, as we have seen in Chapter 3, the choice of direct selling method is largely dictated by the nature of the product. Whichever selling method is selected, there still remains a choice of organization structure. Table 4.1 is a guide to that choice.

Recognition for having built the first successful DSO based on the multi-level concept is usually given to the founders of Nutrilite, a California-based nutritional products business that started trading shortly after the Second World War. However, it was Rich de Vos and Jay

Table 4.1 Organizational options for DSOs

Sales method	Organization structure	
	Conventional (SLM)	Multi-level (MLM)
Big ticket, person to person	Possible	Difficult
Low ticket, person to person	Possible	Possible
Party plan	Possible	Possible

Van Andell who worked with Nutrilite and who later went on to co-found Amway that showed the true potential of this type of DSO. Their family business is still today the largest multi-level DSO with annual sales of more than $6 billion in 1994, achieved in a total of seventy international markets.

The term 'network marketing' came into use in the 1980s as an attempt to distance this type of business from the bad press associated with some of the first MLM businesses and the particular abuses of pyramid selling which will be described in a later section of this chapter. For the 1990s, network marketing is possibly a better description, particularly as the term is now in common parlance as a way of building personal business contacts and, of course, in computer terminology. The concept is much the same. For the sake of brevity I shall, from now on, use the acronym NM to describe network marketing.

In a conventional SLM DSO the selling function is carried out by full- or part-time direct sellers, whose function is to do no more than sell the products marketed by the DSO. The other sales support functions of recruiting, training, motivation, account administration and the delivery of goods are the responsibility of others, who are usually, but not necessarily, employees of the business. This is the way in which most industrial salesforces are organized and was the structure of all the original DSOs. In fact, most DSOs around the world, from low-ticket businesses like Avon Cosmetics, to big-ticket DSOs like Encyclopaedia Britannica, are still organized in this way.

In an NM DSO responsibility for the sales support functions, particularly recruiting, training and motivation, are in effect delegated to independent direct sellers. In a business based on large numbers of part-time direct sellers, this can often be more efficient than using a conventional management structure. It also gives individuals with good organizing abilities the opportunity to put those abilities to good use – from the moment they join the DSO. Without having to wait to be 'appointed' to a management role they can promote themselves.

With an occupation in direct selling now appealing to a wider cross-section of society, the NM concept is steadily gaining in popularity (see Figure 4.1(a) and (b)). In the United States virtually all new DSOs are based on NM principles and many long-established businesses are adopting, at least in part, the NM concept. In the UK, in 1995, 28 per cent of the direct selling industry's total sales were accounted for by NM businesses. In 1990 the proportion was only 17 per cent (see Figure 4.1).

In an NM DSO every participant, from the day they first join the business, is given two quite distinct sources of earnings opportunities. The first is to earn an income, either as a commission on personal sales or

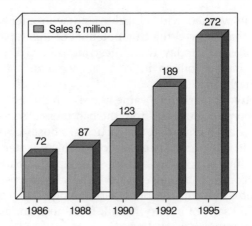

Figure 4.1 (a) *Growth in direct sales achieved by NM DSOs.* (Source: *Direct Selling Association*)

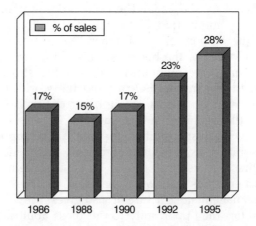

Figure 4.1 (b) *Sales of NM DSOs as a proportion of total direct sales.* (Source: *Direct Selling Association*)

by buying products at a 'trade price', from the DSO and selling them to consumers at a suggested retail price. The second source of income is to build their own network of other participants and to benefit from the retail business that they achieve. The delegated functions that are common to all NM businesses are those of recruitment, training and motivation. With some NM businesses this delegation extends to the collation of small orders and the local distribution of products.

Most NM businesses can be described as those that have the following three ingredients:

> 'First, a DSO supplies products directly to participants who are personally attracted by the products, consider them to be good value for money and are keen to use the products themselves. Second, the DSO rewards participants for sharing their enthusiasm for the products with others who also wish to buy and use the products. Third, and this is the key difference between NM and any other DSO, the DSO rewards every participant for passing on their enthusiasm, both for the products and the business concept, by building and maintaining their own network of other participants, each with their own retail customers.'

Other equally successful NM DSOs can best be described by substituting, for the first two ingredients in the above description, the following:

> 'A DSO provides competitively priced products to participants together with a proven and easily replicable method of achieving retail sales and . . .'

The key words in either of these descriptions are 'consider them to be good value for money', 'are keen to use the products themselves' or 'proven and easily replicable method of achieving retail sales'. If these criteria are missing, then the business is unlikely to succeed – no matter how attractive the financial rewards from introducing or 'sponsoring' others may appear.

The appeal of network marketing

The reason for the recent growth of NM DSOs is that it fits in so well with the changed expectations and demands of society since the early 1980s. No longer can anyone expect a job for life: retailing and trading is now respectable: doing business with friends and within social groups is now much more acceptable: Government policy and tax rules now positively encourage small businesses and, lastly, advances in information technology have made working from home a practical reality. All this has dramatically widened the appeal of a direct selling opportunity to include the higher social groups in society, who would not previously have seriously considered becoming involved in direct sales. NM DSOs also offer a unique opportunity to those with good communication skills and the ability to organize and motivate others. With NM, direct selling is no longer just an occupation – it is a business opportunity. Unlike a conventional DSO, or indeed conventional employment, an individual or a married couple or partners do not have to wait for the management to recognize their abilities and to promote them – they can promote themselves and build a substantial business of their own. It is for this reason that NM has a special appeal to those people with management experience who have either been made redundant in corporate 'downsizing', or who have opted for early retirement.

In Britain the events that perhaps more than any other prompted a wider interest in NM DSOs were the 'Big Bang', the Stock Market collapse in 1987 and the radical restructuring of London's financial institutions. Many able men and women were forced to look for other ways of maintaining the lifestyles they had become used to. A little later, the problems with Lloyd's led to 'Names' who had lost fortunes, looking for other ways of restoring their 'old money'. For those people, and many others who had long cherished the idea of doing their own thing, but have not had the financial resources to start their own business NM DSOs offered just that opportunity.

Yet another appeal of NM is the complete flexibility it offers in terms of time and commitment. In practice, most people become involved on a part-time basis and expand their businesses at a pace which suits them best. From the outset, how many hours they choose to devote to the business is entirely up to them. As an NM business is based on personal contacts, wherever they may be, there is no demand from the DSO that participants make the most use of territories allocated to them – which is the case with some SLM DSOs.

In a way the concept is very similar to that offered by a franchise business. The big differences are the absence of franchise fees, the need for retail premises, expensive equipment, staff costs and territorial restrictions. Conventional high street franchises necessarily demand substantial investments and often additional mortgages on the family home. An NM business opportunity can, for those who are self-motivated, generate the same income from an investment that with many DSOs need rarely exceed the cost of a business kit and a few sample products. The cost need be no more than £100 or, to put it in perspective, the cost of an annual TV licence.

The low entry cost of an NM business does bring with it the problem of maintaining motivation. Every business goes through difficult times. When you are self-employed it is that much more difficult to pick yourself up and press on. Commonly, the high street franchisee is motivated to succeed by fear – the fear of losing their life savings. By contrast, a participant in an NM DSO can easily rationalize their decision to quit when the going gets tough; when orders are hard to get or are cancelled, when their own sponsored participants quit or when faced with a few bad debts. If the investment in the business had been small then it is all too easy to call it a day and write off the small investment to experience! This is a problem for all DSOs and motivation is therefore dealt with in Chapter 5. However, one special feature of the network marketing concept is that the person who introduces, or 'sponsors' as it is usually called, a new participant has an ongoing interest in helping that individual to succeed. It means that although a participant has a business of their own, they are not on their own. Unlike other DSOs, there is always someone to hand, in exactly the same position as themselves, who is able to offer help and encouragement. It is the mark of a well-run DSO that this system of built-in motivation works effectively.

What products are suited to network marketing?

The first general rule is that any product offered for sale through an NM DSO, as with any DSO based on part-time salespeople, should have a mass market appeal. No matter how good and well priced a product may be, if it is not of use to, nor used by every participant, then the business is unlikely to succeed. NM, at its best, could just as well be described as 'referral marketing'. If all participants like the product and use it themselves, and consider it to be good value at the recommended retail selling price, then they do not have to spend too much time thinking how they can sell it. All they have to do is to recommend it to others. In this way sales can easily be the natural outcome of their enthusiasm. This in turn makes it that much easier to promote the business opportunity and build a network of other enthusiastic consumers and participants in the business. Attempting to impart enthusiasm for a product that a salesperson does not use themselves is possible; the problem is that it requires professional selling skills, and these, for a NM DSO, are difficult and costly to impart to a predominantly part-time sales organization. Again, this lack of personal experience, as a user of the product, makes it that much more difficult to pass on the enthusiasm that is so necessary for the building of a network of other enthusiastic participants. Committed advertising executives feel the same about the products they have undertaken to promote. David Ogilvy in *Ogilvy on Advertising* put it this way:

> It's bad manners to use products which compete with your clients' products. When I got the Sears Roebuck account, I started buying all my clothes at Sears. This bugged my wife, but the following year a

convention of clothing manufacturers voted me the best-dressed man in America. I would not dream of using any other travellers checks except American Express, or drinking any other coffee but Maxwell House, or washing with any soap except Dove. When I got the Rolls-Royce account, I followed the rule of using the client's product. As the number of brands advertised by Ogilvy & Mather now exceeds two thousand, my personal inventory is getting complicated.

The second general rule is that the product should have an element of repeat business. Almost by definition, a business implies continuity: either the on-going supply of similar products, or repeat purchases to an established group of clients, or effecting the sale of one-off products to a steady and reliable stream of new customers. Franchises can operate well with both types of product or service. The reason for this is that advertising and high street visibility, usually guarantee the inflow of customers. In any of its forms, direct selling is quite different. It is a proactive business and new customers can only be obtained by a personal approach. Anyone seriously considering putting their energies into an NM business wants to be assured that they can build up some inertia and goodwill from a steadily expanding customer base, to which they can go on and add. Having constantly to replace that customer base makes expansion difficult. Many successful NM DSOs, such as National Safety Associates, have started the business with a repeatable product line, albeit on a three-year replacement cycle, but have later extended the product range with repeatable lines. In the case of NSA, having started with water filters, the range was extended to include nutritional products. Another US company, A. L. Williams, a major supplier of term insurance policies and now part of Primerica Group, built the business on network marketing principles. At first, selling insurance policies does not seem a repeat business. In practice it is. Premium payments have to be maintained and A. L. Williams rewarded their salespeople who encouraged their customers, through regular contact, into maintaining their annual payments.

Network marketing sales plans

In their business manuals NM businesses often describe their payment plans as 'marketing plans' which, of course, is not strictly correct. What they actually mean are payment or sales plans or perhaps, in US terminology, compensation plans – not the overall marketing strategy of the DSO.

A typical NM DSO rewards participants in three ways. The first is a retail profit earned from selling goods to consumers. The second is a wholesale volume profit and the third is a series of bonuses earned on the sales of those other participants they have introduced whose own group sales exceed the volume of sales, in a given period, on which the maximum wholesale volume profit is payable. Let us look at each of these sources of income in turn.

Retail profit

This is the source of income that is offered to salespeople with any DSO. It may be available in a number of ways. With a NM DSO the goods may be offered at trade prices, together with suggested retail selling prices at which those goods should be sold to retail customers. Depending on the nature of the goods, this retail profit may range from 20 per cent to 40 per cent of the RRP excluding VAT. Some DSOs do not make specific suggestions as to RRPs but simply give an overall recommendation on retail mark-ups. In the UK the problem with this approach is that special rules apply to the VAT treatment of direct sales. VAT is considered in more detail in Chapter 7, but the essence of the problem is that it is a DSO's responsibility to ensure that VAT is collected at the full retail price, regardless of whether or not the direct seller is registered for VAT.

It is up to a DSO to decide whether they wish to receive orders and supply goods directly to every participant in the business or, alternatively, to deal directly only with those who have built their business to a certain prescribed monthly sales volume. These are commonly described as 'direct distributors' and it is their function, among other responsibilities, to receive orders and to supply goods to new and less active participants. The decision on whether or not to supply goods directly to every participant may depend on the nature of the goods. This choice of strategy is dealt with in more detail in a section on Distribution in Chapter 6 – 'Managing a direct selling business'.

It is also up to a NM DSO to decide whether or not they wish to deal with all participants as principals in a buyer/seller relationship or to treat participants as agents. The advantages and disadvantages are considered in more detail in Chapter 5, 'Managing a direct salesforce'. Whatever the choice, the principle of offering a retail profit remains the same. In terms of the sales plan there is also no advantage in making any distinction between self-consumption and sales made to non-participating end users. With the exception of big-ticket DSOs, a proportion of all sales can be accounted for by self-consumption by participants or products used in the course of demonstration. With non-NM DSOs this proportion is generally around 10 per cent of total sales, but with NM DSOs it can be as high as 50 per cent. Provided that this proportion of self-consumed sales is genuinely consumed by participants, then that is no bad thing; it is still a sound basis for recommendation to others. One reason why any DSO in the UK may wish to analyse self-consumption is to negotiate with Customs & Excise the rate at which VAT is payable on total retail sales volume. The reason is that it is unreasonable for VAT to be payable on that proportion of sales.

In deciding what percentage level of retail profit to pay, the DSO has to decide whether to make this payable on the full RRP, including VAT, or on the VAT-exclusive price. Some NM DSOs use the VAT-inclusive price in order to simplify the presentation of their sales plan to new participants, but it is more normal to use the price less VAT. The other decision that a DSO has to make is whether or not to pay the same commission or offer the same discount on all the goods in the product range. With some DSOs that offer a wide range of consumer goods, it is often very difficult to justify offering the same margin on every item in the range – if the ultimate RRP is to be competitive with equivalent products offered through retail stores. This is obvious when you consider that retail stores have widely different profit margins on different products. While some retailers make available selected 'loss leaders', they aim to achieve a uniform overall profit margin on a typical 'shopping basket'.

There are several ways in which a NM DSO can overcome this problem. One technique is to allocate to every product in the range a 'sales plan price' or 'business value' (BV) on which all commissions and bonuses are paid. With this approach the BV allocated to one product may not bear the same relation to RRP as the BV allocated to another. Another device is to allocate to every product an additional 'points value', which is a measure of the price difference between one product and another. There are two additional advantages to the latter approach. The first is that it is inflation-proof and does not, over the years, demand that sales plan volumes, required for qualifications and bonuses, are updated in line with inflation. The second advantage of using a points-based sales plan, which again is related to inflation, is that participants maintain a true idea of the extent to which their businesses are expanding. Price increases can all too easily, with any salesforce, lead to a false idea that they are doing better, when in fact the true volume of their business may be static or even declining.

Although it is therefore possible to offset the effects of inflation and variable profit margins, these devices do add an unwelcome complication to a NM sales plan which to the uninitiated is already bound to be seen as complicated and difficult to understand. If it is at all possible, it is preferable for a NM DSO to create a product range that can sustain a uniform commission structure based on retail prices.

Wholesale volume profit

The normal approach to constructing a sales plan for any NM DSO is to offer in addition to a basic retail profit an additional profit based on the volume of sales achieved during a fixed trading period – usually one month. This would offer an additional series of bonuses payable in accordance with a scale of sales up to a specified maximum. This sales volume would be computed as being the addition of personal sales, including personal consumption, to the sales of all those other partici- pants that an individual may have personally sponsored into the business and where each of those sponsored participants have not themselves earned the maximum wholesale bonus. For the purposes of the following illustrations this total will be referred to as being 'personal group volume', or PGV, although the acronym may vary from business to business.

Until now I have referred to 'participants' in a NM DSO. In practice DSOs give participants a business title which they feel is most appropriate to their business; it may be 'agent', 'consultant', 'fashion advisor' or any other such name that suitably reflects their independent status. Perhaps the most common title is the simple term 'distributor' and, for illustrative purposes, that is the term I shall use from now on to describe how a typical sales plan operates.

Within today's NM DSOs there are two basically different approaches to the payment of wholesale volume profit. The first is to make payments at the end of each month in line with a 'performance bonus' scale. This is the approach used by Amway and many of the older-established NM DSOs where the DSO only deals directly with 'direct distributors' – those who have qualified for this position by sustaining for a period of three consecutive months PGV sales at the maximum refund level. For illustrative purposes Table 4.2 shows how the Amway performance bonus operates. These bonuses are in addition to the basic retail profit on their own personal sales which, in the case of Amway, is approximately 25 per cent of retail sales value – excluding VAT.

This maximum bonus of 21 per cent earned on a group achieving 10 000 points is roughly equivalent to retail sales of £12 500. This is the PGV. The actual value of the bonus, based on BV in this Amway example, would represent, approximately, an additional 16 per cent on retail sales achieved in the period.

Direct Selling

Table 4.2   Scale of wholesale volume profits (Amway example)

Sales – based on total points value achieved in one month	Performance bonus – additional % paid out on BV (a monetary figure based on sales, less retail profit and VAT)
200	3
600	6
1 200	9
2 400	12
4 000	15
7 000	18
10 000	21

To illustrate how the volume bonus is calculated, Figure 4.2 represents the case of John Smith, a distributor with a small group in a fictitious but typical NM DSO. We shall assume that the DSO has a bonus scale similar to that shown in Table 4.2 but where, for simplicity, sales are at retail prices and where the performance bonus is based on those sales. Let us also assume that John Smith has directly sponsored five others, 'A', 'B', 'C', 'D' and 'E', and that some of those had themselves sponsored others. The figure beneath each distributor represents their personal sales in one month. The arrows in the figure illustrate direct sponsorship links and point towards the distributor who has been sponsored by the group leader. For distributors A, C, F, G, H, K, L and M, their PGVs are the same as their personal sales as they have not yet sponsored any other distributors.

In this case, John Smith's network has a total PGV amounting to £3000 which qualifies him for a gross bonus of 12 per cent of £3000 – which is £360. However, as every distributor benefits from the sales plan in exactly the same way as John Smith, they are also eligible for refunds according to the same scale. In this case, the PGVs of C, F and L are below £200 and therefore they do not qualify for any bonus. The remaining nine distributors in John Smith's network do qualify for bonuses in their own right and they would be payable as shown in Table 4.3.

The total of the bonuses due to be received by those distributors directly sponsored by John Smith are those payable to A, B, D and E. These are referred to as his 'front-line' distributors. This total to be paid out to them is £135.60 and it is the responsibility of John Smith to pay out these sums from his bonus cheque of £360, leaving him with the balance of £224.40. This may not seem a huge amount but is significant in relation

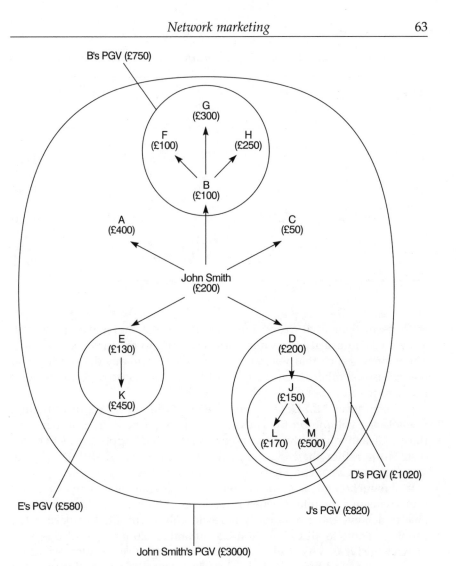

Figure 4.2   *A typical month's PGV for a new distributor – 'John Smith'*

to the retail profit of £40, at say 20 per cent, on his own personal sales of £200. It is his reward for sponsorship and for helping others both to make sales and to start building groups of their own. Sponsorship also provides everyone with the opportunity to make a higher profit on their own personal sales.

In the above example it is the responsibility of each of the distributors B, E, D and J from the sum that they each receive to pay out bonuses due

Table 4.3   Wholesale volume profits earned within John Smith's PGV

Distributor	PGV (£)	Bonus level (%)	Bonus (£)
A	400	3	12
B	750	6	45
D	1020	6	61.20
E	580	3	17.40
G	300	3	9
H	250	3	7.50
J	820	6	49.20
K	450	3	13.50
M	500	3	15

to those in their own 'front lines', i.e. those that they have sponsored. They do so in exactly the same way according to the same bonus scale. The system is such that wherever a bonus is paid to any distributor who has sponsored others then the amount to be paid out to others can never be more than the bonus they have received.

In recent years NM DSOs have developed different ways of providing a wholesale volume profit. These systems are particularly popular with those DSOs that have chosen to receive orders and supply goods to every distributor rather than deal exclusively with 'direct distributors'. The sales plan of Cabouchon is typical of this approach.

In Cabouchon participants are referred to as Consultants and there are four levels of Consultant beneath the level of marketing director who is able to achieve the maximum wholesale volume profit. The basic retail profit available to all Cabouchon Consultants is 20 per cent of the retail price exclusive of VAT. Although Cabouchon's published sales plan does not present the additional wholesale volume profits in quite this way, the structure is, in effect, as shown in Table 4.4.

The essential difference between this plan and that of Amway's is that just as soon as an individual's PGV in any one month exceeds the PGV sales shown in Table 4.4 then they qualify for a permanent appointment at the next level. In this particular DSO there is another way in which any Consultant can attain the next level of appointment and that is to achieve a slightly lower volume of sales over two consecutive months. These individuals will retain their own wholesale volume profit, appropriate to their new appointment, regardless of their future monthly sales volumes.

Table 4.4 Scale of wholesale volume profits (Cabouchon example)

Appointment	PGV sales in one month (£)	Wholesale volume profit (%)	Total profit on personal sales (%)
Consultant	0–229	0	20
Senior consultant	230–699	7	27
Marketing consultant	700–1149	10	30
Marketing manager	1150–2299	13	33
Marketing director	2300 and above	20	40

For comparative purposes let us consider the PGV earnings of, say, Sally Jones with another fictitious sales plan, similar to that of Cabouchon, and compare it with the example for John Smith. For this example let us assume the same PGV sales volume of £3000 and that Sally Jones has five front-line consultants who each have the same PGVs as shown in the case for John Smith. Whereas John Smith is required to pay out the wholesale volume profit out of his own gross refund, Sally Jones will be paid the net amount as each one of her sponsored group are paid their own net volume profits directly by the DSO.

In this case the net wholesale volume profit earned by Sally Jones is shown in Table 4.5. In this case it is assumed that two of the consultants in the group, B and E, have in previous months earned a higher appointment and higher permanent retail profit than their PGVs in this particular month would normally justify. In practice this is a realistic

Table 4.5 Wholesale volume profits earned within Sally Jones' PGV

Consultant	PGV (£)	Net wholesale profit (%)	Profit bonus (£)
A	400	13	52.00
B	750	3	22.50
C	50	20	10.00
D	1020	10	102.00
E	580	7	40.60
Total			227.10

example. This net wholesale volume profit is very similar to the £224.40 earned by John Smith.

Even though a NM DSO may opt to grant every distributor a personal account, to receive orders and payments from them and to pay all bonuses directly to them, it is not necessarily the case that they should all receive goods directly from the NM DSO. Small-order deliveries could be effected through the line of sponsorship. As I shall explain in Chapter 6, this form of distribution serves to ensure better communication and more opportunities for motivation.

No matter how an NM sales plan is constructed, the advantage of gaining a higher appointment through building up a strong PGV, is the effect of increasing the profit earned by every distributor on their own personal sales. The difference between a Cabouchon type plan and that of an Amway type plan is that prior to attaining the maximum wholesale volume profit, where an individual's PGV contains Consultants who have gained the same appointment level as the group leader, they do not make any direct profit on those consultants' personal sales. However, the volume of their sales does influence the size of their PGV and helps in the maintenance of their own appointment level. The motivational effect on participants of granting them a new permanent appointment, on the basis of a one-month achievement, also encourages all participants to strive to reach as soon as possible the appointment appropriate to the highest wholesale volume profit. It is at this point that the third source of income comes into play – royalty bonuses.

Royalty bonuses

When a 'direct distributor' (someone who is earning the maximum wholesale volume profit) sponsors another 'direct distributor', then there is no longer any opportunity for that individual to make a wholesale profit on the other's monthly sales. It is necessary therefore to introduce another form of incentive. The usual system adopted by NM DSOs is to offer a bonus payment or 'royalty bonus' based on the PGVs of sponsored 'direct distributors' and to pay that bonus on a number of subsequent levels of 'direct distributor' sponsorship. It is the reward from these royalty bonuses that represents the major source of income for successful distributors in any NM DSO.

The number of levels on which this bonus is paid can vary, but it is rarely less than three and, with some DSOs, can be down through six levels of sponsorship. The extent to which any direct distributor benefits from his or her downline of other direct distributors is commonly given the term 'payline'.

What can also vary from one sales plan to another is the percentage payment at each level. It can be a sliding scale from, say, 6 per cent on the first level to 1 per cent on the final level. Alternatively, it could be a constant percentage over the set number of levels. Although this pattern can vary from business to business, the aim is to ensure a total payout of royalty bonuses that can be built into a competitive retail price structure. Table 4.6 shows two typical royalty bonus structures.

Table 4.6   Examples of royalty bonus scales

Direct distributor downline	Royalty bonus paid to A on each sponsored direct distributor's PGV (%)	Direct distributor downline	Royalty bonus paid to A on each sponsored direct distributor's PGV (%)
A	Nil	A	Nil
B	5	B	4
C	4	C	4
D	3	D	4
E	2	E	4
F	1	F	Nil
Overall	1	Overall	Nil
Total payout	16	Total payout	16

There are other variations in the way in which royalty bonuses can be paid. Some involve a combination of payments on specific levels plus overall bonuses on groups of levels. This is the approach adopted by, among others, Amway. The overall effect with most NM DSOs is to pay out a total royalty bonus reward equivalent to approximately 16 per cent of the retail pound – although this varies from DSO to DSO.

Both the above systems have proved to be effective in motivational terms. It is simply a matter of choice. However, in both cases it is usual to treat the percentage bonus as a maximum, which is only payable on those PGVs that are equal to, or are in excess of, the qualifying sales volume for a direct distributor. For lower-value PGVs any of the percentage bonuses may be reduced in line with an agreed scale. Having said that, some DSOs either encourage or condone the transfer of monthly sales volume upline. This practice is given the term 'compression'. It has the effect of ensuring that any 'unused' sales volume beneath the 'payline' is used to ensure the qualifying sales volumes for royalty bonuses, at each level, are achieved. This 'compression' can be done in such a way that no individual is disadvantaged in terms of the benefits that they are entitled to receive from their own payline – that is, from the direct distributors immediately beneath them.

Total payout in an NM sales plan

Just to recap, an NM DSO rewards participants in three ways; a retail profit, a wholesale volume profit and a series of royalty bonuses. We have also seen some DSOs consolidate part of the wholesale volume profit into permanent higher levels of retail profit on their own sales when an individual's PGV has expanded to each of a number of appointment levels. Regardless of how an NM DSO devises its sales plan, the maximum total payout for DSOs marketing consumer goods is rarely more than 60 per cent. However, most NM DSOs pay out around 56 per cent of retail sales value, excluding VAT. The breakdown shown below is typical of many UK-based NM DSOs:

Retail profit	20%
Wholesale volume profit	20%
Royalty bonuses	16%
Total payout	56%

In this example, the total payout of 56 per cent is the theoretical maximum. In practice, particularly in the early stages of a new business, it is unlikely that this will be paid out in full. It will depend on the number of distributors who are 'front-line' to the DSO and the size of their downlines. The payout will also depend on the extent to which 'compression' is permitted. The decision on the total payout that a DSO can afford to make, depends on two factors; the competitive retail marketplace for similar products and the expectations of potential direct sellers. Direct sellers, quite naturally, tend to look for 'rich' sales plans. However, if a DSO decides to offer an exceptionally high payout, then this is usually only made possible by inflating the retail selling prices. This may be possible with an exceptional or unique market offer, but the risk is that the product will prove difficult to sell. An analysis of those NM DSOs that have failed in recent years, frequently shows that recommended retail prices were too high and that this competitive disadvantage was not offset by the potential rewards offered by the sales plan.

The basic concept of NM DSOs is that virtually all field salesforce management costs and many administrative support costs are delegated to independent distributors. A typical conventional, non-NM, DSO would offer a sales commission of 25 per cent on retail selling prices, excluding VAT. By deducting this commission from the average total payout of 56 per cent for a NM DSO, and assuming the same retail selling prices, then we are left with 31 per cent. With a non-NM DSO this proportion of the retail pound has to fund the corporate costs of running the field sales operation. For anyone considering setting up a DSO it is a vital exercise to cost out very carefully the two options. Other considerations in making this choice are dealt with in more detail in Chapter 5, 'Managing a direct salesforce'.

Hybrid sales plans

In the United States, in the early 1990s, a number of DSOs were formed which applied networking principles to the party plan sales method. These hybrid sales plans have proved to be remarkably successful.

Traditionally, party plan business, following the Tupperware model, were single-level DSOs. Although Tupperware is organized on a regional distributor basis, most of the other early party plan DSOs were managed centrally. A demonstrator would join the business with one objective in mind – to book and organize sales parties. Although there would be no ongoing rewards for recruiting, they would often be offered prizes for introducing other demonstrators to the business. Those who were successful, would later be offered the opportunity to become a local manager with the responsibility for recruiting, training and managing other demonstrators. The management of the DSO would decide who should be appointed to these field sales management positions. The lower levels of management would be self-employed appointments and there would be an expectation that they would continue to hold their own parties. In addition, they would be rewarded with overrides on the sales of those for whom they were made responsible. Commonly, the higher levels of field sales force management would be employees with basic salaries supplemented by sales performance overrides.

This is a structure which still works well in certain markets, but today, particularly in the United States, it is considered to be a little patronizing by those enterprising women seeking something more than just a selling occupation. The essence of a hybrid sales plan is the introduction of network marketing principles to a party plan DSO. In such a plan, from the day they join the business, a demonstrator has an interest in recruiting others as well as holding sales parties. The main difference between a hybrid plan and other NM DSOs, is that the financial rewards from recruiting are deferred until any individual has recruited a prescribed number of others, usually five or six, and until each has achieved a prescribed volume of sales over a given period, usually two months. Very often, the promotion to the first level of management, which carries with it ongoing sponsorship rewards, is also deferred until an individual has attended a training course in management skills. As with a NM DSO, all senior sales appointments are self-employed and self-appointed – appointments are not conferred by the DSO – they are earned on the basis of personal achievement. However, compared with a NM DSO, it is usual for anyone who has built up even the largest network of other demonstrators, to continue holding sales parties on their own account. At least a minimum commitment to personal sales is often a prerequisite for earning any overrides on a sales group as is, often, the requirement to maintain their own basic, first level, group of five or six demonstrators. The purpose behind this insistence on continued personal sales is that party plan selling is a disciplined approach which requires regular training. Hybrid DSOs have found that one way of ensuring this high standard of training is to ensure that every manager retains familiarity with the core skills of the business.

Figure 4.3 shows the typical field sales organization of a hybrid plan. In this figure, the various management positions are indicated by codes although, in practice, they would be given names such as branch, area or regional manager.

The qualification criteria for each level of management is similar to that in a NM DSO. The principal difference with a hybrid plan is in the M1 qualification, which is more prescriptive. This can also require, from the management of the DSO, a higher level of corporate commitment, and cost, allocated to training and motivation. It is for this reason that the total payout, in a hybrid plan, may be rather less than in other NM DSOs. The following is a typical payout, in commissions and overrides, in a hybrid plan based on three levels of field sales management.

Demonstrator commissions (retail profit)	25%
First level manager overrides	11%
Second level manager overrides	3%
Third level manager overrides	3%
Total payout	42%

It is likely that this type of sales plan will become increasingly popular in Europe for party plan DSOs based on a predominantly female sales force.

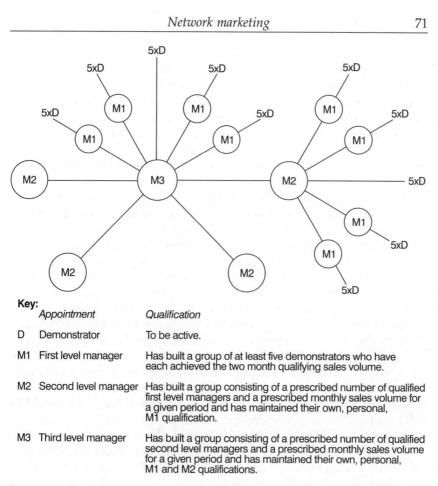

Key:

Appointment		*Qualification*
D	Demonstrator	To be active.
M1	First level manager	Has built a group of at least five demonstrators who have each achieved the two month qualifying sales volume.
M2	Second level manager	Has built a group consisting of a prescribed number of qualified first level managers and a prescribed monthly sales volume for a given period and has maintained their own, personal, M1 qualification.
M3	Third level manager	Has built a group consisting of a prescribed number of qualified second level managers and a prescribed monthly sales volume for a given period and has maintained their own, personal, M1 and M2 qualifications.

Figure 4.3   *Typical field sales organization with a hybrid sales plan*

Sales order values and earnings in network marketing

One of the appeals of NM to would-be participants is that no fixed commitments are demanded of them in terms of time and effort. It is designed to be a truly flexible low-cost business opportunity. There is an opportunity to build a substantial business and to earn an income that is comparable with anything available in salaried employment. Equally, the business has an appeal to someone who just wishes merely to supplement another source of income. For the NM DSO, the management obviously hope that all participants will pursue the maximum earnings opportunity, but they can afford to be equally relaxed about whatever level of commitment a participant decides to choose. No territories are allocated, business kits are rarely subsidized, participants pay up-front for the orders they have obtained. They are also usually required to pay delivery costs on small orders and there are none of the problems experienced by many conventional DSOs in administering credit accounts. Virtually the only fixed cost, associated with maintaining distributors' names on the DSO's records, is the print and postage costs of a regular newsletter. The net effect of this approach to running a DSO, is that the average level of activity of participants and their average order values tend to be lower than those with other types of DSO.

Most successful NM DSOs are based on encouraging every distributor to maintain a consistent, but not necessarily large volume of personal sales. Table 3.2 in Chapter 3 showed that the average annual sales of a direct seller in a NM DSO to be £1623 for 1995. This slightly overstates the true average volume of personal sales, as a number of DSOs record only the annual volumes of those direct sellers with whom they deal directly or whom they consider to be 'active'. The sales recorded for some of these account holders would include the sales of those, in their own personal groups, for whom they are responsible for order collection and product distribution. In 1995 a more accurate average annual sales volume would be nearer £1400. Assuming an average commission of 25 per cent and allowing for a proportion of sales accounted for by personal consumption, then the average earnings are little more than £320 per annum.

The low average earnings achieved by a direct seller in a typical NM DSO leads to the common criticism that DSOs exaggerate the earnings opportunities that are available. This is generally an unfair criticism. The opportunities are there, but it is left entirely to the individual to make a choice as to whether they wish to pursue them. It is a criticism that also discounts the fact that many participants choose to become involved simply as a way of obtaining certain goods at a discounted price. The criticism also discounts the effect of offering a business opportunity with low entry cost. Not having made a significant financial investment, it is all too easy for a participant to delay, sometimes indefinitely, the time at which they decide to start their business. It is not uncommon for an NM DSO to find that as many as 20 per cent of all the participants who sign up to join a business, never actually get around to making sales or attempting to sponsor others. It is for this reason that providing motivational support is of more importance to an NM DSO than to any other type of DSO. This function is dealt with in more detail in Chapter 5, 'Managing a direct salesforce'.

As we have seen in an earlier example, a committed part-time distributor like John Smith, within a few months of starting his business and with average personal sales of £200 per month and a regular personal group volume (PGV) of £3000 per month, could expect the following earnings:

Basic profit on his own personal sales:
20 per cent of £200, for, say, 10 months a year = £40 × 10 = £400

Net wholesale bonus earned on his PGV:
£200 (say, slightly less than the previous one-month example of £224.40) for 10 months a year = £200 × 10 = £2000

While very few distributors in NM DSOs would achieve personal sales in excess of £200 per month, the reward structure from building a substantial PGV, provides an additional incentive to at least maintain their own volume of personal sales. It works in this way. If a group leader has built a PGV which generates a wholesale profit bonus of 21 per cent, this means that he will earn an additional 21 per cent on his own personal sales. It is a part of the gross bonus that does not have to be paid out to anyone else. It is his additional income and would almost double the effective commission on his own personal sales. It is this flexibility of a NM sales plan that appeals to those who enjoy personal sales. Over twenty years ago, when Kleeneze still had in its sales organization a number of good and enthusiastic full-time personal sellers, this was one of the reasons for opting for network marketing in restructuring the sales plan.

In the above example of earnings from a typical distributor like John Smith, the rewards from building a small group are shown as £2000 per year – four times the income earned from personal sales. As a distributor expands his PGV so there will be an increase in the net income earned from his group – although not always in direct proportion to the increase in PGV sales. The reason for this is as follows.

However an NM DSO sales plan is structured, there might at first appear to be an advantage in building a large 'front line'. The reason is that if the PGV were large enough to earn the maximum wholesale volume profit, then the profit earned from those who had been sponsored into the 'front line' would not have to be shared with others. In practice, as with any human organization structure, it is not possible for any one individual to perform an effective job in guiding, training and motivating a group of more than ten others. In building a PGV it is better to maintain a 'front line' of around ten sponsored distributors and to devote any additional time available to encouraging them to do likewise. The objective in making the most of any NM sales plan is to maintain a PGV which earns the maximum wholesale profit and thereafter to aim to build

Table 4.7   Typical distributor earnings

	A new distributor	John Smith or Sally Jones	An established distributor
Total number of distributors in payline	4	12	1 000
Personal sales at RRP excl. VAT (p.a.)	£2 000	£2 000	£2 000
PGV sales (p.a.)	£8 000	£24 000	£30 000
Payline sales qualifying for royalty bonuses (p.a.)	Nil	Nil	£1.5 million
Retail profit at, say, 20 per cent on personal sales (p.a.)	£400	£400	£400
Profit at, say, 8 per cent on PGV sales (p.a.)	£640	£1920	£2400
Royalty bonuses at, say, 4 per cent on each level (p.a.)	Nil	Nil	£60 000
Total annual income (p.a.)	£1 040	£2 320	£62 800

a substantial income from royalty bonuses. As we have seen, these royalty bonuses are earned on sponsored distributors who have themselves each built up PGVs earning the maximum wholesale profit bonus. For a successful distributor in a NM DSO, with an extended downline, the bulk of their annual income would come from royalty bonuses.

Table 4.7 shows the typical incomes that could be expected to be earned from three different distributors. The first is someone who has recently started their business and has sponsored only four others. The second is someone like John Smith or Sally Jones, who have developed their business a little further. The third is a successful distributor whose business may have been been established for several years.

The examples in Table 4.7 are for a typical NM DSO and the proportion of income earned from PGVs and royalty bonuses may vary from business to business. Also, a payline of £1.5 million is by no means exceptional for an established NM DSO. For this reason many top distributors do earn in excess of £100 000 per annum, although they represent a small proportion of the total number of distributors in any NM DSO.

One common ingredient in the sales plans of all successful NM DSOs is the importance placed on personal sales by everyone in the business, whether they be an established distributor or someone who recently joined the DSO. Although the bulk of the rewards earned by the most successful distributors come from royalty bonuses, the business system is based on the cumulative result of every participant achieving and maintaining at least a modest volume of personal direct sales. Without a corporate field sales management team, it is the leading distributors who have to constantly emphasize this point and set an example to others.

A legitimate criticism of some NM DSOs is that they, or more frequently distributors with those businesses, often, at opportunity meetings, exaggerate the potential earnings that can be earned by anyone joining the business. An even more serious criticism is the claim that the greater part of this income is 'passive' income; that it comes from sponsoring other successful distributors who will go on producing a stream of income for the sponsor in return for having done little more than effecting an initial introduction. There are even claims that success in sponsoring can lead to the opportunity for early retirement. In short, the implication is that network marketing has some of the features of a lottery. If you sponsor enough people then the chances are that some of them will make you rich. It is these false claims that have contributed to a widespread and poor public image of network marketing. It is a problem that has been addressed in the drafting of the DSA's Code of Business Conduct. Enforcing this code is a high priority for the CEOs of reputable NM DSOs.

As I have shown, the proportion of those who do succeed in achieving a substantial income is small. Having said that, in any good NM DSO the opportunity to earn a substantial income is there. Furthermore, in practice it has been proved that it matters little at what stage in the NM DSO's development an enterprising participant joins the business. However, any analysis of the working patterns of the top earning distributors in ethical and well-established NM DSOs, clearly shows that their earnings are anything but 'passive'. Maintaining a downline of several thousand distributors demands considerable powers of organization and motiva-tion – as it would in any business. Apart from ensuring that every distributor maintains at least a minimum volume of personal sales, the entire organization requires constant motivation. This means not just motivating a small front-line group, but helping those with their own front-lines to do the same.

The opportunity to enjoy an early and comfortable retirement is equally illusory. Many NM DSOs, quite sensibly, demand that any benefits from sponsorship can be earned only if the sponsor maintains a minimum monthly volume of PGV sales. This reinforces the importance of personal sales and ensures that the sponsor keeps in touch with the business. It is therefore possible for a distributor who reaches retirement age to maintain a residual income, but a substantial retirement income would depend on everyone else in the sponsor's payline remaining fully motivated. For this reason, talk of early retirement presents another problem which is self-generating. The strength of network marketing is in encouraging others to replicate a pattern of doing business, in other words, for the sponsor to help others by saying 'do as I do'. If a sponsor were to announce that he or she was taking early retirement, then there would be a strong possibility that his front-line would be encouraged to do the same. If that pattern of intentions were further replicated, then the earnings from a payline would quickly degenerate.

Pyramid selling and potential abuses of network marketing

In PR terms the biggest problem faced by NM DSOs in the UK has been that of disassociating themselves from pyramid selling. Around the world, the term 'pyramid selling' is synonymous with schemes that are, at best, commercially unsound and, at worst, illegal. This is certainly the view of the general public. However, for over 20 years, from 1973 until a change in law in 1997, the British public had good reason to be confused. The reason for this confusion was that virtually every DSO in which a direct seller had an interest in introducing others was legally bound to comply with the Pyramid Selling Regulations.

The only similarity between a pyramid scheme and an NM DSO is that both offer an incentive to every new participant to introduce others. However, this incentive carries with it two principal opportunities for abuse. The first is the promotion of a scheme which, while it may offer rewards to the first participants, is commercially unsustainable. The characteristics of this type of pyramid scheme are, first, that rewards are offered to anyone who encourages another person to join the scheme, and to make a payment to the promoter of the scheme, in the expectation that they will receive other rewards from a subsequent series of similar introductions and payments to the promoter. The second characteristic is that the rewards offered under the scheme can only be paid out by using the income generated from the initial payments made by a steadily expanding pyramid of investors.

The second opportunity for abuse is in offering participants a quick and easy route to success, based on a substantial initial investment in stock. This is a practice which distinguishes an unsound scheme from any good DSO. The reason for the success of direct selling is that it is a business opportunity which demands no more than a very modest investment – rarely more than the cost of those products that are required for demonstration. There is no such thing as a 'quick fix' in direct selling. It is a business based on building a sales organization from the bottom up – not from the top down. 'Buying' a higher-level appointment in a distributorship structure, or purchasing large quantities of goods at a higher than normal discount, is not just bad practice, it is needlessly risky.

In an NM DSO all direct selling participants are encouraged to introduce others but they receive no rewards for the simple act of introduction – even if a new direct seller is required to purchase a business kit. The only rewards from introducing or sponsoring others come from the subsequent sale and consumption of consumer goods and services supplied by the DSO and where those rewards are earned by allocating, to commissions, a realistic proportion of the retail selling price of each one of the goods and services that have been sold to consumers.

The term 'pyramid' scheme first came into use in the United States in 1920 when Charles Ponzi started selling promissory notes offering a 50 per cent return within 90 days. For a few months he was able to honour these notes by using the revenue received from a rapidly growing number of investors. Possibly the first 'pyramid selling' scheme involving some sort of product was the Swastika Note Case scheme which initially was unsuccessfully prosecuted against in Britain in 1934. In an appeal to the High Court it was later ruled to be a fraud. In this scheme small leather note cases were sold through a network of participants who were offered commissions on downline sales on each unit sold that exceeded the selling price of the note case. Again, the rewards were paid out, for a short while, using the revenue generated from the number of participants entering the scheme, which grew, again for a few months, in an exponential pattern.

In the UK pyramid selling returned to the public's attention in the mid-1960s. At that time a number of schemes, for example Holiday Magic and others originating in the United States, were introduced into the UK. At first these business opportunities resembled NM DSOs in that they did offer consumer goods at suggested retail prices which, if perhaps a little on the high side, seemed realistic. At business opportunity meetings it was explained to would-be participants how they could benefit from the direct selling of the products on offer, and how they could also benefit from the sales of others they introduced to the scheme. The presentations at many of these meetings were no more than a straightforward explanation of the NM concept.

For many naive participants the abuse of the concept usually came in the form of a personal proposition put to the participants on an individual basis straight after the meeting. The proposition would have been made, by the promoter or another leading participant, in something like the following terms:

> 'Now I can see that you are just the sort of person who will do well in this business. In my experience I just know that someone like you will quickly attract a group of others and that you will build a substantial business in a very short time. For that reason, we are able to offer you a quick-start programme in which you are permitted to purchase straight away an amount of stock which will enable you to buy these goods at the maximum retail discount. The risk is very low, as I just know that you will be recovering your investment within a few days by supplying them to others you have introduced to the business. The advantage to you is that you will be benefiting from the maximum retail margin on all the sales you make, from your very first sale onwards. You will not have to wait until you have built up your group. Not only that, you will have the added advantage of gaining an immediate appointment as one of our direct distributors.'

Commonly this proposition was put to just about everyone who attended the opportunity meeting. Many fell for this line and the result was that garages and front rooms all over the country were filled with stock that most participants found they were unable to sell or to pass on to other participants. In some of the worst cases the promoters arranged for representatives of fringe banks, which were booming in the late 1960s, to be on hand at opportunity meetings to arrange second mortgages on the homes of those participants who were not able to pay cash for the suggested investments – which, at today's values, were often around £10 000. Virtually none of these early schemes offered participants any form of contract or guarantee that all or part of their investments in stock could be recovered. Those that did, had often failed before the participant could recover the sums they had paid out to the promoter.

It is hardly surprising that the government took action to deal with this growing problem. They did so in Part XI of the Fair Trading Act 1973. This Act made it an offence to offer rewards for the recruitment of participants into defined schemes, and provided regulations which discouraged imprudent investments; by limiting the maximum initial investment that could be made within the first seven days; specified certain contract terms; provided for buy-back rights and outlawed exaggerated earnings claims; and misleading advertisements. The Direct Selling Association, which was worried by the negative effect these schemes were having on the overall image of the industry, was consulted by the DTI and actively supported the new legislation. However the liability for NM DSOs was the name given by the government to the regulations – Pyramid Selling and Similar Trading Schemes Regulations. The practical effect of this was that all NM DSOs, including some non-direct selling franchises in which participants benefit from introducing others, have for over twenty years been required to abide by regulations bearing the pejorative label 'pyramid selling'.

This legislation was partially effective; it certainly controlled the worst problem of 'front-end loading' – the purchase of excessive amounts of stock in anticipation of future sales. However, the most serious weakness was that some schemes could be devised in such a way that they did not fall within the description of a regulated scheme. Regulated schemes were those that embodied certain features, one of which was that the promoter offered a product or service. If one of these features was missing, then the scheme was unregulated.

The most blatant examples of this loophole were 'money games' which did not involve a product, but where participants made regular payments to the promoter in the expectation of earning substantial sums from payments made by others they had introduced. Shortly after the opening up of Eastern Europe an outrageous pyramid scheme was started in Romania which defrauded millions of naive investors of their savings. This was followed in 1992 by an almost identical scheme in Russia, MMM, involving shares and bonds. Again this was targeted at naive and greedy investors at a time of uncontrolled capitalism. Both schemes differed little from the original Ponzi scheme. Many of the 'investors' knew perfectly well that the potential earnings were unsustainable, but thought that if they got in early enough, there would be some 'rich pickings' while it lasted. Between 1993 and 1996 a spate of similar schemes were started in Britain – FPW, Alchemy, Titan and many others. All exploited a basic weakness in the Fair Trading Act 1973. Given the weaknesses of this Act, and its supporting regulations, the government was forced to appeal to the courts that these money games should be closed down on the grounds that their continuing operation was against the public interest.

There were also other weaknesses in the legislation. Offering buy-back rights with no time limit had the effect of inducing a feeling of false security in the case of an unsound business which could fail at any time. The law was also unsatisfactory in that it implied that pyramid selling was not unlawful – merely that it was subject to regulation. Since 1990 the

Direct Selling Association has been in the forefront of a campaign to persuade the government to make further substantial changes to the law, both to overcome this confusion and to deal with the problem of money games. The DSA's aim was to bring the UK into line with the United States and some other countries, by defining and banning unsound practices and to label them pyramid selling schemes – and so separate them more clearly from NM DSOs. In the most recent new UK legislation, the Trading Schemes Act 1996, this has largely been achieved by widening the scope of the 1973 Act and through new and better Trading Schemes Regulations (see Appendix 2). However, although there is a strong case for the introduction of a more clearly understood pyramid selling offence, this has yet to be introduced.

Matrix, binary and other networking schemes

Apart from 'front-end loading', another problem that has tarnished the NM concept has been a persistent and widespread belief that all that is necessary to make a substantial income from an NM DSO, is to join a business in its early growth stage, recruit or sponsor a few others, and then just sit back and wait for the business to grow. The belief is that the built-in dynamics of the sales plan can somehow do the work for you. Any earnings opportunity which appears to offer a passive income, in return for no more than a token commitment in sponsoring a few others, has an obvious appeal. This is just the appeal of matrix schemes. Since 1990 dozens of magazines and subscription newsletters have appeared in circulation which are devoted to advertising the very latest NM opportunities. They have a special appeal to 'multi-level junkies' who are quite happy to try one scheme and, if it does not work, to move on to the next. Of course, with a product of doubtful value, with no commitment to using it oneself, and with no interest in selling or recommending it to others, the scheme certainly would not work. But to many it still seems worth a try.

Promoters of schemes designed to market consumer goods through direct sales have often tended to encourage this passive involvement by the use of a 'matrix' sales plan. In these plans they show, through a geometric progression, how with little effort, large numbers of people can be sponsored in a short space of time. These schemes are often described as in Table 4.8.

The extent to which you would benefit from the sales made at each of the various levels in your downline would be set out in the promoter's sales plan. It may be a fixed percentage over a given number of levels, or it may be a reducing percentage. Table 4.8 shows six levels and may be described by the promoter as a '4 wide–6 deep' matrix plan.

Table 4.8   A typical matrix sales plan

Action required	Total numbers from whom you benefit
You sponsor just 4 others	4
and they, in turn, each sponsor 4 others	16
and they, in turn, each sponsor 4 others	64
and they, in turn, each sponsor 4 others	256
and they, in turn, each sponsor 4 others	1024
and they, in turn, each sponsor 4 others	4096

To someone without any previous experience in direct selling or in managing and motivating others, it is easy to see why this type of plan could seem attractive. It is simple and seems to require only a modest level of involvement – just the sponsoring of four others. If it were a '2 wide' plan it would seem even simpler. The practical reality is that this type of scheme rarely, if ever, works or becomes a soundly based NM DSO. In some of the worst schemes, participants are offered the opportunity, by increasing their own payments to the promoter, to re-enter the matrix at a point at which they can double-up on their anticipated rewards from their downline. In Britain the life span of most matrix schemes has over the past few years been measured in months. The reason is quite simple. People are different and tend not to respond to any business opportunity in the same way. For example, even if the product or service on offer were marketable and fairly priced, not everyone is able or willing to sponsor a prescribed number of others. In a soundly based NM DSO, sponsorship patterns tend to vary widely. Some will be very successful in sponsoring, others less so.

If this point is put to the promoter of a matrix plan, then they may respond by saying that if any participant, at any level, is unable to sponsor the prescribed number of others, then their own sponsor could do so on their behalf. This betrays an unawareness of human nature. If someone offers to do something difficult on your behalf, then there is a natural tendency to let them go on doing so! When this starts to happen in a matrix scheme, it would soon end up with a few individuals attempting to do all the work in building a group. This would be impossible and the plan would fail. This also illustrates another vital ingredient for the success of an NM DSO. It is the integrity of a sponsorship relationship. Sponsorship differs from corporate recruitment in one fundamental way. It is a relationship between two individuals in which one person has taken the step of introducing to another, exactly the same business opportunity as their own. Thereafter it is not a matter of saying 'now do as I say', but is all about saying 'now try to follow me and do as I do'. At its best, sponsorship in the most successful NM DSOs leads to bonds of friendship, trust and gratitude that remain unbroken from the time of that first introduction. I mention this to explain why sponsoring on behalf of others can easily lead to resentment and impermanent relationships. This is an aspect of motivation that I shall deal with in more detail in the next chapter.

'Binary' sales plans are another group of 'simplified' networking schemes. In a binary plan, the aim is to do no more than sponsor two others, to encourage them both to make personal sales and sponsor two others and to replicate this pattern in an endless chain of sponsorship (see Figure 4.4).

In many of these schemes, in addition to retailing profits, participants are offered rewards for specified sales achievements that are duplicated in both sides or 'the left- and right-hand legs' of their group. Furthermore, these rewards may be offered throughout an infinite payline. It is a scheme that seems at first disarmingly simple, even though, if there is

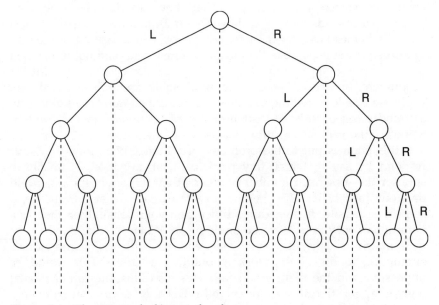

Figure 4.4   *The pattern of a binary sales plan*

activity only in one leg, then no reward is paid out. In practice, such duplication is not easy to achieve. As with a matrix scheme, any binary plan demands an artificial pattern of sponsorship and has exactly the same basic weaknesses. Many of these binary plans also offer the opportunity for participants to re-enter their own downline in the hope of 'gearing up' their rewards from sponsorship.

An even more unattractive feature of some binary plans, is that some promoters offer bonuses on incremental sales that exceed the sales revenue of those sales. They feel able to do so on the basis that a significant proportion of total sales, i.e. that represented by the sales of participants who are unable to recruit others in the required pattern, will attract no liability for bonus payments. Any networking scheme that offers bonuses on incremental downline sales that exceed a reasonable proportion of those sales is flawed. Whether such a structure is likely to form the basis of a sustainable business is, as yet, unproven.

In addition to matrix and binary plans there are many other variations of simplified networking sales plans. Uni-level and 2-up plans are two examples. While businesses based on simplified plans have traded relatively successfully for several years, there is no evidence as yet, that they can form the basis of a sound and substantial NM DSO.

What has served to further discredit matrix and other simpified networking plans, has been their use by the promoters of a variety of pyramid schemes. During the 1980s and 1990s countless schemes were promoted in the UK involving a grossly overpriced product or subscription to a publication or some other service. The attraction was that the rewards from recruiting others, more than compensated for a participant's own regular contributions. Some schemes involved regular monthly payments to a promoter who offered the prospect, to any participant who was able to recruit a certain number of others, of leasing a motor-car on a monthly rental that was well below normal commercial leasing rates. All of these schemes were based on matrix plans, as they appeared to offer participants the minimum level of personal commitment to recruiting. As with the original Ponzi scheme, none were sustainable businesses, as they required for their survival a constantly growing number of new participants.

Even under the UK government's 1996 revision of the Fair Trading Act, and the supporting Trading Schemes Regulations, the continued operation of matrix schemes may not be illegal – unless the rewards are offered simply as the result of recruiting participants. However, such schemes, despite their apparent simplicity, cannot be recommended as the basis for direct selling businesses based on the sound network marketing principles that have been described earlier in this chapter.

Key points

- Network marketing is a method of organizing a DSO. It is not an alternative to direct selling. Any NM DSO that is not based on good direct selling principles in retailing products to consumers, is likely to fail.
- The success of network marketing is largely due to the ability of the structure to enfranchise those direct sellers with good organizing abilities and to enable them to be fairly rewarded for their achievements.
- Most successful NM DSOs are based on the principle of personal recommendation of a product or service.
- Network marketing is not suited to marketing big-ticket product lines.
- In creating a sales plan for an NM DSO, an easily replicable selling method has more lasting appeal than the potential payout, in terms of discounts, bonuses and royalties.
- Any NM DSO that offers a payout of more than 60 per cent of the RRP of the products on offer, is likely to be uncompetitive in relation to retail competition.
- An NM sales plan is flexible to the extent that it is able to fairly reward high personal sales, in addition to building a group of other direct sellers.
- The most serious abuses of network marketing are practices whereby participants are encouraged, or even permitted, to take 'short cuts' to higher discount or bonus levels by investing in stocks of product in advance of making sales to consumers or recruiting others.
- Although simplified networking plans have an obvious appeal, the most successful NM DSOs are based on rewards from three sources; retail profits, wholesale volume profits and a series of royalty bonuses.

5

Managing a direct salesforce

The principal trading asset of a DSO is its salesforce. In comparison with any consumer goods business, marketing its products through conventional retail stores, a DSO is totally dependent on its salesforce to provide its 'shop window', its advertising medium and its retail and distribution outlets. A substantial part of the total assets of high street or out-of-town retailers are in property; not only the fabric of the stores, but also their location. Of course, to retailers, a reputation for quality and service is vitally important, but stores in prime sites can, mainly through their location, generate a guaranteed volume of prospective customers. This assured 'footfall', from the time the store opens until it closes in the evening, determines to a large extent their volume of trade. DSOs, by contrast, have no such assurance. If an established DSO, with a fine and well-known brand name and with well-priced and marketable products, loses its salesforce, it has lost its business – instantly. Even those DSOs with loyal customers for repeat purchases have no practical alternative to serving those customers without a salesforce. For most DSOs this vital but predominantly self-employed and therefore independent asset is composed mainly of a large number of people, each of whose working commitment is part-time and whose financial commitment and risk is small. Each night this human asset goes home to bed, with the DSO hoping that the following morning they will wake up with renewed enthusiasm for their own small business. Managing a DSO in anything other than an economic climate in which no other jobs are available, requires exceptional skills in management, recruiting, training and motivating this asset. This chapter deals with each of these key functions. As a separate aspect of motivation, I shall also consider salesforce communications and recognition programmes.

Managing direct sellers

With the exception of NM DSOs, managing the field salesforce of a DSO requires much the same organizational structure as any commercial operation set up to sell the company's products. Apart from high-ticket DSOs, where the recruitment and initial training of direct sellers is usually a central management function, low-ticket DSOs usually make these functions the responsibility of field sales management. This is logical, given the low level of commitment required and the inherently high turnover rates of direct sellers. In a company such as Avon Cosmetics, where a manager may be responsible for several hundred representatives, a very high proportion of field management time is spent on recruitment, although they are also responsible for local training and motivation.

Direct selling is a numbers business. The management skills required are not just in maintaining numbers of direct sellers – that is relatively easy. The essential skills are in maintaining the number of presentations made by those direct sellers every week. With good products and a well-thought-out sales plan, sales volume can be in predictable proportion to the number of presentations made.

Single-level party plan DSOs, for reasons that have been explained in Chapter 3, demand a higher level of commitment than most other DSOs. Every party plan demonstrator has to be trained and motivated to hold at least one party a week and to aim to book at least two parties a week. This imbalance allows for the fact that between 20 per cent and 50 per cent of all parties booked are likely to be cancelled. Apart from training in how to organize parties, and in how to demonstrate the goods, they have to learn that the first priority in holding a party is to book other parties and that this is best done at a party. If every party held does not yield the booking of at least one other party then the business will not expand. If, over a period, the ratio of parties booked to parties held, is in excess of 1.5, then that is the best indication that the business will expand. It is more important than attempting to influence average party sales values. With conventional single-level party plan businesses, it is much easier than with most other DSOs to predict future sales. A common sales management discipline is to encourage every demonstrator to maintain a permanent 'string' of at least six future party bookings. If these bookings are reported to a manager, then the data it provides are a clear and reliable indication of future business. SLM party plan DSOs find that it needs one local manager to supervise and maintain a team of ten demonstrators. This management function is usually performed by an experienced self-employed demonstrator, who is rewarded in the form of commissions on the sales of his or her team, in addition to the rewards from holding parties on their own account. Training and motivating first-level area managers is usually the responsibility of regional managers in the ratio of 1:4 to 1:6. These regional managers are also usually self-employed and are rewarded by overriding commissions on the total sales of demonstrators in their region.

The basic concept of an NM DSO is that the DSO delegates to everyone, from the day they join the business, the responsibilities for managing, training and motivating others. To some extent this is a self-adjusting formula. While an NM DSO may not prescribe the number of participants that any individual may sponsor into their own front line, it is difficult for any individual, particularly if their involvement is part-time, to perform an adequate management function for a group of more than ten others. If they sponsor any more than that number into their front line, then the chances are that more will quit the business for lack of regular help and encouragement. The best advice that the NM DSO can offer is that group leaders use any extra time they have available to help and encourage a small team to develop their own sponsorship lines.

Recruiting direct sellers

The current working population in the UK is 22 million. This includes 3.2 million full-time self-employed. In addition, although not accounted for in official government statistics, it is estimated that 1.8 million have part-time self-employed earnings occupations, the majority of which are in addition to other paid employment. While big-ticket DSOs do recruit full-time direct sellers from the ranks of the unemployed, it is those seeking part-time occupations that represent the main recruitment market for DSOs. The DSA's 1996 annual survey of all UK DSOs showed that the total number of independent direct sellers was 400 000. This indicates that direct selling currently accounts for 26 per cent of all part-time self-employed occupations. Although this may seem a high proportion, it should be seen in the context of the growing number of people in employment who are now looking for ways of supplementing their incomes. At present this proportion is under 10 per cent, but with changing work patterns it is certain to increase.

Within this growing market for part-time occupations, those that choose to work with a DSO make that choice for a variety of reasons and they are not all to do with the need for an extra income. Neil Offen, the president of the US DSA which accounts for 200 substantial DSOs and annual sales of almost $18 billion in 1995 has recently analysed the reasons why people are attracted to direct selling occupations in the

United States. This motivational pattern is almost identical in the UK and the following analysis is based on the categories that Offen has identified in the United States:

1 *Short-term goal seekers*. These are people who have a specific objective in mind. For example, a woman may decide to join a DSO in the autumn with the specific aim of earning sufficient cash to pay for her family's Christmas presents. Another may be someone who wishes to make a specific purchase; a holiday, an expensive household appliance or even to pay the airfares to visit a relation living on the other side of the world. This group may also include those who wish to raise money for a charity. For these people this goal may be a one-off objective or it may be repeated year after year.

2 *The underpaid*. These are those people who are employed, but whose income does not match their desired expenditure. They may not be able or even wish to change their jobs, but have sufficient spare time to use for some other earnings opportunity which to become involved does not demand a significant financial outlay. This would also include those who have retired on inadequate pensions and who feel that they still have the energy for a part-time occupation.

3 *Career direct sellers*. These are those for whom direct selling is their prime source of income. It is an occupation that appeals to them and one in which they are prepared to devote anything from 40 to 80 hours a week. They are people who are particularly attracted to the concept of being rewarded in direct relation to what they have achieved. In the United States, as in Britain, these people account for little more than 5 per cent of the total numbers involved in direct selling, although, both directly and indirectly in organizing groups of others, they can account for up to 80 per cent of a DSO's sales revenue. This category is of particular appeal to women who are able to match, without any gender prejudice, the earnings of men. This category includes students who during the summer months look to direct selling as a source of funds to support their college education and as a valuable addition to their CVs. In the United States this is a long-established practice, and it is only recently that DSOs in the UK have recognized this potential source of highly motivated direct sellers.

4 *Recognition seekers*. Women, particularly those who have spent many years running the family home and bringing up children, have good reason to feel that they have not received the recognition they deserve. This category therefore includes those women for whom direct selling offers an ideal opportunity to return to work on terms that suit their family commitments. It also includes men who, despite many years of

conscientious employment, may never have received any recognition, on stage, in front of others, for a job well done.

5 *Product enthusiasts.* Successful DSOs tend to be those that concentrate on the marketing of quality and often novel products that are not readily available in retail stores. This feature attracts some individuals who have a passionate personal belief in the products and a desire to introduce the benefits of these products to others. Frequently, this may represent more of a motivation than the desire to make money. This category may represent only a small proportion of the salesforce of any DSO, but they are of huge value to the business as a whole.

6 *Discount seekers.* This category is represented by those enthusiasts for the products of a DSO whose main purpose in joining the salesforce is to gain the opportunity of purchasing the products at the discounted rate available to participants. This may include those whose original purpose in joining the DSO was to earn a part-time income but who, for a variety of reasons, may have ceased being active direct sellers. Their wish to remain with the business is based on their continued enthusiasm for the product and to have the opportunity to communicate that enthusiasm to others.

7 *The unemployed.* In the United States and in most EU member states direct sales does not today represent a particularly good earnings opportunity for the unemployed. This is for two reasons. The first is that the sales plans of most DSOs are based on offering part-time occupations to new participants. Although these opportunities can, over a period of time, be built up to be a source of full-time income this is rarely a practical option for someone seeking an immediate full-time income. The second reason is that most of today's sales plans are based on introducing the DSO's products and the business itself to their peer groups. For many of the unemployed, particularly in the lower social groups, this can represent a problem. There are, of course, exceptions. One of these is that group made up of the 'white-collar' unemployed, and those experienced managers faced with redundancy or enforced early retirement, who can sustain themselves while they build up a business, and whose peer groups still represent useful contacts. Another exception, although outside the UK, is that represented by many of the new market economies in Eastern Europe where Western standards of retailing have yet to be developed. Multinational DSOs are currently having great success in recruiting highly qualified and enterprising professional people who are finding it difficult to get jobs with incomes that can match those available from direct selling.

In planning a recruitment strategy, or in training NM distributors how to sponsor others, it is important to recognize the potential of all these groups. Just as any good marketer must segment the market according to different customer needs, NM DSOs and their distributors must recognize the potential of all these groups. DSOs should adapt their sales plans to meet their needs.

Most non-NM DSOs recruit direct sellers by placing classified advertisements in the 'Business Opportunities' sections of local newspapers. The Code of the Advertising Standards Authority, and local newspaper policy, usually prevents these ads appearing in the 'Situations Vacant' columns. Placing these ads and responding to the enquiries is usually the responsibility of local field sales management who themselves, may be either employed or self-employed.

Recruiting part-time direct sellers with press campaigns organized centrally by a DSO is rarely practical, mainly because it is difficult and costly to respond quickly and to arrange a personal visit to the applicant to answer the inevitable questions that are raised. This is equally true with regional TV recruitment ads. Corporate recruitment ads, in support of a sales plan which is based on providing in-built incentives to direct sellers to recruit others, can also lead to two further problems. The first is the problem of being seen to be fair in the distribution of leads: the second is the risk of weakening the resolve of direct sellers in establishing their own contacts and of becoming too dependent on the DSO for leads.

The most effective recruiting technique is by referral or by personal recommendation. Party plan DSOs rely heavily on finding recruits from among those who have attended a sales party; particularly those who appear to have enjoyed the occasion and who may have indicated an interest to the demonstrator in having a need for a part-time occupation. Most non-NM DSOs offer some sort of incentive to all their direct sellers to recommend others who they feel may be interested in the opportunity. For those who join, the reward to the person who made the recommendation may be a small cash bonus or a gift.

Whatever form it takes, salesforce recruitment, including both the cost of media advertisements and time spent in interviewing applicants, represents a major cost item in the budgets of non-NM DSOs and can account for up to 10 per cent of gross sales revenues. The nature of direct selling in that it is based on part-time activity is such that a high turnover rate of direct sellers has been considered to be an inherent feature of the business in even the best-managed DSOs.

The average turnover rate in the UK exceeds 100 per cent per annum. The same is true in the United States (Biggert, 1989). The cost of this turnover is not only that incurred in recruitment costs, but also the intangible costs of possible consumer dissatisfaction caused by the loss of their direct seller contact. Constantly looking for ways of reducing this wastage is top priority for every well-run DSO. From studies carried out in the United States (Wotruba and Tyagi, 1991–1993) the suggestion was that low met expectations, poor job image, and inadequate job satisfaction produced a tendency to quit, leading to turnover. More recent work in Europe (Brodie, 1995), focusing on the UK and France, supported this hypothesis and suggested that the primary factors influencing the decision to quit related to 'work hours', 'operating costs and expenses', 'prestige of the job in the eyes of the family and friends' and 'rejection by prospects'. Research work by Brodie, at the University of Westminster, involves the creation of a model of movements 'in' and 'out' of DSOs.

Reducing salesforce turnover rates is a high-priority task for all DSOs. Finding methods of doing so requires meticulous research. In 1996, the DSA encouraged the first of a series of collaborative projects, involving both academics and its member companies, with the aim of producing guidance on how to reduce salesforce turnover.

Table 5.1 shows, for 1995, the average annual attrition rates for various types of DSO in the UK. This analysis shows that apart from big ticket direct sales, which demand a high level of sales activity, the highest turnover rate is with party plan businesses. The main reason for this is that many party plan DSOs either rent or make a loan of a sales kit to demonstrators and subsidize this investment. In these circumstances it is not unreasonable for the DSO to demand a certain level of commitment. If a demonstrator does not choose to be sufficiently active, then it is common for the kit to be withdrawn and the demonstrator agreement terminated. By contrast, the lowest turnover appears to be with NM DSOs. The explanation is that an NM DSO makes virtually no financial

Table 5.1 Recruiting activity needed to sustain a DSO

DSO type	Annual number of recruits needed to maintain a part-time salesforce of 100 direct sellers
Big ticket – person to person	432
Low ticket – person to person	119
Low ticket – party plan	130
Network marketing	110

Source: Direct Selling Association

investment in participants, neither do they have territories which need be reallocated. For this reason there is no need for the DSO to terminate any direct seller unless they become so inactive as to make even the mailing of a periodical newsletter uneconomic.

A constant turnover of salespeople is a fact of life that has to be accepted by the management of any DSO and by those distributors who are responsible for their own recruitment. Although every effort should be made to keep this turnover rate to a minimum, it is unrealistic to expect that every new participant will either find the occupation to their liking, or be able to maintain their commitment. The first management challenge is to ensure that each new direct seller does at least give the business opportunity a chance to prove itself. It is a sad fact that a high proportion of those who take up a direct selling opportunity, never get around to starting their own small business. With NM DSOs this proportion can be as high as 20 per cent. The reason is usually fear of the unknown or fear of rejection, and this problem is dealt with later in this chapter in the section on training.

For whatever reason a direct seller decides to quit, it should be a high priority for a well-managed DSO to try to ensure that the parting takes place on good terms. This is as true for a direct seller, who has been with the DSO for some years, as it is for an individual who was only active for a short time – or who perhaps never became active. In each case it is important to remember that the individual at one time made a decision to start a business of their own, and in doing so made an investment in that opportunity. In practice, it is very difficult to know exactly why any individual did not pursue the opportunity. It may have been because it was too socially demanding; or that they were unsuccessful; or that changed family commitments made it impossible for them to pursue a part-time occupation.

Whatever the reason, it is in the DSO's best interests to ensure that every individual who quits does so feeling good about themselves and good about the business in which they have been associated. The DSO's best interests are these: that the individual remains a positive ambassador for the business and that they remain enthusiastic consumers of the DSO's products. The UK direct selling industry as a whole recruits, and loses, over 400 000 direct sellers every year. Inevitably, many will be in a position to influence others who may be considering taking up a similar occupation. It is much better in recounting their own experiences that former direct sellers give positive reasons for ceasing their own involvement. One good sales management approach is for the CEO, or sales director of the DSO, to write to everyone leaving the business, thanking them for their contribution and making it easy for them to return – should they ever wish to do so. Encouraging former direct sellers to remain enthusiastic users of the product is something that Amway, for example, do very well by offering membership of the 'Connexions Club' which has a range of special offers.

Some other sound reasons why it is so important for DSOs to retain good relationships with their former direct sellers are highlighted in a market research study carried out in 1996 by Wirthlin Worldwide for the US DSA. This survey showed that while 43 per cent of the public have positive views of direct selling as a distribution channel, three out of every four Americans have, to some extent, negative views about direct selling as an occupation. Interestingly, this public attitude has changed little from those expressed in a similar Harris poll conducted in 1976. However, a strong positive survey finding was that those who had experience of direct selling were far more positive than those who had not. The recent survey showed that 4 per cent of all adults were currently involved with a DSO and that 14 per cent of the population reported previous experience as a direct seller. The overall findings showed that negative attitudes to direct selling were inversely proportional to experience as a direct seller. The latest survey showed that 41 per cent of those who had no previous experience had, at some time been approached to become a direct seller and that only 6 per cent of those who had been approached expressed any likelihood of their becoming involved in direct selling. However, those who do become involved find the experience agreeable for a variety of reasons and 93 per cent of current direct sellers expressed positive views about the chances of their continuing. Over half of all current direct sellers in the United States became involved because of a recommendation from a relative, a close friend or an acquaintance.

In 1996 a BMRB/Mintel survey on public attitudes to network marketing in the UK showed that 2 per cent of all adults were currently involved in direct selling, half the number reported as being involved in the United States, and that a further 8 per cent had been involved at some time in the past.

Both the UK and US research findings reinforce the need for ensuring that all those who leave a DSO remain positive ambassadors for the business when, and for whatever reason, they cease their involvement.

One of the most effective recruitment techniques is for one direct seller to have an ongoing incentive to share the opportunity with others. This is the essence of network marketing. With a NM DSO it is often suggested to participants that they start their business in a very small way and then go on and build it up at a pace with which they feel comfortable. This introduction to direct selling put across by someone just like themselves who may be a friend or an acquaintance and who is doing exactly the same thing, can often be less intimidating, particularly if the friend is also new to the business and not yet totally familiar with the intricacies of the sales plan. It can be an easier recruitment task than that required of a manager in a non-NM DSO following up leads from an advertisement.

The essence of direct selling is that instead of advertising, a direct seller gives a 'live commercial' for the DSO's products. The same is true for 'selling' the business opportunity. Advertising is the least effective method of recruitment and this is one of the reasons why NM DSOs generally discourage participants from attempting to sponsor others by advertising. Apart from negating the basic principle of 'networking' within an expanding number of circles of personal contacts, the cost of doing so can needlessly dissipate the profits to be earned from sponsorship. There are at least two other risks.

The first is that if a distributor in a NM DSO advertises, then it could convey the message that advertising, despite what it may say in the DSO's sales manual, really is the established way of building a network. The obvious cost involved in having to advertise can have the effect of deterring others from becoming involved. The only people who might see this method of sponsorship as being an advantage are those who are either unable or unwilling to pursue personal contacts and see advertising as the soft option. In practice these are the very people who are unlikely to succeed in any DSO. It is a group that is well represented by those 'MLM junkies' who purchase or rent mailing lists in a vain attempt to build a business by direct mail.

There is another big risk in encouraging distributors in an NM DSO to advertise the opportunity in the local press. It is that a proliferation of advertisements, placed by different distributors, can all too easily convey the false impression to a potential applicant that the business is already overcrowded. This method of recruitment tends to fuel the widespread misconception that unless you become involved in a NM DSO, in its early growth stage, then your prospects of achieving a useful income are limited. That this is just not true for a soundly based NM DSO is borne out by the fact that in 1995 among the most successful distributors with NM DSOs in the UK are those who joined Amway not at the beginning but fifteen years after the business commenced trading in the UK. That this DSO recognizes that the most effective way of building a business is by personal contact is the fact that rarely, if ever, do Amway distributors advertise the business opportunity.

Another good reason why DSOs should discourage non-corporate advertising as a recruiting technique, is that the most effective marketing plans are those that are based on sales and recruitment techniques that are capable of being duplicated, at a modest cost, by every new participant. This applies to both the method of achieving retail sales and the methods by which new participants are introduced to the business. It is true for every DSO, but particularly so for NM DSOs. This does not mean that special sales and recruitment methods cannot be used from time to time; it simply means that a DSO should develop, test and prove standard methods that can be relied upon and easily duplicated. Advertising for recruits in a NM DSO cannot be duplicated for the reasons I have explained. The same is true for business opportunity meetings held in expensive hotels. Occasionally, a professionally run opportunity meeting organized by a senior distributor can help the sponsoring efforts of a new participant in a NM DSO. If, however, that new participant gets the impression that the only way to convince others of the merits of the opportunity is to duplicate that expense, then the likelihood is that they will very quickly become discouraged.

However a DSO is structured, the keys to its commercial success are an attractive and marketable range of products and an ability to recruit direct sellers – the retail outlets of the DSO. Of the two, the latter represents the biggest challenge to the management of a DSO; ensuring that those in whom the responsibility for recruitment is invested do so in the right way. This means providing them with a proven formula for developing their businesses.

Many of the entrepreneurs who have set up NM DSOs in the UK over the past ten years opted for the NM structure for the wrong reasons. They did so on the basis of what appeared to be a very modest requirement for working capital. There is no requirement for a salaried field salesforce and both distributors and front-line direct sellers pay up-front for their orders. Furthermore, many of the sales support and distribution responsibilities are provided by independent distributors within the terms of an NM sales plan. And yet, a high proportion of these entrepreneurs failed. The main reason for these failures was a total lack of appreciation of the risks involved in delegating to others the total responsibility for recruitment and the managing of a sales organization.

In a conventional DSO, that is one in which the salesforce is managed either by employees or self-employed distributors who are given territorial rights and other concessions, it is possible to control recruitment, the geographic spread of the business and, to some extent, sales volume. The problem is that it is expensive, and there is no guarantee that a 'managed' sales organization will be successful – or profitable. Bob King, a former CEO of two major multinational US DSOs, puts it this way: 'If you wish to control every single aspect of a DSO, then it is possible to design such a sales organization. This way you will have the business run exactly as you wish – for the brief period before it goes bust.' The point he makes is that for the majority of DSOs, no matter whether the business is a conventional 'single-level' DSO or a NM DSO, the selling function is the responsibility of independent self-employed direct sellers. In a NM DSO this responsibility extends to recruitment and motivation. Their success depends on giving a certain amount of 'free rein' to those who are prepared to use their entrepreneurial skills. At the same time, the DSO has to ensure that all direct sellers do their business in a way which conforms to clearly laid-down general rules which should be fair and reasonable, and that every new participant is properly trained.

Training direct sellers

In managing the salesforce of any DSO, there are three quite distinct training tasks: how to sell the products; how a direct seller should manage their own business and promote it to others; and, finally, how those with an opportunity to build a group of other direct sellers can best motivate them to succeed. Training responsibilities can be delegated, but for a DSO to abdicate complete responsibility to an independent salesforce for any of these tasks is a recipe for commercial disaster. The only training task in which it is sensible to permit any significant measure of free expression by independent direct sellers in creating training programmes is that of motivation. This is dealt with in the final section of this chapter. Let me deal first with product sales training.

Before it commences trading, every DSO should have researched and tested a selling method that has been proved to be successful. A typical new recruit to a DSO, who may have never before sold anything to anyone, will want to know which is the best way of going about the task of selling. For big-ticket DSOs this management commitment to training is an essential and substantial investment. For low-ticket sales the task is easier, but one which still requires meticulous attention to detail in ensuring that the method is understood by every new direct seller. Offering several optional selling methods without adequate training, such as saying that the new recruit could use personal one-to-one sales or party sales, is risky. If proven to be possible, and if training is provided, that is fine; if not, it can all too often be interpreted as being a sign of weakness in the management of the business. These new direct sellers may well be inclined to say; 'I have only a few hours available each week, so please show me the best method of achieving sales'. That method therefore should be as simple as possible.

The other reason why a DSO should dictate and monitor the way in which their products are sold, is that direct selling in the UK and in most countries, is subject to statutory regulation and industry codes of practice. In the UK these regulations and codes are set out in Appendices 2–4. They cover the way goods are sold, the times at which cold calls are acceptable, product claims and the provision to customers of order-cancellation rights. In the case of credit transactions there are further responsibilities required under the Consumer Credit Act. These regulations and codes are not onerous, but non-compliance can have serious financial and negative PR consequences for a DSO.

Low-ticket person-to-person DSOs, as we have seen earlier, have developed the simplest selling techniques which can be explained in a few minutes. Wearing or using a product in such a way that it invites interest is one approach, as is a system based on delivering catalogues with the proven expectation of receiving a certain proportion of orders when the catalogues are collected. Some NM DSOs marketing their own brand of regularly used household and personal products have a sales strategy based on encouraging self-use by their direct sellers and suggesting that they should simply ask prospective customers to switch brands for a while. If a direct seller does use the product to the point where they have developed their own positive enthusiasm, then this process of suggestion becomes quite natural. The direct seller need hardly think of having to sell. Sales become the natural outcome of shared enthusiasm. It is for this reason that successful NM DSOs devote substantial effort to 'selling' the product benefits to their salesforce and not looking upon them as an intermediary in the selling process. Yet another approach is based on lending samples of a product to prospective customers in the expectation that when the sample is collected the product will have sold itself to a certain proportion of those prospects. No matter how simple the selling method may be, it needs to be tested and the DSO needs to develop a reliable system by which they can guarantee that it is understood by every new direct seller.

Party plan sales training is more demanding. It is a selling process that requires careful training in every stage of the process: finding a hostess, helping her to invite guests and to organize the event, how to introduce the DSO to the guests, preparing a product display, making product demonstrations, how to collect orders and how to book further demonstrations. Expecting even the most extrovert direct seller to make an effective demonstration on the basis of a verbal explanation, or by being asked to refer to a sales manual, is unreasonable. Successful DSOs, based on party plan or group demonstration techniques, put great emphasis on regular training sessions and also in giving new direct sellers the opportunity to do their first demonstration with some supervision or assistance. Thirty years ago the early success of Tupperware was, to a large extent, based on their emphasis on weekly morning meetings, at which every demonstrator was expected to attend. This was an opportunity for those who had achieved successful parties to tell others in the team how they had done it. Such an event is motivational, but also valuable in training terms. It is a system still used by big-ticket DSOs with full-time direct sellers. However, in the 1990s, with an increased proportion of party demonstrators having other daytime jobs, it is not practical to expect every direct seller to attend regular daytime meetings. For this reason party plan DSOs now have to devise more flexible meeting programmes which may often include role-playing sessions. A simple guide for a party plan demonstrator in how to run a party is shown in Appendix 7.

In the direct selling industry big ticket, as I have earlier defined it, is an expression used in a business where the average order value exceeds £75. For the industry as a whole, as I have shown earlier, the average order value is under £20, which means that as a method of marketing it is most successful with low-ticket transactions. The reason is simply that there is no requirement for professional selling skills. However, training in these skills is essential in making any sale that exceeds the value of an impulse purchase. DSOs have shown that virtually anyone, with a modest level of commitment, can be trained in these skills, but it is rarely possible to do so in less than two weeks. Even if the direct seller receives no payment during their training period it is, for the DSO, a substantial investment in management time and resources. Encyclopaedia Britannica provides all new recruits with a six-day sales training course. At the end of that initial training, those who survive the course, are judged to be competent to receive orders, although not sufficiently competent to deal with all the challenges they can expect in the field; these skills are learned in supervised sales calls over a further period of two months. In the United States the Southwestern Company, whose method of selling books is described in Chapter 3, provides all recruits with a two-week residential sales training course. Those who pass this course go off to various parts of the country in groups, each under the supervision of another more experienced student, who is able to continue the training process. This DSO has now started, trading in the UK with an identical direct selling format and with products designed for the British market.

The second aspect of training is in how to run a small business. Even if a direct seller's function is to do no more than sell products on a part-time basis, they are, as independent contractors, in business for themselves. This means that there is a need for some basic training in managing their own accounts and in how best to separate their sales income and associated costs from their domestic accounts. Responsible DSOs also provide direct sellers with advice on their responsibilities with regard to income tax declarations. This information can usually be provided by a well-prepared manual and by advice provided by field sales managers. Where a direct seller's business opportunity extends to recruiting and training others, then the task is more complicated and is one which a responsible DSO has to remain accountable. The Trading Schemes Regulations, which in 1996 replaced the earlier Pyramid Selling Regulations, apply to any DSO where there is an opportunity to recruit others. As with the regulations governing the selling of goods, some of the Trading Schemes Regulations, such as Statutory Warnings and the provision of contracts, are the direct responsibility of the DSO in ensuring that direct sellers are provided with the correct paperwork. However, others, such as local advertising and the maximum size of initial investments in a business opportunity, may be delegated to those direct sellers wishing to build a group of other direct sellers. For this reason it is vital that a DSO takes all reasonable steps to ensure that all new direct sellers are aware of their responsibilities.

Comprehensive training manuals and company-sponsored training meetings are the only way that this can be achieved. In NM DSOs it is common for responsible DSOs to invite those who have achieved a certain level in the business to attend an extended business development meeting – perhaps over a weekend. Apart from receiving training in motivating and managing others, it is a good opportunity to emphasize further their legal responsibilities.

Motivation

The key to the long-term success of any DSO is the ability of a company to motivate its self-employed salesforce. The graveyard of failed DSOs contains many that had first-class and competitively priced product ranges, together with sales plans that offered fine income-earnings opportunities. They failed for one simple reason: an inability to motivate their direct sellers. In essence, this means that, having recruited an individual, the DSO needs to maintain that initial enthusiasm and help the individual overcome all the setbacks and disappointments that come with any small business opportunity. As a business opportunity the great strength of that offered by most DSOs is also its greatest weakness: the start-up cost is low but it is very easy to rationalize a decision to quit. By contrast, many of those who start other businesses, whether it be in manufacturing or trading of any sort, are motivated by fear of losing the capital or borrowed money they have agreed to sink into their project.

Anyone who has taken up a high street franchise and mortgaged their home to do so, does not need much in the way of day-to-day encouragement from the franchisor. They have a built-in rationale for self-motivation.

In direct selling it is quite different. The start-up investment in any of today's DSOs is rarely more than £50 or so. It is for this reason that there is a strong demand for direct sales opportunities. Many are prepared to have a go. Equally, for many, while it may seem a good idea at the time, it is all too easy to say, when the first few problems, disappointments or rejections occur, 'Do I really need this hassle?' This is the challenge for DSOs and all those with a responsibility for helping others develop their businesses. Even when a direct seller has managed to overcome their initial doubts, problems and lack of confidence; motivational programmes are equally important in providing longer-term security. This is particularly important when the earnings from direct selling begin to form a substantial part of a family income. The specific motivational tasks for the management of any direct salesforce are:

1 Self-motivation
2 Maintaining trust and confidence in the product, the earnings opportunity and the DSO
3 Providing personal recognition for achievements
4 Creating job satisfaction.

Let me start with the task of instilling self motivation in a direct seller. The great majority of those who join a DSO do so on a part-time basis, with a modest level of commitment, in the hope and expectation of supplementing a family income. At the time they join the business they may be open-minded as to whether it is the sort of business worth pursuing seriously. Commonly the unsaid attitude is 'If it works out, that's fine. If it doesn't, then I have nothing much to lose and I'll write off the small investment to experience.' The smaller the initial investment, the shorter the time it will take to make that judgement. As I have already said, this small investment is both an asset and a liability. If a DSO does nothing to forestall this problem then, no matter how simple the selling method may be, the business will face a high drop-out rate. This is a particular challenge for NM DSOs where the corporate investment in that new recruit is modest. The result is that not only will their growth rate be slow, but those who are sufficiently self-motivated to start sponsoring others will also become demotivated. Without a strategy for instilling self-motivation, an NM DSO can find that as many as one in three of all those who invest under £50 in a business opportunity, will never even get around to attempting to make their first sale. Many never open their business kits! It is just too easy to procrastinate.

The first stage in developing a self-motivation strategy is to help every new recruit to establish some clear personal goals. Setting long- and medium-term objectives, in the form of accumulating quite specific amounts of cash to pay for a second car, a holiday or future school fees is fine. The problem is that, in the first week or so, after the first few setbacks, they can very quickly seem unrealistic. The answer is to gain a commitment to devote a specific amount of time on specific days of the week, and to set a modest initial goal divided into easy 'bite-sized' steps. I do not intend going into this subject in any more detail, as there are many excellent books available on self-motivation. Such generic books and tapes can be valuable tools to be used at every stage in building an independent direct selling business and many DSOs make them available as business aids.

Generally, the most powerful source of self-motivation is that provided by the person who introduced a direct seller into the business, or who is someone with whom the new recruit can readily identify. Unlike field sales management in a conventional commercial business, motivation in direct selling is more about saying 'do as I do' not 'do as I say'. If new direct sellers are recruited into a DSO by people just like themselves; roughly the same age, in the same social network and perhaps with the same family commitments, then it is that much easier to persevere in achieving similar goals, and to cope with the inevitable setbacks. This is just as true with an NM DSO as it is with a party plan business, where managers are encouraged to continue holding their own parties as well as managing a team of others.

Very rarely will new direct sellers, recruited into any DSO, have sold anything to anyone. Most will not think of themselves as having what they may consider it takes to be a 'salesperson'. They may be scared by the prospect of having to prove themselves and may only have signed up on the understanding that it is easy and that orders automatically result from making presentations. To some extent this may be true and it is up to a DSO to ensure that the basic selling method is tried and tested and as simple as possible. It is also vitally important that they become, and remain, personally committed to the DSO's products. A high level of motivation can result from a DSO's management using all the skills and resources they can muster to 'sell' the products to their direct sellers. This can and should be done by encouraging direct sellers to use the products themselves, taking every opportunity to explain the interesting facts behind how products are designed, formulated and made, by arranging company demonstrations and by publicizing all customer and technical endorsements.

Reinforcing a strong personal belief in the product has the effect of turning the selling process into an almost involuntary urge to share that enthusiasm with someone else. A strong streak of product evangelism by their direct sellers is a characteristic of every successful DSO. The converse is equally true. No matter how good the product and no matter how attractive the earnings plan, it is virtually impossible for a DSO to succeed without the salesforce having a high level of personal enthusiasm for the products they are selling. It is certainly impossible to exaggerate the importance of encouraging this personal product commitment. Over the years I have met many of the most endearing direct sellers, who have given me the impression that they looked upon telling the world about their products as one of their missions in life. I have often felt that if they were told that their commission rates were to be reduced it would have made little difference to their commitment to the DSO. Such people are, of course, a minority, but they have a strong motivational effect on others. This is a characteristic of direct selling that is rarely (if ever) found in any other type of business and is something that has continued to motivate me during almost a lifetime in the direct selling industry.

Although the earnings potential offered by a DSO is not the only reason why people join and stay with a DSO, it is the cornerstone of every business plan. The earnings opportunity must be clearly seen to be realistic and attainable. This means that an important motivational task for those with management responsibilities is to provide direct sellers, both new and long serving, with constant reminders of what sales and earnings can and have been achieved by others. This is the main purpose of any sales meeting. To an outsider it may appear that DSOs spend an inordinate amount of time and resources organizing company meetings and encouraging leaders to hold meetings of their own. The fact is, they are right to do so; they are vital. A DSO can produce the finest sales manuals with examples of what can be done. They can, and should, also publish examples of what other direct sellers have achieved. However, nothing is as powerful a motivating influence as hearing at first hand how someone else has achieved success. Every successful DSO employs this approach to motivate others. Big-ticket DSOs, with full-time direct sellers, commonly have regular morning meetings at which those who have done well the previous day recount their successes. Those with part-time direct sellers do the same at evening meetings. A sales meeting can be used to impart information and to provide training, but the greatest benefit is in motivation. The motivational effect is simple. Just consider a busy married woman with family commitments who has found it difficult to make sales and who has faced what she considers to be unsurmountable problems in making a success of her business. When given the opportunity to hear how someone much like herself has succeeded, with much the same problems, the chances are that she would leave the meeting feeling that 'If that person can do it, then so can I'. Without that opportunity to meet and talk to other ordinary successful people, the chances are that she would think that all the success stories she had been told about were either exceptions or were achieved by those with superior gifts of salesmanship. Occasionally, listening to a super-salesperson can be motivating as well as entertaining and instructive – particularly for full-time direct sellers. However, to reinforce a belief in the DSO's earnings opportunity, there is no motivational substitute for making arrangements for direct sellers to meet one another.

At the point at which most direct sellers consider joining a DSO, their decision is likely to be based on their judgement of the earnings opportunity, the product and the credibility of the DSO – usually in that order. At the outset, the proposition is, unlike a franchise, a modest investment and there is little financial necessity to check out the standing and public reputation of the DSO – although many very sensibly do so. The more sophisticated, particularly those considering an NM DSO and who are aware of the past problems of pyramid selling, do tend to rank the reputation and past performance of the DSO rather higher. Whatever their initial views on the DSO, and despite the influence of the person who introduced them to the business, the way in which the DSO projects itself to a direct seller becomes an increasingly vital motivating force.

> Avon Cosmetics reinforce this confidence in the company at an early stage by telephoning a high proportion of their new representatives shortly after they have received delivery of their first order. The DSO's outbound telesales team is trained to detect any incipient problems and to advise the local manager so that they can provide immediate help and encouragement.

This demand for confidence in the DSO becomes stronger, the longer direct sellers stay with the business, and the more reliant they become on their income from direct selling. It is not just the support they get from the DSO in terms of quality of goods and reliability and promptness in the delivery of orders. It is a demand for long-term confidence and trust in the DSO.

This is a good stage at which to re-emphasize one important effect of the difference between an NM DSO and a conventional direct selling business; it is in management disciplines and expectations. I am making this point because there has been, over the past few years, a widespread belief that network marketing is 'the modern way' of organizing a direct selling business. Certainly, it meets many of the demands in today's society. It can also be an efficient distribution structure, but it has one big drawback – the difficulty of exerting direct management control over the pace at which the business develops. An NM DSO relies on distributors using their entrepreneurial skills. Sometimes management is faced with a problem of 'reining in' this entrepreneurial activity. Even more of a problem can be in getting the business to grow when sales stagnate.

I have shown that in an NM DSO management delegates to independent direct sellers virtually all the key sales management functions and responsibilities that in any other business are under direct management control – recruitment, training, advertising, sales promotion and motivation. To some extent it is an act of faith – which can often be misplaced. It is this problem that accounts for a high proportion of the failures of NM DSOs after their first year of trading.

Consider, for a minute, a new NM DSO that has been been formed by investing in stocks of a fine product and in preparing an appealing sales plan with excellent business support material. The proprietor will also have funded the cost of finding a small group of front-line distributors. This could be through advertising or by selling the idea to a small group of personal contacts. It is that group who will collectively have to accept the challenge of passing on the corporate message and developing the business. Starting with a small group of personal contacts is how virtually all the large NM DSOs were established. If it is a good product and a good sales plan, then it is perhaps not unreasonable to expect that the business will succeed. But what happens if this new business develops well for the first few months and then stagnates – or worse still, fails to develop at all. What can the management do? The answer is very little - at least, not directly.

To illustrate my point let us consider an NM DSO that was formed in the south of England and through the efforts and contacts of the first distributors produced sales groups in the West Country and in East Anglia, but then stopped growing. In a field management structure based on employed managers, the company, if they wanted to expand into the North West or Scotland, would simply appoint local managers and start recruiting in those regions. In an NM DSO the options are much more difficult. Either the management has to exhort their existing distributors to invest more of their own time and money in travelling to underdeveloped parts of the country, or they could attempt to create more front-line distributors. Either option is fraught with difficulties. The first is time consuming, and the second runs the risk of demotivating the existing distributors. Even if there is a good geographic distribution of distributors, but the business still begins to stagnate, the management is faced with much the same problem. In running any conventional business the usual way of dealing with a fall-off in demand is to reassess sales effort, advertising and sales promotional expenditure. With an NM DSO it is not so easy to throw money at the problem. The costing of the sales plan means that they cannot afford to advertise to stimulate demand. Any tinkering with the sales plan can be seen as a sign of weakness and leads to insecurity. Nor can management take direct control of recruitment. To do so can lead to resentment or worse; a feeling by the distributors that they can stand by and let management do their job for them.

Let me return for a moment to the starting up of a new NM DSO. Some entrepreneurs are tempted to get off to a flying start by poaching some leading distributors from another NM DSO, in the hope that they will bring with them a substantial number of their downline distributors from the other business. Not only is this unethical, it rarely, if ever, seems to work out in practice. The reason is this: the concept of network marketing is based on the principle that everyone who joins a NM DSO has a business of their own, on exactly the same terms as their sponsor. Each new distributor has just the same chance of building a network and a payline as large, if not larger, than that of the person who sponsored them. In a good NM sales plan it is the integrity of the DSO and the price and quality of the products that has most influence on a decision to join a business. Although some successful distributors become convinced that their success is due mainly to their powers of leadership, they soon find on defecting to another business that very few of their downline are prepared to follow them. Unlike an SLM DSO, the most successful NM DSOs have been built up slowly from a group of personal contacts – preferably those with no previous experience of network marketing.

Given the lack of direct management control, the only way in which an NM DSO can stimulate continued growth, apart from concentrating on the essentials of the business, is to develop a strong motivational programme outside the sales plan; contests, awards and recognition programmes. These can be organized by the DSO and also by the leading distributors. The latter become a progressively more important source of motivation as the business grows. The largest and most successful NM DSOs are heavily reliant on their top distributors in ensuring that motivational programmes work effectively. Whoever provides this motivation needs to adopt a slightly different approach in dealing with problems than they might in any other type of business. In short, hours spent in meetings analysing the reasons for lack of growth are rarely worth while. From my own experience, and by observing the success of other businesses, it is far better to spend more time accentuating the positive, than attempting to eliminate all the negatives. In practice this means analysing every motivational campaign and identifying those campaigns that worked – and why. With this information it is possible to replicate success; to find the buttons which, when pressed, produced results, and then to go on pressing them! This is a principle that works well for any DSO, but for a business organized on a network marketing basis is absolutely vital.

Salesforce communications

For a typical DSO marketing low-ticket consumer goods and with annual sales of, say, £5 million, the business is likely to involve the part-time activities of over 2000 direct sellers. For such a business to be successful, it is vital that the DSO maintains some sort of regular direct and personal contact with all those direct sellers. Doing so often represents their biggest motivational challenge. For different reasons, this contact is just as important for full-time direct sellers as it is for those whose involvement is limited to an hour or so a week. For a DSO offering good-value products and an attractive earnings proposition it is just not realistic to imagine that periodic visits or telephone calls from a local manager or sponsoring distributor are all that is required to maintain continuing commitment to a self-employed earnings opportunity.

Direct selling can be a lonely business. We have already seen that as a part-time occupation, with a modest financial commitment, it is easy to rationalize a decision to give up after just a few setbacks or to decide that some other business or occupation might be better. Working from home, only rarely meeting other direct sellers and perhaps never having seen the DSO's headquarters, it is also easy on a bad day to question the substance of the business. On such days it is natural to wonder whether everything is going well elsewhere – even to question whether next month's commissions will be paid!

I first learned this lesson in my early days with Kleeneze. It happened when I had started to examine the cost of running our transport fleet, which made weekly deliveries to all our mainly full-time agents. It was immediately apparent that the drivers on regular routes around the country were making far too few drops per day. Having asked someone to find out what was going on, the explanation proved revealing. Far from being idle, many of the drivers were frustrated by the time they had to spend on each call, which were made on predetermined days. Having unloaded their orders, the agents would invite the drivers into their homes, offer them tea or coffee, and pump them for information on what was going on down at the factory in Bristol and with other agents around the country. The drivers knew little about how the business was going and could no more than pass on gossip. Clearly we had a communications problem! In this case it was one that we were able to resolve temporarily by putting these enforced 'tea breaks' to good effect. I arranged for all the drivers to be given a weekly briefing on good news and exciting developments in the company. It was something that we should have been doing anyway for men who worked unsociable hours – leaving the warehouse at dawn and returning at night, later in the week. Rarely did they have a chance to meet management or any other employees. However, in this case, the solution to the problem gave the drivers satisfaction in being able to pass on good news – and how we were dealing with the occasional problems and shortages. They were happier and, with more informed and concise messages to pass on, delivery times were also reduced.

Today, DSOs have many more and better opportunities for effective communications. Many direct sellers now place their orders by telephone. A telephone order operator is in an ideal position to cement a good relationship between the DSO and the direct sellers. It is a sound policy to fully brief and motivate all staff who have regular telephone contact with the salesforce, by letting them know the important role they play in salesforce communications. The same is particularly important for all those who have to deal on the telephone with accounts queries from direct sellers.

Knowing that all is well with the business is obviously important to a direct seller whose involvement is full-time and whose family's income depends on the success of the DSO. A part-time direct seller needs this constant reassurance for another reason. Most of the country's working population, whether they be full- or part-time, leave home each day to work in offices, stores or factories. At work they are surrounded by strong physical evidence of a substantial and reliable source of future income. They may not be aware of the financial strength of their employer, but their working environment, in the company of others, can give a feeling of security, confidence and pride in the business they work for – even if sometimes that confidence may be misplaced.

Some part-time direct sellers choose an earnings opportunity with a DSO because they dislike all that goes with conventional employment – but not many. The majority of today's direct sellers choose direct selling because the hours are completely flexible; they can work from home; they like going out and meeting people and their rewards are directly related to what they are able to achieve. This does not mean that they would not welcome the opportunity to meet others in the business, and to have pride and confidence in the DSO. As would an employee, they need to feel that the business is well managed and that promises to supply goods and pay bonuses will be met.

Expecting the trust and confidence of a direct seller, who has never seen any concrete evidence that the DSO actually exists, or who may even have been told is operated out of a small rented warehouse, requires a great act of faith. It is a confidence that is easily shattered when things go wrong – as they will with any business from time to time. It is up to the management of a DSO to work hard at building up this confidence. Good sales literature and corporate videos can go a long way to achieve this aim, although, for a new small direct selling business, giving direct sellers the opportunity to visit the head office of a DSO is even better. Provided such visits are arranged at weekends, many of those for whom direct selling is still a part-time occupation, but who have made a personal commitment to succeed, will be quite prepared to travel a hundred miles or more to visit the headquarters of business and meet the staff.

Over the years I have changed my views on the need for a DSO to have a smart headquarters building. At one time I thought that many of those I had visited in the United States were extravagantly self-indulgent. Some were, but I am now convinced that for a retail business with no other real estate, there is a good case for a DSO having an impressive physical focus – something with which direct sellers can identify themselves and see the part they play in its day-to-day operation. For any direct seller who is totally committed to the business, and whose future family income depends on the ongoing success of the DSO, it is even more important. If the management of the DSO show in every way they can, that they too are committed to the long-term success of the business, then they are more likely to gain the loyalty of their direct sellers. A solid investment in a headquarters building is one way of showing that commitment.

In the mid-1980s an innovative NM DSO was set up in Britain which totally disregarded this advice. The founder was a clever and honest man who had a strong personal aversion to ostentatious offices and what he considered to be superfluous staff functions. He made a point of emphasizing that the business had modest warehouse facilities, the leanest possible management team and that he did not waste money on either a personal secretary, or even an office of his own. His was an ascetic corporate style that might have found favour with some City analysts, but it did not impress his direct sellers. They had the impression, wrongly, that he did not take the business seriously. After a few years a group of distributors defected to form a rival business. Through the lack of a strong team to help him weather the storm the business failed shortly afterwards. So too, did the rival business.

Corporate newsletters are another way in which any DSO can maintain a strong motivational link with every direct seller in the business. In an SLM business it is the responsibility of a corporate management team to keep in contact with every direct seller for whom they are responsible. For this reason, a newsletter, while helpful, is not vital. Similarly, in many party plan DSOs, one day a week is strictly reserved for making telephone contact with every demonstrator to record sales and party bookings and to give help, advice and encouragement. By contrast, for NM DSOs where management cannot insist on such a disciplined approach, a corporate newsletter is essential. While it is suggested and assumed that distributors will have a vested interest in making frequent contact with those they have sponsored, it cannot be guaranteed that they will. Nor is it reasonable or realistic to expect a clear message from the DSO to be passed on through a network from one distributor to another.

With the rapidly improving facilities of IT some major DSOs are finding even better ways of communicating with all their direct sellers. In 1995 Herbalife introduced Herbalife Broadcast Network. HBN is already one of Europe's largest private television networks offering the company, through a satellite, the opportunity for corporate staff and leading distributors to communicate live with their distributors all over Europe. Also, at preannounced times, by assembling distributors in certain locations, they are able to hold discussions and training sessions that can be seen by others in every European country in which this DSO is trading.

Two final points to remember about salesforce communications are the old adages that no news is bad news, and that nothing travels so fast as bad news. For any DSO with several thousand direct sellers, often with their own interwoven lines of communication, the reasons for even the most minor product shortage can all too easily be distorted by rumours into a crisis and lack of confidence in the DSO. It is an essential role of sales management to anticipate and forestall problems by communicating clearly and often.

Recognition programmes

Long before I became involved in direct selling, I worked for a few years with Raleigh Industries, at that time part of the TI Group, which I had joined as a management trainee. After going on an excellent sales training course, I was sent to Glasgow to manage a team of salesmen selling bicycles, wheeled toys and mopeds to dealers around Scotland. An additional responsibility of mine was for the major house accounts. In that first year our little team did well and, in personal recognition for signing up a particularly large house account, the sales director presented me with what I thought was a rather fine Parker pen. I still have it, rather battered now, in my desk at home. In fact I treasure it – as being my very first sales award.

I mention this tale as illustrating the power of recognition. For anyone becoming involved in sales their first achievement award is a memorable occasion. In my view the very best DSOs appreciate this power of motivation better than any other business. It is one of the strongest and best influences of the US multinational DSOs; and it is not just in direct selling. On countless occasions during visits to the United States, I have been impressed by how much more attention US management pays to recognizing special achievements by employees; not just in sales, but in manufacturing, administration and in every part of every type of business. Evidence of this is the large number of businesses who specialize in producing award plaques of a quality that it is still rarely seen in Britain.

Further evidence of how much more British industry and commerce needs to learn about the power of recognition, is the reaction of those who win an award in a DSO. One of the indelible memories of my time with Kleeneze were the comments of grown men who had joined the business following redundancy, or after retiring from another occupation. Many a time I was told, often with tears in their eyes, that it was the first time that anyone had ever thanked them, or recognized them in public, for a job well done.

Certainly, most people join a DSO with the aim of supplementing their income. However, the opportunity for recognition, particularly on a stage in front of their peers, is an immensely powerful motivator. We all strive for recognition. Some will work hard to produce quite remarkable achievements for little else. It is not the value of the award that matters, it is the thought behind it. Recognition awards are quite separate from the financial rewards of a sales plan. They are a permanent reminder of a personal achievement: a confidence booster: a reminder that, despite some current difficulties, they can do it again.

Recognition in public motivates any recipient to strive to do even better and achieve the next level of recognition. What motivates everyone else at an awards event, is to hear from the recipient how they achieved that award. Hearing these personal success stories still has a powerful effect on me. On those occasions today, when I am invited to attend company meetings, I always come away with a renewed conviction that direct selling is not only a great way of doing business, but that it has that unique ability to bring out the best in people.

The one essential ingredient of any worthwhile recognition programme, is that the award must be sincere. Recognition without the
clearly perceived sincerity of the person or DSO making the award, is
absolutely worthless. Some DSOs have recognition programmes that start
with an award for a very modest achievement in sales, or an equally
modest achievement in building up a group of other direct sellers. In
direct selling I believe that such awards are well justified. For the majority
of those who join a DSO, never previously having sold anything to
anyone, it is a real achievement – even more so if, at first, they had been
terrified by the prospect of selling. The same is true of anyone organizing
a group of others who has never had any experience of management or
supervision.

Apart from formal recognition programmes involving award pins and
certificates, the manager or leader of a group of direct sellers can and
should recognize achievements in other ways. During the years that
Mary Kay built up her great cosmetics business, she devoted many hours
a week to writing personal letters to those who had achieved something
special. A personal note of thanks and congratulation from the founder,
chief executive or sales director of a DSO can be as good a form of
recognition as any award. It is permanent and can be a treasured record.
For the chief executive of even the largest DSO, finding the time to write
personal notes is time well spent – but they must be personal. If not
handwritten, then, at the very least, a typed letter must have an added
handwritten note. Anything less can imply that the recipient is just one of
others on a list, and would have as much warmth and sincerity as an
unsigned Christmas card.

Although I have referred to what a director or CEO of a DSO should do
to recognize special achievements, these principles are just as applicable
to any manager or top distributor in an NM DSO. Within any DSO there
is the opportunity for groups of direct sellers to rally behind the leader of
a group in friendly rivalry with other groups.

> Anyone attending the Annual Rally of a successful party plan DSO,
> such as Princess House, would see astonishing signs of loyalty by
> sales ladies to their own sales group – with each group in
> competition for the top divisional award. These events are wonder-
> fully inspiring, charged with emotion, with each team waving flags
> and banners and willing their team on to be announced as the
> winner. Although this is a business based on the efforts of self-
> employed direct sellers, they are competing for an award that brings
> with it no additional financial reward. It is the recognition of being
> a member of the winning team. Throughout the year the leaders of

the sales divisions in that business use all the same skills of leadership, and recognition of the achievements of their group members in their efforts to win the award.

It is not just self-employed direct sellers who respond well to public recognition. Avon Cosmetics has a larger employed sales organization than any other industrial or commercial organization in the UK. These are the field managers who recruit, train and motivate Avon representatives. Every year almost 700 of these managers attend an event at which the leading managers are recognized in front of their peers. It is an emotional and highly motivating event, with the winning managers being cheered on by those others in the same divisional team. Again, although the winners may be rewarded by attending a special overseas event, it is not the prospect of extra income that spurs them on to win; it is recognition.

Even in an NM DSO, it is just as possible for a top distributor to generate the same team spirit. In addition to a corporate recognition programme, many successful distributors devise recognition programmes for their own downlines. Everyone likes the idea of being part of a winning team. It is a sound policy for any DSO to encourage direct sellers to identify themselves with a group.

The sales plans of the best NM DSOs are based on the principle that every distributor has exactly the same opportunity to build a substantial business – no matter when they joined. One result is that an individual could sponsor another, whose own group and payline could expand to the point where it provided a higher level of recognition and financial reward than that of his or her sponsor. This means that in terms of recognition the roles can sometimes be reversed.

Some years ago, in the United States, I attended a major sales event at which the leading distributor, after receiving his own recognition, invited up on stage the man who, many years ago, first sponsored him into the business. The leader explained to the audience how much he owed to his sponsor, not just for being introduced to the business, but for his initial help and encouragement in the early days. Although the leader had gone on to achieve higher recognition and financial rewards, his sponsor still received, through the sales plan, some financial benefit from the success of his prodigy. It was a powerful example of what sponsorship in the form of a permanent umbilical link can, and should, mean in a good NM DSO. It was also a good illustration of the reason why matrix schemes, where no such links exist, rarely work for very long.

Many DSOs offer the opportunity to travel to a seminar, held in some exotic overseas location, as the ultimate reward and recognition for their top achievers. In practice, particularly with an established DSO, it can be exceptionally difficult to decide on the criteria for winning any top award, such as foreign travel where for cost reasons the numbers of award winners have to be limited. There is a real risk of motivating a few and demotivating many more. The management challenge is in deciding precisely what it is that deserves reward. Is it being one of a group of consistently high performers, or rewarding those who have achieved remarkable growth over a given period? Both deserve recognition, but they are difficult to mix in a single recognition programme. Recognizing a percentage increase in sales or an achievement against a set target can all too easily demotivate those who have achieved higher but more consistent sales. It is generally better to separate the two.

The best and most powerful recognition programmes are those which set standards of achievement that are common to everyone, and in which everyone has the same opportunity to be a winner. Such programmes need not be costly. These criteria are just as applicable to a group leader in motivating his or her own group as they are in the overall sales management of a DSO.

In *The Direct Option* Dick Bartlett likens the importance of recognition in direct selling to the importance of location in valuing real estate. If the three most important factors in judging the value of a property are location, location and location then the three best ways of motivating direct sellers are recognition, recognition and recognition! There is nothing patronizing in a good recognition programme; we all respond well to being recognized for an achievement. It is as true for those who achieve a national honour for service to their country, as it is for those who are publicly recognized for an achievement in direct selling. Financial rewards are important, but recognition is longer lasting. As a method of motivation, recognition, sincerely given, is a method that cannot be used too often.

Key points

- The appeal of an earnings opportunity in direct selling is the low entry cost. It is also its biggest weakness – in that it is easy to justify a decision to quit. Providing motivation is the key criterion for the success of any DSO.
- Most direct sellers join a DSO to make money. They will only stay with the business if they enjoy the experience.

- Although the prospect of earnings is the attraction for most direct sellers, many others will join and stay with a DSO for other reasons – recognition, a passion for the product and the opportunity to buy the products at a discount.
- Direct selling is a numbers business; not just numbers of direct sellers but also the number of presentations made regularly, every week, by direct sellers. A belief that sales are in proportion to the number of presentations is the motivational aim of every DSO.
- In low-ticket direct sales, the major training task is in the first two steps of making a sale – attracting the attention, and gaining the interest of a prospect.
- In big-ticket direct sales the key requirement is for a single, well-proven demonstration method.
- In party plan sales the first objective in holding a party is to book two more parties. This is more important than maximizing sales at a party.
- A high turnover of direct sellers is an inescapable feature of any DSO. Ensuring that former direct sellers remain ambassadors for the DSO is a top sales management priority.
- Personal recommendation or referral is a much better recruitment technique for any DSO than media advertising.
- The most successful DSOs 'sell' their product to their direct sellers. Testimonials from direct sellers who are enthusiastic users of the DSO's products is easier to engender and more effective than personal selling skills – particularly with NM DSOs.
- Direct selling can be a lonely occupation. Good communications, directly with the DSO, and providing confirmation that the business is soundly based, is vital to motivation. It is more important than the potential rewards from the sales plan.
- Of all the motivational tools available to a DSO, the most important is the sincere recognition of achievement.

6

Managing a direct selling business

The purpose of this chapter is not to cover every aspect of managing a DSO, most of which are similar to operating any business. My aim is to focus on those aspects of managing a retail distribution business that are peculiar to the direct selling channel. These are pricing, inventory control, product distribution and credit control.

Pricing policies

Unlike conventional retailing, with any type of DSO it is very difficult to influence the mix of products sold. A high street retailer can influence both the value of an average 'shopping basket' and sales product mix, by the siting of products on gondola shelves, special displays, dump bins and special price offers. In direct selling it is much more difficult. A DSO using regularly changed catalogues can use mail order illustration techniques to steer customer choice, and can feature special offers. However, the problem for the DSO is that special offers are unlikely to result in any increase in the value of a customer's average purchase order. Special offers simply replace regular lines that they might otherwise have selected. The biggest influence on customer choice is the direct seller. What appeals to a direct seller is what they are most likely to sell. For these reasons, the safest pricing policy is to ensure that every product item on offer yields the same gross contribution. This way, if any new item introduced into the range results in a reduction in the volume of sales of another line, which it almost certainly will, then the change in mix will not affect overall profitability.

Another popular misconception is that the direct selling channel of distribution offers, or at least should offer, manufacturers the opportunity to supply consumer goods at retail prices below those at which they would be sold through conventional retail outlets. Without having to bear the costs of advertising and wholesale distribution, this has regrettably led many NM DSOs to claim that network marketing does offer price advantages to retail consumers. Rarely, if ever, can these claims be justified. While this may be possible for a very small DSO, any substantial business demands other overhead costs that match those required in conventional distribution. If those other overheads, particularly those associated with motivation and account administration, are not built into the retail price structure, then the business is unlikely to succeed. This does not mean that the direct selling distribution channel is more expensive; it is much the same. To illustrate this point, Table 6.1 is an analysis of the cost build-up for a typical housewares product sold through a conventional retail store and through two types of typical DSO. In the case of the conventional retail store this is assumed to be a multiple retailer who deals directly with the supplier. Had supply been through a wholesaler to a small retailer, with margins of 25 per cent and 33 per cent respectively, then the overall margin would be much the same as the 50 per cent discount available to a multiple store.

For the purpose of this comparison, the aim, in each case, is to produce a contribution towards profit and finance costs of 10 per cent on the total volume of retail sales achieved.

The cost breakdowns shown in Table 6.1 are intended to be no more than a rough guide to the pricing policies that should be adopted by DSOs marketing other consumer goods. For example, warehousing and distribution costs for a DSO selling fragile items of tableware, would be very much higher than for a business selling either jewellery or fashion wear.

On the face of it, it would appear that a traditional, single-level, party plan business can operate on a much lower cost price multiplier than an NM DSO. In practice, a multiplier of 3.5 is the very minimum on which any business which aims to become a substantial DSO should attempt to operate. The party plan example in Table 6.1 is more typical of a small DSO with limited buying power. Many would-be entrepreneurs start small party plan businesses by buying goods from a local wholesaler and selling them through a small network of home demonstrators. They can operate on a low mark-up because they are not having to fund the substantial cost of rewarding field sales management. Traditional single-level DSOs also have to finance the working capital needed to support higher non-variable sales costs and the cost of offering demonstrators credit accounts.

These are some of the reasons why many party plan DSOs in the United States are opting for semi-NM 'hybrid' sales plans. In these

Table 6.1   Comparison of cost build-ups for a houseware product –
conventional retail v. direct selling

	Supplier to a multiple retailer (%)	NM DSO (%)	Single level party plan DSO (%)
Sales (less VAT)	100	100	100
Basic discount on RRP	50	–	–
Advertising charge	5	–	–
Settlement discount	2.5	–	–
Retrospective discount	1.5	–	–
Retail profits	–	25	–
Wholesale volume profits	–	20	–
Royalty bonuses	–	12	–
Demonstrator commissions	–	–	22
Field sales management commissions	–	–	9
Dating gifts and hostess gifts	–	–	6
Sales aids and sample kit subsidies	–	–	4
Bad debts	–	–	0.5
Sales force motivation costs	–	2	3.5
Sales management and training	1	1	3.4
Marketing	1	1.5	1.5
Salesforce recruitment costs	–	–	1.5
Sales admin. and management information systems	1	1.3	1.3
Warehousing costs	2	2	2
Transport and distribution	2	2	4
Property and other central services	3	3	3
Contribution towards profit, finance and other operating costs	10	10	10
Cost of products sold	21	20.2	28.3
(Multiplier from cost to RRP)	(× 4.76)	(× 4.95)	(× 3.53)

plans there are virtually no corporate field sales management costs, and greatly reduced product distribution costs. Direct sellers pay for goods when they place orders, which commonly include the cost of delivery, and demonstrators are encouraged to sponsor others from the day they join the business. The only difference between these plans and other NM DSOs is that the rewards from sponsorship are usually deferred until an individual has sponsored a given number of others and has satisfied the DSO that they are competent to take on training responsibilities. Hybrid party plan DSOs are more 'dynamic' and attract the same type of enterprising direct sellers who join other NM DSOs. However, the price of offering higher earnings opportunities is the demand to select products that can bear a higher product cost multiplier.

Inventory control

Stock availability of the current range of products is of crucial importance to any DSO. While conventional retailers do not generate customer hostility by being temporarily out of stock of certain lines, and while mail order businesses frequently advise those who have ordered a certain product that there will be a delay of a few weeks before their order can be fulfilled, such treatment of a self-employed direct seller spells trouble. The distribution of low-ticket direct-sold products is usually through the direct seller or, in the case of a party plan DSO, through a party hostess. If a product is not available, or is delivered late, then the direct seller has to waste time making an extra visit to the customer, or runs the risk on the first delivery that the order for the outstanding item will be cancelled and that they will lose commission. In the case of a party hostess who may have collected cash from her party guests prior to delivery, non-availability presents her with an unwelcome problem and a strong disincentive to host another party.

Dealing with back orders also presents a DSO with serious logistic and administration problems. Many find it easier to delete the order and request the direct seller to reorder the item at a later date. In an NM DSO such a policy presents additional problems, as a direct seller may have relied on a cancelled order to qualify for a specific monthly volume bonus. To some extent, this can be overcome by substituting the out-of-stock line with some other item of equivalent value. However, these are all problems that every DSO should endeavour to avoid. If they do not, then they are likely to lose their direct sellers.

Product distribution

Having made a sale there are a number of ways in which a DSO can supply goods to the customer. I shall examine these in the four main categories of DSO.

Big-ticket person to person

In the UK the majority of big-ticket sales are made under credit agreements and it is therefore essential that the DSO fulfils its legal obligations under the Consumer Credit Act. This Act provides for a five-day cooling-off period, from the day of receipt by the customer from the DSO by post of a credit agreement. This demands of the DSO that they are informed immediately that a sale has been made. It also makes good sense for a DSO to ensure that the goods are not delivered until the cooling-off period has expired. It is also logical for the DSO and not the direct seller to be responsible for delivering the goods to the customer. This is the approach used by double-glazing companies and results in the direct seller having no further contact with the customer after an agreement has been signed.

DSA member companies commonly adopt a slightly different approach. Encyclopaedia Britannica, for example, require the salesperson to be present when the books are delivered and to be assured that the customer is still happy with their purchase. Only when the direct sellers get this confirmation, which may even require that the benefits are 'resold', do they receive their commission. This policy has the added advantage of giving the direct seller another opportunity to ask for leads to other potential customers.

Quite apart from credit sale considerations, the distribution cost to the DSO of delivering a big-ticket product to a consumer is usually modest in relation to sales value and is a sensible strategy.

Low-ticket person to person

In businesses such as Avon, sales representatives are independent contractors. Avon ladies collect orders from their customers and place orders with the company on their own account at the end of each three-week sales campaign. These goods are delivered directly to the representative, and it is their responsibility to deliver orders to each of their customers and to receive payment. Betterware salespeople selling household goods operate in much the same way, except that orders are placed and goods are delivered via their local manager. One factor that can dictate which method to use, is the nature of the product. Housewares tend to be heavier and bulkier than cosmetics and therefore local distribution is more cost effective.

Party plan

Traditionally, the most common product distribution arrangements for party plan DSOs have been systems which involved the following stages:

1 The demonstrator collects orders from each guest at a party and collates them into one order which she sends to the DSO.
2 Over the following two weeks the party hostess collects individual payments from each of the guests, and either:
   (a) Retains the money until the goods are delivered, or
   (b) Remits the money by bank giro to the DSO.
3 After a period of approximately two weeks, or after the money has been received by the DSO, the company dispatches the goods ordered at the party in one consignment, to either:
   (a) The party hostess, or
   (b) The demonstrator who, in turn, delivers the goods to the hostess.
4 If, as in the case of 2(a) the hostess retained the cash collected from the party guests, then the DSO would deliver the party order to the hostess on a COD basis, either:
   (a) By a national carrier or by using special delivery agents, or
   (b) Via the demonstrator to whom the consignment had been sent.
5 If the hostess had already remitted the money to the DSO, then delivery would be directly to the party hostess.
6 On receipt of the goods, the hostess would advise her guests that their orders were available for collection and she would retain from the consignment either a hostess gift, or her own order which, as a reward for holding the party, would be purchased at a discount. This reward is commonly valued at between 10 per cent and 12.5 per cent of the party sales value.
7 The demonstrator is rewarded in one of two ways:
   (a) If the hostess remits the full retail value of the goods ordered directly to the DSO either by bank giro, or through a COD payment collected on delivery, then the DSO would send the demonstrator a commission cheque.
   (b) Alternatively, if the money were collected by the demonstrator then that demonstrator would deduct the commission due to her, and remit the balance to the DSO.

For a party plan DSO it is a matter of choice which of these procedures they adopt. A decision can be influenced by the nature of the product, such as the cost and difficulty of delivering bulky or fragile goods.

Traditionally, the reasons for making a delivery as much as 28 days after the goods were ordered have been both to give the customer the statutory and DSA code-demanded cooling-off period in which to cancel an order, and also to give the customer time to obtain the money to pay for her order. In the 1990s, particularly with the increasing use of credit cards, the latter is becoming a less important consideration. Many customers are now quite prepared to pay for their order either by cheque or by credit card at the time they place the order – in just the same way as they would in a direct mail transaction. This acceptance of paying up-front has forced many party plan DSOs to rethink their distribution strategy. It is one of the reasons for the development of NM hybrid party plan DSOs.

Another reason why some party plan DSOs require payment, either by COD or by bank giro, before they release goods to the hostess is to avoid the credit risk involved in relying on the demonstrator to remit the correct balance to the DSO. Hybrid DSOs overcome this problem by demanding that demonstrators pay up-front for the party order sent to the DSO. This procedure is referred to in the next section on NM DSOs. If a direct seller does pay in advance of delivery, then this imposes an extra discipline on the DSO – which is to ensure that the goods are dispatched promptly.

Network marketing

An important difference between traditional party plan demonstrators and those direct sellers working with an NM DSO is that for the majority of the latter their involvement is on much more of a part-time basis. An NM DSO is all about a lot of people each accounting for a small volume of personal sales each month. A minority make a decision to take the business seriously not so much by increasing their own volume of personal sales, but by organizing groups of other part-time direct sellers. In planning a distribution strategy this has several implications.

As the average monthly sales volume is low, it has been proved acceptable to participants in NM DSOs that they pay for the goods when they place an order with the DSO. An accepted practice is for cheques payable to the DSO to be held for a few days before banking, to enable the goods to be delivered to direct sellers and for them to make deliveries to their customers, who would pay when they receive their goods. In those cases where a direct seller pays using a personal credit card, DSOs would also delay the credit card transaction for a few days.

Another approach, which is accepted by some banks, is for those direct sellers who have an account with the DSO to enter into a direct debit agreement with the DSO. In this way any direct seller when they place an order would be advised of the amount to be debited within a few days.

It is becoming increasingly common for DSOs to receive orders, not by post or fax on handwritten order forms, but by telephone. Apart from speeding up the order-fulfilment process this enables the DSO to check the availability of each of the products ordered and, in the case of out-of-stock lines, to gain the immediate agreement of the direct seller to a product substitution. It also enables the DSO to advise the direct seller immediately of the precise amount that will be either debited from their bank account or charged to their credit card. Such procedures require sophisticated order-processing software which can create warehouse order-picking lists at the time the order is received. A further current demand is for software which enables the orders department of an NM DSO to advise the direct seller of their current position regarding both volume and downline bonuses at the time a telephone order is received. Calculating bonus payments through a complex genealogy of sponsorship links, particularly if it involves international sponsorship, is a major data-processing challenge and there are now several software companies specializing in this field.

When establishing an NM DSO the first distribution decision that has to be made is whether or not to give purchase order accounts to every participant and whether it is practical to make direct deliveries to every participant. The original NM DSOs, such as Amway, opted for a system whereby new participants placed orders with their sponsor. Only when a participant had built their own sponsorship group up to a certain volume of monthly sales, would that individual become a direct distributor with the opportunity to deal directly with the DSO. To some extent this decision should be based on the nature of the product. Household goods, particularly liquids and aerosols, are difficult and costly to ship and therefore low-value direct deliveries are uneconomic – even if they attract a small order surcharge.

Even if small orders are distributed via direct distributors, and thereafter through the sponsorship line, this does not mean that an NM DSO cannot receive small orders and payments from every participant. From a data processing point of view, current software now makes this quite feasible and there are many advantages in doing so. The first is that the DSO is able to provide direct motivation, and to keep much better records of the activity rates of all direct sellers. It also makes it possible for the DSO, and not the direct distributor, to calculate the bonuses due to every participant and to make direct payments. This avoids delays, disputes and misappropriation of bonuses with an improvement in the morale of the organization as a whole.

The only major disadvantage in both receiving orders and making deliveries to every direct seller in the network, is that it can lead to the isolation of a new participant at a time when they most require motivation from their sponsor. Having to meet their sponsor every week or so to place orders and to receive goods provides a natural opportunity for them to receive help and encouragement which, in an NM DSO, is a sponsorship obligation in return for receiving bonuses. If such a distribution system is adopted, then it is of vital importance to the NM DSO that they find other ways of ensuring that a sponsor maintains close contact with those they have sponsored.

Other distribution issues

For most direct sellers, regardless of the type of DSO with which they are working, product distribution is seen as a chore and an unproductive use of their time. Some direct sellers overcome this problem by arranging for other members of their family to make deliveries of goods and collect payments, and so give them more time for the more important task of collecting orders. In devising a distribution strategy, it is sensible therefore for a DSO to consider whether it is feasible for pre-paid goods to be delivered directly to retail customers. The following is a list of the issues that need to be considered:

1 Is the nature of the product and the size of average order values such that the cost of direct distribution would be more than the cost of delivery via the salesforce and could any excess cost be charged to a direct seller as a delivery fee? In the United States it is accepted practice for variable delivery costs, based on the distance delivered, to be charged on all deliveries. Although this is becoming more common in the UK, most UK DSOs do not normally make delivery charges and do so only on small orders.
2 When a direct seller makes a delivery to a customer there is an opportunity to reinforce a good relationship between the two – and sometimes the chance of collecting another order.
3 Athough mail order purchases require pre-payment, the opportunity to pay on delivery is still regarded by most customers as a more attractive feature of the direct selling channel. It also overcomes to some extent consumer dissatisfaction in the case where goods ordered are not available or where substitute products are offered.

4 Both the law and the DSA Code provide consumers with the opportunity to cancel orders obtained through direct sales. Mail order experience, where delivery is impersonal and where cancelled orders or returned goods commonly exceed 10 per cent of total orders, shows that there is a greater chance of cancelled orders than with direct sales, where cancellations rarely exceed 1 per cent. If a direct seller makes a delivery, then there is also an opportunity for that direct seller to resell the product at the point of delivery.

5 Advances in IT now make it possible to obtain and put to good use information on individual consumers. It is also possible to process 'consumer to DSO' credit card payments as part, or all, of a direct seller's order. However, to take advantage of either of these opportunities requires great care if there is to be no breakdown in the esential trust that must exist between a DSO and its direct sellers.

Credit control

The following comments apply mainly to those single-level DSOs which offer their direct sellers credit accounts, and particularly where there are direct sellers whose earnings from direct selling represent all, or a substantial part, of their total family incomes. Many of the older DSOs were founded at a time when there were more opportunities for promoting jobs in direct selling, from the outset, as being a source of full-time income. For direct sellers who submitted orders to a DSO on a weekly basis it was usually three weeks before they would be in a position to receive the goods they had ordered, make deliveries and obtain cash from their customers. At that point the direct seller would deduct their commission from money collected, and remit the balance to the DSO together with their next order. For the first three weeks they would receive no income and credit accounts were considered to be an essential aid to recruitment.

For those DSOs that still offer credit accounts, the usual credit control procedure for orders placed weekly is not to release any order until the cash due on the order placed three weeks earlier had been received. Unfortunately, such a procedure does not always work quite so smoothly. Frequently, orders are submitted without any cash, or with a part-payment, together with plausible and sometimes implausible explanations as to why no payment has been made. Sales departments are often tempted to accept such orders particularly if, the following week, an order is received with cash, but still without full payment for the previous order. In my experience dealing with problems of this sort can consume a large and unnecessary amount of management time. The problems become even greater if it is decided to allocate suspense accounts against which direct sellers can pay off their outstanding debts over a future period of time. A direct seller may initially welcome this concession, but very soon begins to resent their treatment. Such concessions are also demotivating to those others who pay their accounts promptly. The best advice to any DSO which chooses to offer credit accounts to their salesforce, is to establish a fair policy and to abide rigidly by those terms.

Corporate advertising and public relations

For any DSO, regardless of whether or not it has achieved full national coverage, deciding on the extent to which they should advertise or even commission a PR campaign is difficult. Direct selling is all about building a channel of distribution for consumer goods in which media advertisements are replaced by 'live commercials'. For FMCG manufacturers it is a golden rule of marketing that you should never advertise without first ensuring that the product has already been distributed, and is easily available to those who see the advertisement. If advertising takes place in advance of distribution, then not only is the advertisement wasted but it is likely to generate a high level of customer annoyance and disaffection. The same is true for product-based PR campaigns. For a DSO this is even more true when the business is not geared up to meet direct demand from consumers and where it is difficult, if not impossible, for a consumer to make contact with an unknown local direct seller. For different reasons, explained in Chapter 5, it is usually equally inappropriate for a DSO to embark on national or even regional advertising campaigns for direct sellers.

Having said that, some large DSOs do advertise. Avon Cosmetics has advertised on TV from time to time and, in 1995, Amway placed some high-profile corporate advertisements in some high-circulation consumer magazines. Although such advertising does result in some direct response, that is not their purpose. The strategy is usually to recharge the morale of the company's direct sellers, and to influence the response of those who may subsequently be approached to join the sales organization. Such advertisements may not at first appear to be recruitment advertisements. They are just as likely to feature the quality of the products and the corporate image of the DSO and, almost as an aside, state that the products are available through a direct seller. The latter is not even necessary for the advertisement to have the same effect on recruitment. The same is true for national PR campaigns. While I have described the advertising strategy of DSOs in the UK and in other

Western countries, those operating in Eastern Europe have to contend with different consumer attitudes.

> At a joint WFDSA/FEDSA symposium on direct selling held in Prague in 1995, Professor Sarkissov of the Moscow Academy of National Economy and Professor Poliakova of St Petersburg University, presented an unusual perspective on the case for a DSO allocating funds for corporate product advertising. With the advent of democracy, they explained the effect on the population of the novelty of being exposed to powerful consumer advertising – particularly for good-quality products from the United States and other Western countries. The effect has been that of advertising becoming associated with quality. If any supplier does not advertise, then the quality is likely to be perceived as being as suspect as that of locally produced non-advertised goods. This consumer attitude will no doubt change, but for the next few years multinational DSOs operating in Russia and some of the former Warsaw Pact countries may well have to consider advertising as an essential form of PR.

However, in the UK, the greatest benefit from a corporate press advertising or PR campaign is not in the size of their initial readership, but can come in another way. It is the use to which those press clippings can be put by direct sellers. A quality advertisement in a national magazine or a good PR story is a powerful sales aid. Added to the DSO's own sales literature, they create a strong impression that the DSO is both substantial and well recognized for the quality of its products. While direct sellers may use clippings they have obtained themselves, DSOs should take great care in reproducing magazine editorials. Many newspapers take a relaxed view of this practice, but with some magazines there is a risk of copyright infringement.

Earlier in this chapter in the section on recruiting, I explained the difficulty and dangers of either allowing direct sellers to place recruitment advertisements or even attempting to mount a corporate recruitment campaign. It is even more dangerous to permit direct sellers to place advertisements for the DSO's products. Local PR, on the other hand, is less of a problem to delegate to direct sellers. Regional newspapers like to feature local success stories. If any direct seller has achieved a company or even a DSA award, then this is a story that is relatively easy to place. Many DSOs have a PR department with the resources to help direct sellers to get this local publicity. They provide direct sellers with names and contact details of reporters and editors in their local press and supply photographs and other editorial material to assist in the making of a good story. Other DSOs manage local publicity centrally or retain an agency to do it for them. Either way, PR, whether it be national or local, is the most cost-effective way of creating a warm market in which direct sellers can operate.

Multinational direct selling operations

For reasons that I have already explained, virtually every DSO is based on marketing products under a brand name that is exclusive to the DSO. Most of the products on offer differ in some way from those available through conventional retail outlets. Again, most are formulated and manufactured by, or supplied to, a DSO under a specification set by the DSO. Furthermore, the method by which the goods are direct sold is also clearly specified by the DSO as is the field sales organizational structure. What this means is that a DSO is totally accountable for the complete supply chain, from conception to retail consumption. It is for this reason that any DSO wishing to exploit business opportunities in other markets is faced with a much bigger challenge than that which confronts any other FMCG supplier or manufacturer. In exploiting export market opportunities, the manufacturers of goods for conventional retail distribution have to do little more than find a suitable importer, wholesaler or multiple retailer in selected markets and leave to them the problems of dealing with many of the local trading and licensing requirements. Such businesses should consider, in advance, local labelling, formulation and technical specification requirements, but they will have a trading partner who can help provide that advice. For DSOs it is entirely up to them. Establishing a multinational direct selling operation is a major undertaking.

This is one of the reasons, as I have pointed out in Chapter 2, that most of today's multinational DSOs are US-based corporations who have pioneered and developed the most effective organizational formats and direct selling techniques. In 1995 these US businesses accounted for international sales of over \$20 billion. Excluding Japan, where a similar volume of direct sales is achieved within the Japanese home market, this is almost half of total worldwide direct sales of \$72 billion. Apart from the United States the only other countries outside the UK from which are operated substantial multinational DSOs are:

Australia   Nutri-Metics (CTP), PRO-MA Systems (CTP)
Austria   Pierre Lang (jewellery)
Belgium   Oriflame (CTP)
France   Groupe Cita (books)

Germany   Vorwerk (household electrical appliances), Eismann (frozen
            foods)
Spain   Planeta (books)
Sweden   AB Lux (vacuum cleaners)
Switzerland AMC (cookware), Deesse (CTP)

In 1996 the list of those substantial British DSOs who had already
established overseas direct selling operations and the countries in which
they were operating is as follows:

Ann Summers Ltd	Germany, Denmark and Holland
Betterware PLC	France, Germany, Spain, Mexico (in a joint venture with Avon), Argentina, and in Australia
Cabouchon Ltd	All EU member states (excluding Luxembourg and Portugal), Finland, Switzerland, USA and Japan.
Dorling Kindersley Family Library	United States, Australia and Russia

During the next decade this international activity is likely to increase.
Throughout the Western world and in the newly emerging market
economies of China, India and South-East Asia, the direct selling channel
is thriving – for much the same reasons as it is in Britain and the United
States. In certain EU member states, notably France and Germany, the
channel is even stronger than in Britain, despite having to contend with
more prescriptive consumer protection legislation and more difficult tax
and social security burdens on direct sellers. In virtually every overseas
market it has been proven that despite cultural differences, the selling
methods and organization structures used in the UK work well. The
opportunities for a British DSO to develop overseas operations are
therefore excellent. However, this is nothing new.

My final reference to Kleeneze in this book concerns a period long
before I joined the company. Before the Second World War, in the 1930s,
Kleeneze maintained a salesforce of over 300 full-time, locally recruited,
door-to-door salesmen in France, Holland and Belgium. Every week, they
posted their orders to Bristol. The following week trucks were sent over
on a Channel ferry to deliver the goods and collect payments for the
previous week's orders – in local currencies. In most respects the
European direct sellers were administered in just the same way as were
other salesmen in the villages and towns around the UK – they even
featured in the lists of top sellers who appeared in the company's

monthly newsletter. We tend to forget that, at that time, there were no exchange control regulations, no passport controls, no labelling laws, no laws and regulations governing direct selling and no duties on imported goods. Doing business in Europe was very simple. It began to get difficult in the immediate post-war years, as each European country strove to revive and protect their battered economies. I use this little story to illustrate the fact that the creation of the EEC, and now the European Union, is not so much a revolutionary development in free trade but more of a return to the trading conditions that existed over sixty years ago.

The 1957 Treaty of Rome was dedicated to the progressive removal of all barriers to the free movement of capital, goods, services and people and the encouragement of entrepreneurship between European member states. It could not be a better charter for DSOs. Today a number of NM DSOs are already taking full advantage of the opportunities on offer. Enterprising distributors with European contacts are all too eager to take advantage of the international sponsoring facilities offered by most NM DSOs. The building through sponsorship of strong bonds of friendship between individuals and their families across national borders is a development that I suspect would have been warmly welcomed by the founding fathers of the EU. However, this long-term opportunity for developing European DSOs still presents major management problems. Although there are no longer any export duties, there is still a wide disparity in national trading law, licensing, consumer protection legislation and local taxation as it affects direct sellers.

The Federation of European Direct Selling Associations (FEDSA) was created to promote common high standards in direct selling: to enable a better understanding of the direct selling channel, by opinion formers and legislators throughout Europe: to protect the industry from ill-considered EC legislation and to encourage the harmonization of national laws. A more recent objective of FEDSA is to ensure that cross-border trade is carried out in an orderly manner. Local DSAs are now able to provide advice to DSOs wishing to trade in their markets and a directory of FEDSA members appears in Appendix 5.

The World Federation of Direct Selling Associations (WFDSA) has similar objectives on a worldwide basis, although without any aspirations to harmonize international legislation. After two years of negotiations and debate, led by former FEDSA chairman Kurt Bressler, the WFDSA obtained international agreement in 1995 to a World Code for DSOs. The provisions of this code are now incorporated into a FEDSA Code and in the UK DSA Codes, which are set out in Appendices 3 and 4.

Particularly within Europe, the introduction of international free trade agreements has led to an increased interest in multinational operations.

An even greater influence has been the growth of NM DSOs and the opportunities for international sponsorship. Keeping under proper control an excess of entrepreneurial initiative by distributors with NM DSOs has become a major challenge for management.

One dangerous practice for a DSO that has not established a proper business in an overseas market is to permit or even to condone a direct seller privately exporting goods to those who may resell those goods to consumers in overseas markets. Even in Europe, there are still wide variations in the regulations governing direct selling. For example, in Italy nearly all direct sellers must have a licence: in Denmark cold door-to-door direct selling is banned: in Sweden any direct selling transaction has to be accompanied by the issue of a cooling-off notice in the form of a special document only made available by an official consumer body: in Germany it is an offence in an NM DSO for goods to be supplied in transactions between one direct seller and another. A final example is in France, where it is an offence to accept cash at the time a direct sales transaction is effected.

Any contravention of these, and other national regulations, can lead to the prosecution of a local direct seller and can seriously prejudice the future prospects of a DSO, if and when they decide to set up a business in that market. These uncontrolled direct selling activities, and the bad publicity they receive, is also damaging to the public reputation of well-ordered DSOs operating in those markets. This does not mean that the prospects for direct selling businesses in other countries are any less attractive than they are in both the UK and the United States. In some respects they are better, but any DSO has to be vigilant in its observance of local legislation. It is for these reasons that the WFDSA has drawn up sound practical advice for those DSOs wishing to embark on cross-border sales. It is advice which covers both direct selling and the building of a sales organization through local recruitment and is as follows:

1 Before permitting any direct selling activity of a DSO's products in another market, the DSO should:
   (a) Be fully familiar with the product and labelling requirements in that market and ensure compliance
   (b) Be willing and able to offer consumers the opportunity to exercise their local market rights under consumer protection legislation, product warranties and guarantees and after-sales service
   (c) Make arrangements to provide all customers with details of a local point of contact for the purposes of service, complaint and order cancellation

(d) Have appointed an individual or suitable body resident in the local market and with knowledge of local laws and regulations (if not an employee, then a local lawyer or law firm) with responsibility for receiving legal notices, queries from government, consumer bodies, the media and also consumer complaints and enquiries

(e) Seek advice from the local DSA and provide the DSA with information on their future marketing intentions. (This is important as some DSAs have been invested by their national governments with a degree of self-regulatory authority)

2 Before any recruitment takes place, either by the DSO or by independent distributors, the DSO should appoint a suitably qualified manager, either locally or at the headquarters of the DSO, with responsibility for ensuring compliance with all local legislation with regard to direct selling.

3 In most international markets the majority of direct selling activity is accounted for by DSOs that are members of their national DSA. It is sensible therefore for any DSO wishing to enter a new market to apply to join the local DSA, or at least to agree to comply with the provisions of that DSA's local code. Any DSO which is a member of a DSA, affiliated to WFDSA, is, as a minimum requirement, required to comply with provisions of the WFDSA code. This is a code requirement which applies whether or not the DSO is accepted into local DSA membership.

Conforming to this advice does not necessarily demand that a DSO should establish a corporate entity in every market in which they choose to operate. Many choose to do so for fiscal and taxation reasons and in some markets a corporate entity is a statutory requirement. Apart from their own tax and legal advice, every DSO should also seek advice from the local DSA.

The flexibility also applies to the creation of an international product distribution strategy. Although a decision may depend on the geographic proximity of the DSO's headquarters to the market in which they intend to trade, it does not mean that the DSO should have a physical corporate presence in that market. Particularly within the EU, developments in IT, and in efficient international delivery services, make it quite feasible to receive orders and to dispatch even small consignments of goods to individual direct sellers across national borders on a regular weekly basis. This can produce dramatic savings against the cost of maintaining local warehouses and overall inventory levels. This is an approach now adopted by several UK-based DSOs.

Both Herbalife and Cabouchon have central ordering, warehouse and dispatch facilities servicing all their European markets. Direct sellers, in every country in which these DSOs now operate, are able to place orders on the telephone using a local number. These calls are trunked through to the UK at no extra cost to the caller. Speaking to a UK-based national from their own country, in their own language, they are able to make payments using a local credit card in their own currency. Goods are dispatched the following day.

This approach to operating a multinational DSO is likely to become common over the next few years.

Legal issues

Although legislation that is specific to DSOs is dealt with in detail in the following chapter, there is one particular issue that should be borne in mind in the financial management of a NM DSO. It is the legal right of a direct seller, when they terminate a contract, to receive a refund for returned goods. Although the codes of all DSAs within the WFDSA require that a DSO should refund the net price paid for returned goods in saleable condition, in the UK it is also a legal rquirement for NM DSOs.

From 1973 until 1996 this liability was open-ended. Provided goods were in saleable condition, they could be returned at any time after they were purchased. The practical effect of this statutory regulation was that unless a DSO could prove to its auditors that goods had been sold to consumers, then the revenue from the sale of those goods represented a contingent liability on the business. In fact, numerous small NM DSOs failed when large volumes of unsold goods were returned by direct sellers. The terms of this regulation were unreasonable, and, under the 1997 Trading Schemes Regulations, the period after purchase, during which goods may be returned, has been reduced to 90 days. Despite this reduction, any NM DSO, particularly a business which is growing rapidly, still faces a significant contingent liability. It is therefore vitally important, for the sound management of a DSO, to ensure the volume of sales to direct sellers not represented by retail orders already received by those direct sellers is closely monitored and kept to a minimum.

Key points

● Introductions into a DSO's product range invariably replace sales of existing lines. The safest pricing policy is a common gross profit margin.

- For similar categories of consumer goods, the multiple between prime cost and RRP is the same for direct selling as it is for conventional retail distribution.
- Overall distribution margins in direct selling are similar, regardless of the way in which a DSO's sales plan is structured.
- Stock shortages in a DSO are more damaging to a business than in other distribution channels.
- DSOs, wherever possible, should aim to distribute goods directly to every participant. If this practice is adopted in a NM DSO, then it is important to ensure that there are other opportunities for a direct seller to keep in contact with their sponsor.
- While it is feasible for a DSO to distribute goods directly to consumers, this can prejudice good consumer relations and can result in a higher cancelled order rate.
- Offering credit facilities to direct sellers does no one any favours.
- The only justification for a DSO to commit funds to corporate advertising is to improve the morale of direct sellers.
- Cross-border trade, particularly within the EU, represents an easy and attractive opportunity for expansion for enterprising direct sellers – particularly with NM DSOs. However, a DSO should never permit goods to be resold in other markets without first establishing a mechanism for monitoring compliance with local legislation.
- Orders for stocks of products placed by a direct seller on an NM DSO, that are not covered by orders from consumers, can impose a serious financial liability on a DSO.

7

Direct selling legislation and industry codes

This chapter deals with the practical effect of legislation that is exclusive to DSOs, and with established industry codes. As with any channel of retail distribution, there are other, more general, legal responsibilities. This legislation will be referred to, and should be observed by all DSOs.

Many DSOs have sales plans in which the pattern of product distribution involves contracts of sale between the DSO and their direct sellers, prior to those direct sellers selling the goods on to retail consumers. In NM DSOs distributors also have legal responsibilities in the recruitment of others. Compliance with legislation is not just a DSO's management responsibility. It is the duty of management to ensure that all their direct sellers are fully aware of their own legal responsibilities and that they are provided with relevant, updated information on all aspects of consumer law.

The following is a list of the most important Acts and Regulations that are relevant to DSOs. There are civil responsibilities under:

Misrepresentation Act 1967
Consumer Credit Act 1974
Unfair Contract Terms Act 1977
Sale of Goods Act 1979
Supply of Goods and Services Act 1982
Consumer Protection Act 1987 (Part 1 – product liability)
Sale and Supply of Goods Act 1994
Control of Misleading Advertisements Regulations 1988
Consumer Protection (Cancellation of Contracts concluded away from Business Premises) Regulations 1987 (as amended in 1988)
Unfair Terms in Consumer Contracts Regulations 1994

There are also criminal liabilities arising under:

Trades Descriptions Act 1968
Administration of Justice Act 1970
Fair Trading Act 1973 (as amended by the Trading Schemes Act 1996) (Part XI)
Prices Act 1974
Business Names Act 1985
Consumer Protection Act 1987 (Parts II, III, IV, and V)
Consumer Transactions (Restrictions on Statements) Order 1976 (as amended in 1978)
General Product Safety Regulations 1994
Trading Schemes Regulations 1997

'Cooling-off' regulations

Cooling-off regulations in consumer contracts made by direct sellers in prescribed circumstances arose from an EC Doorstep Selling Directive. In the UK they were introduced under the Consumer Protection (Cancellation of Contracts concluded away from Business Premises) Regulations 1987 (Appendix 1). The key features of these regulations are:

> With certain exceptions, the regulations apply to:
>
> (a) any unsolicited transaction effected away from a trader's business premises. This would include sales made during an excursion organized by a trader. For DSOs this would normally mean at a consumer's home or at another's home (party plan sales are included even though guests may previously have been given an invitation making clear that it is a sales party) or at places of work and other social gatherings; and
> (b) where the transaction involves a payment of £35 or more.

Transactions excluded from regulation are those:

> (a) that involve, land, buildings, most repairs to buildings, financial services within the meaning of the Financial Services Act and those involving food, drink and other household goods where they are supplied by regular roundsmen such as milkmen; or

(b) where the terms of contract:
   (i)   contain a minimum seven-day cooling off period; and
   (ii) are contained in a trader's catalogue which can be examined by the customer, in the absence of the trader, before a contract is concluded; and
   (iii) are based on an ongoing relationship between the customer and the trader.

This exclusion is intended to cover mail order agents, although it may also exclude some DSOs whose sales method is to leave catalogues for subsequent collection, together with an order, by a direct seller.

The regulations provide that:

(a) the trader offers customers a minimum seven-day cooling off period in which to cancel any order; and
(b) all customers shall be provided with a receipt that includes prescribed information and a prescribed 'notice of cancellation'.

The cooling-off regulations were intended to protect consumers from entering into ill-considered and substantial transactions resulting from a cold call by a direct seller. In practice, the threshold of £35 (which was the sterling equivalent of the 60 Ecus specified in the EC Directive) is unreasonably low and embraces most DSOs marketing low-ticket consumer goods, where there is a low record of consumer complaint. At the same time, the majority of current consumer problems either relate to categories of excluded transactions, or are those which result from encouraging potential customers to respond to advertisements, telesales calls or leaflets requesting a visit or demonstration from a direct seller. Any prior agreement to a sales call, which resulted in a transaction, could mean that the transaction would be excluded from the scope of these regulations. For these reasons there is a strong likelihood that the regulations will be amended.

Network marketing regulations

In Chapter 4, in a section on the abuses of network marketing, I described the background to the first pyramid selling regulations, which were enabled by the Fair Trading Act 1973, and which were revised in 1989 and 1990. In controlling 'front-end loading' these regulations were partially successful – at least to the extent that the DTI, who have direct responsibility for enforcing the regulations, have never had to make any prosecutions. However, over the past twenty-three years, other abuses have occurred which have defied any further regulatory control. The reason is that certain schemes managed to circumvent control under the 1973 Act. This is the background to the Trading Schemes Act 1996 and the consequent changes to the Fair Trading Act 1973 (see Appendix 2).

Part XI of the 1973 Act defined regulated schemes as those which contained all of a number of features. If one feature was missing, then the scheme was not subject to regulation. The 1996 Act amends Part XI of the Fair Trading Act 1973 and the effect is as follows.

1 Scope

The amended Act, in simple terms, applies to any scheme in which participants are involved in effecting transactions for the supply of goods, services or selling aids, provided by the promoter, through transactions involving consumers or other participants and where the scheme involves any of the following:

(a) introducing other participants;
(b) the continued participation of those who have been introduced;
(c) the promotion or change of status of those who have been introduced;
(d) the supply of goods or services;
(e) the acquisition of goods and services.

2 Exclusions

Excluded from control are schemes regulated under the Financial Services Act 1986, and certain other schemes with features that are defined in the supporting Trading Schemes (Exclusion) Regulations 1997 (see Appendix 2).

3 Offences

The criminal offences remain unchanged. In simple terms, they are:

(a) to receive rewards for doing no more than recruiting others who pay money to join the scheme; or
(b) non-compliance with regulations provided for under the Act.

4 Regulations

The Trading Schemes Regulations 1997 (see Appendix 2) replace the previous Pyramid Selling Regulations all of which were cancelled under the amended Part XI of the 1973 Act. As before, they cover the promotion and advertising of schemes, the form of contracts, the size of initial investments, cooling-off rights, the cancellation of contracts and the right to recover payments for goods made to the promoter.

Some of the previous regulations provided doubtful benefits to participants, and others presented unreasonable burdens on the promoters of ethical DSOs. These have been either amended or dropped. For example, the previous regulations provided for warnings on contracts and promotional literature in a prescribed form headed 'Statutory Warning'. Experience has shown that these were often perceived as being marks of official recognition, rather than as warnings. Another example was the requirement for a DSO to offer an open-ended buyback provision in respect of returned goods. Not only was this an unreasonable financial burden on an ethical DSO, it also tended to convey a false feeling of security to any participant who overinvested in a business opportunity – particularly if the DSO were to fail. The provisions of the new regulations, again in simple terms, are:

(a) Exclusions
   The following types of scheme are not subject to the regulations:
   (i)   where there is no benefit from recruiting others, or where the benefit is no more than £50 per participant introduced. [This is designed to exclude those SLM DSOs where gifts or cash rewards are offered to those direct sellers who introduce others.]
   (ii)   where the benefits to participants come from sharing expenses or profit distribution. [This exclusion is designed to cover certain franchise schemes.]
   (iii) where the taxable turnover of participants is above the threshold which requires VAT registration. [This is intended to cover certain franchise schemes and non-direct selling businesses.]

(b) Promotion and advertising
   (i)   All recruitment advertisements, or any advertisement featuring the earnings opportunities in a regulated business opportunity, in newspapers, magazines, directories, radio and television, must be legal, honest, decent and true. All advertisements must

comply with the Special Rules set out in the British Codes of Advertising and Sales Promotion. These rules require that advertisements shall:

- give the name and contact details of the advertiser;
- make clear that the business opportunity is self employed – if that is the case;
- where possible, give a clear description of the business opportunity;
- where possible, disclose any required investment;
- not make any exaggerated or unrepresentative earnings claims.

(ii) All advertisements, other than those placed in the media, and all other promotional material, shall be subject to the same rules as for media advertisements, but, in addition, are required to:

- carry two statutory warnings (see Appendix 2). The first is a statement making it clear that high earnings cannot easily be achieved. The second is a statement making it clear that it is illegal to persuade anyone to join a trading scheme by promising benefits from getting other people to join the scheme (as opposed to promising benefits earned as a result of future sales and purchases of products). These warnings have to appear in the promotional text and must have no more and no less prominence than any other part of the text;
- show the name and address of the promoter, (this must be the full postal address and not a PO Box number);
- disclose the nature of the products being marketed by the scheme.

These regulations cover all handbills, brochures, audio and video tapes, the internet and similar promotional material. (They do not cover small, interest generating devices, such as stickers and lapel badges, although these should not be created so as to mislead in any way.)

(c) Contracts
  (i) All participants in a regulated trading scheme must be provided with a written contract that must be signed by the participant and an authorized representative of the promoter of the scheme.

(ii)   The contract must include the name and address of the promoter; a description of what the participant will acquire, or be supplied with, as a result of signing the contract, and a clear reference to the participant's role in the scheme. [The latter would include the sales plan of the scheme, and the terms and conditions associated with participation. While this information need not form part of the contract, they must be made available to the participant before the contract is signed.]

(iii) The contract must include details of a participant's right to a cooling-off period of fourteen days. This information must appear on the contract immediately above the space for the participant's signature. During this cooling-off period a participant has a right to cancel the contract without penalty; to recover any money paid to the promoter for participation in the scheme; to be repaid the full amount paid for goods supplied by the promoter provided that those goods are returned in a resaleable condition; to cancel any orders for other services and to recover any money already paid for those services. [The goods that a participant is entitled to return, for a full refund, include all sales promotional material in resaleable condition.]

(iv) The contract must include details of a participant's rights to terminate a contract at any time, subject to his giving fourteen days' written notice of his intention to do so. These rights must include the right to be released from all future contractual obligations; to return any goods purchased in the previous ninety days and to recover the full price paid, less a reasonable handling charge. [The cost of returning the goods would be borne by the party terminating the contract. In the case of a participant terminating the contract, this cost of returning goods would be limited to costs incurred in delivery to a point in the UK.]

(v)   The contract must include details of any financial obligations, of a participant in the first twelve months, and provide for sixty days notice of any changes to these obligations. [This is designed to cover payments for training courses and material, sample products, demonstration kits and any annual registration fees.]

(vi) The contract must include a statement which makes clear that it is an offence to persuade any person to make a payment, by promising them benefits from simply recruiting others. [This means that the contract of a NM DSO should make clear that benefits from sponsorship derive solely from sales achieved by others.]

(vii) The contract must include full details of the terms under which any commissions paid may be subsequently recovered.

(d) Initial investments

(i) The maximum amount which any participant may pay, or promise to pay, to a promoter, within the first seven days of signing a contract, is £200. [This means that it is an offence to receive more than this amount, or post-dated cheques which, with other payments, exceed £200.]

(ii) It is an offence for a promoter to take any guarantee or security from a participant, in return for supplying goods, unless this is accompanied by a written promise to refund the payment if the goods are returned undamaged. [This is to discourage participants from risking their homes or other assets through participation in a scheme.]

(e) General trading conditions

(i) Participants must be provided with an invoice or a receipt for all purchases made under the scheme.

(ii) On termination of a contract, a promoter is not able to recover any commissions paid to a participant relating to returned goods, unless the promoter has refunded all other money due and that the commission was paid less than 120 days previously.

(iii) Neither in writing, nor by any other means, may a promoter make any statement or promise that a participant will benefit from the continued participation of others, other than rewards related to sales that they may have accounted for. [This is intended to provide added protection against the promotion of money circulation schemes, and certain buying clubs where participants are encouraged to make regular payments to the promoter and where those payments are used to benefit other participants.]

(iv) If a promoter commits any breach of the regulations, then a participant will not be liable for any payments required to be made under a contract.

Summary of UK legislation governing network marketing

1 **Relevant Act of**   Fair Trading Act 1973, Part XI, as amended by the
  Parliament   Trading Schemes Act 1996 (the Act).

2 **Definition of a**   Any scheme where a promoter supplies goods or
  regulated   services which are supplied:
  scheme   (a) to other persons under transactions effected
                              by participants, or
  Section 118   (b) to persons introduced by participants and, in
  of the Act   either case, where the prospect of benefits is
                              offered to participants in respect to any of the
                              following:

                          ● introduction of other participants
                          ● continued participation of participants
                          ● change of status of participants within the
                            scheme
                          ● acquisition and or supply of goods and or
                            services to or by any person.

3 **Exclusions**   These include direct selling businesses where:

                          ● all participants are VAT registered
                          ● the sales plan is single level and the maximum
                            reward for recruiting another participant is
                            £50.

4 **Trading Schemes**   (a) *Promotional material*: All recruitment material
  Regulations 1997   other than newspaper, magazine advertise-
                              ments and on radio or television, but includ-
  Section 119 of   ing video and the Internet, must include the
  the Act   following:

                          ● the name and address of the promoter
                          ● a description of the products and or ser-
                            vices offered
                          ● prescribed references to the recruitment
                            offence and earnings claims.

                          (b) *Advertising*: All recruitment advertisements in
                              newspapers and magazines must comply with
                              the ASA Code.
                          (c) *Contracts*: All participants shall be provided

with a written and signed contract which shall include:

- name and address of the promoter and a description of the products and or services
- description of the participant's role and financial obligations for 12 months, which the promoter can only change by giving at least 2 months' notice
- statements giving a 14 days cooling off period and, thereafter, 14 days in which to terminate a contract without penalty
- terms under which goods can be returned for refund and under which previously paid commission and bonuses may be recovered
- prescribed warning relating to the recruitment offence and earnings claims.

(d) *Initial investments*: No more than £200 may be received or promised by a participant within 7 days of signing a contract.

(e) *Rights on termination of a contract*: On termination of a contract, a participant has a right to:

- be released from all future obligations other than 'poaching' and any non-competing obligations specified in a contract, and to
- return goods in good condition and recover the sum paid inclusive of VAT, if purchased within 90 days of termination. This would be the full sum paid where the promoter terminated the contract. On termination by the participant, then the sum would be reduced by diminution in value caused by the participant and by a reasonable handling charge.

(f) *Recovery of commissions*: On termination of a contract, a promoter may only recover those previously paid commissions relating to returned goods that were paid within 120 days of termination.

(g) *Sales records*: A promoter must supply participants with an invoice or receipt in respect of all purchases of goods and services.

5 **Offences**

Section 120 of the Act

It is an offence for anyone who is a promoter or participant in a regulated scheme to:

- invite anyone to make payments to the promoter or to a participant in a scheme by promising benefits in respect of the introduction of other participants into the scheme
- contravene the Trading Schemes Regulations 1997.

Taxation of direct sellers

Income tax and social security

In the UK, direct sellers are treated in terms of income tax and National Insurance contributions, in exactly the same way as any other category of employed or self-employed people. For those in full-time employment, and for whom direct selling is a part-time occupation, and also for those whose only income comes from a part-time occupation with a DSO, it is their responsibility to declare their earnings in their annual tax return. The Inland Revenue normally monitors this activity by requiring DSOs to submit a periodic return showing the commissions paid to any direct seller over a certain amount in the period. This threshold, and the period between returns, is usually agreed between a DSO and their local tax office.

For the tax year 1996/7, for those direct sellers whose sole earnings are from self-employment, and where they are less than £3430 per annum, which accounts for the majority of direct sellers, there is no liability for any social security payments. For those whose self-employed earnings are in excess of £3430, then they are required to pay a flat rate Class 2 contribution of £6.05 per week. A Class 4 rate of 6 per cent of profits applies to all profits between £6860 and £23 660 per annum. For those direct sellers who also have employed occupations, where they pay Class 1 contributions, then they may possibly incur an extra social security liability up to the maximum Class I rate. Direct sellers in that category should seek advice.

Similarly, for tax purposes, DSOs are treated, with the one exception of VAT, no differently from any other type of business.

Value Added Tax

In 1985 a UK derogation of the 5th VAT Directive required DSOs to pay VAT on the full retail price paid for goods by a consumer – regardless of whether or not the transaction was effected by the DSO or one of their non-VAT-registered direct sellers. This ruling is at odds with the rules in most other EU member states, where VAT is payable on the price charged to independent direct sellers. The only way in which some DSOs have overcome this ruling is where goods are supplied to direct sellers, at wholesale prices, without any recommended retail selling prices. In these cases DSOs have claimed that they have no knowledge of what retail prices are charged by their independent direct sellers. Although many DSOs could supply products in this way, it invites investigation into what may be commonly accepted retail margins. It is a practice which also presents other problems relating to a DSO's obligations to accept cancellations and pay refunds for goods returned under guarantee claims.

Another ongoing dispute, with Customs & Excise in the UK, concerns the current ruling that hostess gifts offered by party plan DSOs to a party hostess as a reward for holding the party, attract VAT payable at the full retail price of the goods offered. The DSO's arguments, which as yet have not been upheld in UK courts, is that the incentive offered to a hostess, which is commonly a discount of between 10 per cent and 12.5 per cent on goods of their choice, is in return for a service rendered. The current ruling is that the DSO has to pay VAT at the full retail price. Similarly, any facility offered to a hostess to buy one or two items at 50 per cent of the normal retail price also requires the DSO to pay VAT at their full retail price.

However, where products are supplied in a direct seller's business kit, or where goods are supplied at a discount for demonstration purposes only, then VAT is payable only on the net price charged to the direct seller.

Depending upon a DSO's method of achieving retail sales, it is also acceptable for a DSO to negotiate a reasonable overall reduction in the VAT rate paid on their overall volume of sales to allow for the consumption of products used by direct sellers in the course of demonstration. This reduction can usually be agreed in negotiations with the DSO's local Customs & Excise Office who are also prepared to take into account the proportion of goods sold to direct sellers, at wholesale prices, and which are used, or consumed, by direct sellers and not sold at a profit.

Other legislation

Direct selling businesses in the UK are relatively free of any other special legislation. In the UK mainland neither DSOs, nor most direct sellers, have to be licensed to trade. For direct sellers the only exceptions are those itinerant pedlars and hawkers who offer goods for sale at the doorstep in return for immediate payment. In these cases the direct seller is still required, in most parts of the country, to have a pedlar's licence issued by the local police authority. No substantial UK DSO operates in this way. The only other places in the UK where a DSO should advise its direct sellers to seek a licence are the Isle of Man, and in some of the Channel Islands, where licensing was introduced to protect certain local retail traders.

The Direct Selling Association

The DSA was founded in 1965 as the Direct Sales and Service Association. Its original mission was, and still is, to promote the direct selling channel of distribution and to protect the interests of its member companies from unreasonable legislation.

At the time the DSSA was founded there was not only some ill-informed criticism of the direct sales method from consumer groups, but also allegations that direct selling represented unfair competition to local retailers. If direct selling did pose any threat to small retailers in the 1960s then it paled into insignificance over the following two decades with the growth of superstores and multiple retailers. It was, however, consumer criticism that prompted the DSSA to create the first consumer code for direct selling.

The Direct Selling Association, as it was later named, first obtained an endorsement for its code from the Director General of Fair Trading in 1985. This endorsement specifically related to party plan sales. The code successfully dealt with the concern that guests might unwittingly be invited to what was a selling occasion and that, once there, were placed under moral obligation to make a purchase. In 1987, in consultation with the OFT, the code was revised to cover all the selling methods used by DSA members. At each stage of its evolution, the DSA Code has been updated to ensure that consumers are offered a degree of protection, when they make a purchase from a direct seller, that is equal to if not better than the protection they would get from a purchase made from any other retail channel. Furthermore, as with any good code, a consumer is offered better protection than that afforded under UK law.

In 1991 the DSA introduced a new code, the Code of Business Conduct, to cover a DSO's dealings with direct sellers. DSOs, in effect, 'sell' a business opportunity. As with the consumer code, the business code offers a degree of protection to direct sellers, that is not only fair and reasonable, but which exceeds that which is provided by law.

The UK DSA was was one of the first DSAs to introduce an independent code administrator. Any disputes which cannot be resolved by the DSA are referred to the code administrator, whose judgment is binding on a DSA member company. This is one of the commitments that the CEO of every member company is required to make on an annual basis when they sign a code compliance certificate. In 1997 both the consumer and business codes were further strengthened to keep ahead of consumer expectations, the requirements of the 1997 Trading Schemes Regulations and the provisions of the WFDSA's World Code.

The DSA's policy is to encourage all soundly based DSOs in the UK to join the Association, or at least to abide by the DSA's codes. All applicants for DSA membership are vetted for legal compliance and, after a one-year period as a prospective member, are required to undergo an audit by the DSA's code administrator. This audit includes making contact with both the DSO's retail customers and former direct sellers. Well-run DSOs invariably find this audit to be both helpful and positive.

The DSA is active in promoting the DSA logo, which can be used by all full members, as a sign of fair trading. Journalists, writing feature articles on part-time earnings opportunities available in direct selling, normally like to refer to an organization that gives further advice. The DSA fulfils this role by making available, free of charge, an advice pack containing the DSA's codes, help on what to look for in selecting a sound business and a full list of DSA member companies which highlights the DSO's product speciality, their method of organization and their method of direct selling.

In a channel of distribution which still accounts for a relatively small proportion of total retail expenditure, DSOs tend to compete not with one another, but with other distribution channels. For this reason, DSA members find it helpful at seminars and annual conferences to share information on their experiences and current practices.

The DSA's aim is to enhance the overall level of both competence and fair trading in running a direct selling business. In this way the image and good reputation of direct selling is improved in the eyes of the consuming public, consumer bodies and those in government who are responsible for legislation. A further aim is to achieve a proper recognition for direct selling as a significant channel of retail distribution. In the absence of any government statistics on the size of this channel, the DSA commissions an annual survey of all DSOs operating in the UK. Since 1990, these data are used by all the UK's major market research organizations in their studies of retailing in general and home shopping channels in particular.

The DSA is administered by a director who is responsible to a Council composed of up to ten members elected by the DSA membership. Council members are normally the CEOs of member companies and their businesses represent the full spectrum of activities within the DSA in terms of size, method of direct selling and organization structure.

The DSA consumer code

The precise terms of the consumer code are set out in Appendix 3 – the DSA Code of Practice. The main provisions of this code with which every DSA member has to comply are as follows:

Responsibilities of a DSO on appointing a direct seller.
1 Provide adequate training, advice and printed sales material to direct sellers, which shall include advice concerning their responsibilities to the public, and their own liabilities as independent contractors.
2 Provide protection to the public, through the provision of insurance policies covering the demonstration and use of products.
3 Provide a copy of the code to all direct sellers.

Prospecting for sales
1 All advertisements and promotional activity shall comply with other relevant codes recognized by the Office of Fair Trading.
2 Invitations to any event at which goods will be offered for sale, must make clear the purpose of the event.

Selling practices
1 Direct sellers shall:
   (a) immediately identify themselves, and the name of the DSO, to a prospective customer, and shall ensure that they know the purpose of the call and the nature of the products on offer;
   (b) be truthful and accurate in describing any aspect of a product and its price and answer customers' questions, honestly and clearly;
   (c) respect rights of privacy and any request to bring a sales contact to an end; and
   (d) provide customers with an order form which must include clear details of any guarantee and service provisions provided by the DSO, the customers' right to cancel any order within fourteen days, and full contact details of the DSO and the direct seller.

2 Direct sellers shall not:
   (a) use misleading, deceptive or unfair sales practices, and
   (b) exploit the customer in any way.

Self-regulation of a DSO
It is the responsibility of the CEO to ensure that the DSO:
1 makes regular audits of all compliance provisions; and
2 keeps records of all customer complaints and actions taken.

Code administration
1 The code is administered by a legally qualified independent administrator appointed by the DSA.
2 The Code Administrator:
   (a) conducts regular compliance audits of member companies;
   (b) deals with all consumer complaints that cannot be resolved, within a set period of time, by the DSA director and his staff;
   (c) makes judgments that are binding on member companies and direct sellers, but which do not prevent customers, who do not accept his findings, from seeking redress in other ways;
   (d) reports his findings to the DSA Council, with recommendations, in the case of non-compliance, for appropriate action, and publishes an annual report which is made available to government and all consumer bodies in the UK.

Code publicity
1 The DSA logo may only be used in material produced by a DSA member.
2 DSA members are required, wherever possible, to promote the fact, in written and other material, that they are members and therefore comply with the code.
3 It is a mandatory requirement that all customer order forms, used by member companies, feature the DSA logo.

The DSA business code

The full provisions of this code are set out in Appendix 4 – The DSA Code of Business Conduct. The principal provisions of this code, with which every DSA member has to comply, are:

Recruitment of direct sellers
1 DSOs and direct sellers shall not, either verbally or in writing, make exaggerated or misleading earnings claims, nor be misleading in regard to the nature of the business opportunity.
2 All recruitment material created by independent direct sellers must be approved by the DSO, prior to its use.
3 Recruitment material must not denigrate any other DSO nor feature the names of other DSOs.
4 All face-to-face presentations of an earnings opportunity, or invitations to attend a presentation which incur a cost in attendance, shall clearly identify the name of the DSO.

Investments in a direct selling opportunity

1 DSOs and direct sellers shall not encourage any direct seller to make unreasonable investments in products or services. In particular, investments in goods, prior to their resale, shall not be permitted to be made in order to attain a higher appointment in a DSO, or to benefit from any higher discounts on purchases.

2 On termination of a contract, a DSO shall buy back any saleable inventory at the price paid, less any commissions or bonuses paid on the inventory, and less a reasonable handling charge of up to 10 per cent.

Training

1 DSOs shall ensure that all new direct sellers are provided with a reasonable level of training in the DSO's products and business, and that a basic level of training and advice is made available as part of any investment, made by a participant, in taking up that business opportunity.

2 Where DSOs permit independent direct sellers to create training material, then:

(a) it must be approved by the DSO prior to its use, and

(b) where direct sellers are required to pay for such training, it must be made clear that any charges levied are optional, and are not a condition attached to a direct seller's right to receive a reasonable amount of basic help and advice as part of their initial investment.

3 DSOs and direct sellers requiring fees to be paid for training may only do so subject to the fees being refundable in the case of dissatisfaction expressed within fourteen days of receiving the training.

International trade

Any DSO which wishes to trade in any market outside the UK, or permits its direct sellers either to direct sell, or to recruit in other markets shall:

(a) observe the WFDSA rules on international trade; and

(b) observe either the code of the DSA in that market or the WFDSA code.

Code administration and publicity

The responsibilities for administration and publicity of this code are the same as those for the DSA Consumer Code.

Appendix 1

The Consumer Protection (Cancellation of Contracts Concluded away from Business Premises) Regulations 1987*

Made	*7th December 1987*
Laid before Parliament	*16th December 1987*
Coming into force	*1st July 1988*

The Secretary of State, being a Minister designated(a) for the purposes of section 2(2) of the European Communities Act 1972(b) in relation to matters of consumer protection in respect of contracts negotiated away from business premises of the trader, in exercise of the powers conferred on him by that section and of all other powers enabling him in that behalf, hereby makes the following Regulations:

Citation and commencement

1 These Regulations may be cited as the Consumer Protection (Cancellation of Contracts Concluded away from Business Premises) Regulations 1987 and shall come into force on 1st July 1988.

Interpretation

2–(1) In these Regulations–
'business' includes a trade or profession;
'consumer' means a person, other than a body corporate, who, in making a contract to which these Regulations apply, is acting for purposes which can be regarded as outside his business;

---

*Reproduced with the permission of the Controller of HMSO
(a) S.I. 1986/947.
(b) 1972 c.68.

'goods' has the meaning given by section 61(1) of the Sale of Goods Act 1979**(a)**;

'land mortgage' includes any security charged on land and in relation to Scotland includes any heritable security;

'notice of cancellation' has the meaning given by regulation 4(5) below;

'security' in relation to a contract means a mortgage, charge, pledge, bond, debenture, indemnity, guarantee, bill, note or other right provided by the consumer, or at his request (express or implied), to secure the carrying out of his obligations under the contract;

'signed' has the same meaning as in the Consumer Credit Act 1974**(b)**; and

'trader' means a person who, in making a contract to which these Regulations apply, is acting for the purposes of his business, and anyone acting in the name or on behalf of such a person.

(2) In Scotland any provision in these Regulations requiring a document to be signed shall be complied with by a body corporate if the document is properly executed in accordance with the law of Scotland.

Contracts to which the Regulations apply

3–(1) These Regulations apply to a contract, other than an excepted contract, for the supply by a trader of goods or services to a consumer which is made–

(a) during an unsolicited visit by a trader–
  (i) to the consumer's home or to the home of another person; or
  (ii) to the consumer's place of work;

(b) during a visit by a trader as mentioned in paragraph (a)(i) or (ii) above at the express request of the consumer where the goods or services to which the contract relates are other than those concerning which the consumer requested the visit of the trader, provided that when the visit was requested the consumer did not know, or could not reasonably have known, that the supply of those other goods or services formed part of the trader's business activities;

(a) 1979 c.54.
(b) 1974 c.39; the sums mentioned in section 17 were amended by S.I. 1983/1878.

(c) after an offer was made by the consumer in respect of the supply by a trader of the goods or services in the circumstances mentioned in paragraph (a) or (b) above or (d) below; or

(d) during an excursion organised by the trader away from premises on which he is carrying on any business (whether on a permanent or temporary basis).

(2) For the purposes of this regulation an excepted contract means

(a) any contract–

    (i) for the sale or other disposition of land, or for a lease or land mortgage;

    (ii) to finance the purchase of land;

    (iii) for a bridging loan in connection with the purchase of land; or

    (iv) for the construction or extension of a building or other erection on land: Provided that these Regulations shall apply to a contract for the supply of goods and their incorporation in any land or a contract for the repair or improvement of a building or other erection on land, where the contract is not financed by a loan secured by a land mortgage;

(b) any contract for the supply of food, drink or other goods intended for current consumption by use in the household and supplied by regular roundsmen;

(c) any contract for the supply of goods or services which satisfies all the following conditions, namely–

    (i) terms of the contract are contained in a trader's catalogue which is readily available to the consumer to read in the absence of the trader or his representative before the conclusion of the contract;

    (ii) the parties to the contract intend that there shall be maintained continuity of contact between the trader or his representative and the consumer in relation to the transaction in question or any subsequent transaction; and

    (iii) both the catalogue and the contract contain or are accompanied by a prominent notice indicating that the consumer has a right to return to the trader or his representative goods supplied to him within the period of not less than 7 days from the day on which the goods are received by the consumer and otherwise to cancel the contract within that period without the consumer incurring any liability, other than any liability which may arise from the failure of the consumer to take reasonable care of the goods while they are in his possession;

(d) contracts of insurance to which the Insurance Companies Act 1982**(a)** applies;

(e) investment agreements within the meaning of the Financial Services Act 1986**(b)**, and agreements for the making of deposits within the meaning of the Banking Act 1987**(c)** in respect of which Regulations have been made for regulating the making of unsolicited calls under section 34 of that Act;

(f) any contract not falling within sub-paragraph (g) below under which the total payments to be made by the consumer do not exceed £35; and

(g) any contract under which credit within the meaning of the Consumer Credit Act 1974 is provided not exceeding £35 other than a hire-purchase or conditional sale agreement.

(3) In this regulation 'unsolicited visit' means a visit by a trader, whether or not he is the trader who supplies the goods or services, which does not take place at the express request of the consumer and includes a visit which takes place after a trader telephones the consumer (otherwise than at his express request) indicating expressly or by implication that he is willing to visit the consumer.

Cancellation of Contract

4–(1) No contract to which these Regulations apply shall be enforceable against the consumer unless the trader has delivered to the consumer notice in writing in accordance with paragraphs (3) and (4) below indicating the right of the consumer to cancel the contract within the period of 7 days mentioned in paragraph (5) below containing both the information set out in Part I of the Schedule to these Regulations and a Cancellation Form in the form set out in Part II of the Schedule and completed in accordance with the footnotes.

(2) Paragraph (1) above does not apply to a cancellable agreement within the meaning of the Consumer Credit Act 1974 or to an agreement which may be cancelled by the consumer in accordance

---

(a) 1982 c.50.
(b) 1986 c.60.
(c) 1987 c.22.

with terms of the agreement conferring upon him similar rights as if the agreement were such a cancellable agreement.

(3) The information to be contained in the notice under paragraph (1) above shall be easily legible and if incorporated in the contract or other document shall be afforded no less prominence than that given to any other information in the document apart from the heading to the document and the names of the parties to the contract and any information inserted in handwriting.

(4) The notice shall be dated and delivered to the consumer–
   (a) in the cases mentioned in regulation 3(1)(a), (b) and (d) above, at the time of the making of the contract; and
   (b) in the case mentioned in regulation 3(1)(c) above, at the time of the making of the offer by the consumer.

(5) If within the period of 7 days following the making of the contract the consumer serves a notice in writing (a 'notice of cancellation') on the trader or any other person specified in a notice referred to in paragraph (1) above as a person to whom notice of cancellation may be given which, however expressed and whether or not conforming to the cancellation form set out in Part II of the Schedule to these Regulations, indicates the intention of the consumer to cancel the contract, the notice of cancellation shall operate to cancel the contract.

(6) Except as otherwise provided under these Regulations, a contract cancelled under paragraph (5) above shall be treated as if it had never been entered into by the consumer.

(7) Notwithstanding anything in section 7 of the Interpretation Act 1978**(a)**, a notice of cancellation sent by post by a consumer shall be deemed to have been served at the time of posting, whether or not it is actually received.

Recovery of money paid by consumer

5–(1) Subject to regulation 7(2) below, on the cancellation of a contract under regulation 4 above, any sum paid by or on behalf of the consumer under or in contemplation of the contract shall become repayable.

(2) If under the terms of the cancelled contract the consumer or any person on his behalf is in possession of any goods, he shall have a lien on them for any sum repayable to him under paragraph (1) above.

(a) 1978 c.30.

(3) Where any security has been provided in relation to the cancelled contract, the security, so far as it is so provided, shall be treated as never having had effect and any property lodged with the trader solely for the purposes of the security as so provided shall be returned by him forthwith.

Repayment of credit

6–(1) Notwithstanding the cancellation of a contract under regulation 4 above under which credit is provided, the contract shall continue in force so far as it relates to repayment of credit and payment of interest.

(2) If, following the cancellation of the contract, the consumer repays the whole or a portion of the credit–

(a) before the expiry of one month following service of the notice of cancellation, or

(b) in the case of a credit repayable by instalments, before the date on which the first instalment is due,

no interest shall be payable on the amount repaid.

(3) If the whole of a credit repayable by instalments is not repaid on or before the date specified in paragraph (2)(b) above, the consumer shall not be liable to repay any of the credit except on receipt of a request in writing signed by the trader stating the amounts of the remaining instalments (recalculated by the trader as nearly as may be in accordance with the contract and without extending the repayment period), but excluding any sum other than principal and interest.

(4) Repayment of a credit, or payment of interest, under a cancelled contract shall be treated as duly made if it is made to any person on whom, under regulation 4(5) above, a notice of cancellation could have been served.

(5) Where any security has been provided in relation to the contract, the duty imposed on the consumer by this regulation shall not be enforceable before the trader has discharged any duty imposed on him by regulation 5(3) above.

(6) In this regulation, the expression 'credit' has the same meaning as in the Consumer Credit Act 1974.

Return of goods by consumer after cancellation

7–(1) Subject to paragraph (2) below, a consumer who has before cancelling a contract under regulation 4 above acquired possession of any goods by virtue of the contract shall be under a duty, subject to any lien, on the cancellation to restore the goods to the trader in accordance with this regulation, and meanwhile to retain possession of the goods and take reasonable care of them.

(2) The consumer shall not be under a duty to restore–
   (i) perishable goods;
   (ii) goods which by their nature are consumed by use and which, before the cancellation, were so consumed;
   (iii) goods supplied to meet an emergency; or
   (iv) goods which, before the cancellation, had become incorporated in any land or thing not comprised in the cancelled contract,

but he shall be under a duty to pay in accordance with the cancelled contract for the supply of goods and for the provision of any services in connection with the supply of the goods before the cancellation.

(3) The consumer shall not be under any duty to deliver the goods except at his own premises and in pursuance of a request in writing signed by the trader and served on the consumer either before, or at the time when, the goods are collected from those premises.

(4) If the consumer–
   (i) delivers the goods (whether at his own premises or elsewhere) to any person on whom, under regulation 4(5) above, a notice of cancellation could have been served; or
   (ii) sends the goods at his own expense to such a person,

he shall be discharged from any duty to retain possession of the goods or restore them to the trader.

(5) Where the consumer delivers the goods as mentioned in paragraph (4)(i) above, his obligation to take care of the goods shall cease; and if he sends the goods as mentioned in paragraph (4)(ii) above, he shall be under a duty to take reasonable care to see that they are received by the trader and not damaged in transit, but in other respects his duty to take care of the goods shall cease.

(6) Where, at any time during the period of 21 days following the cancellation, the consumer receives such a request as is mentioned in paragraph (3) above and unreasonably refuses or unreasonably fails to comply with it, his duty to retain possession and take reasonable care of the goods shall continue until he delivers or sends the goods as mentioned in paragraph (4) above, but if within that period he does not receive such a request his duty to take reasonable care of the goods shall cease at the end of that period.

(7) Where any security has been provided in relation to the cancelled contract, the duty imposed on the consumer to restore goods by this regulation shall not be enforceable before the trader has discharged any duty imposed on him by regulation 5(3) above.

(8) Breach of a duty imposed by this regulation on a consumer is actionable as a breach of statutory duty.

Goods given in part-exchange

8–(1) This regulation applies on the cancellation of a contract under regulation 4 above where the trader agreed to take goods in part-exchange (the 'part-exchange goods') and those goods have been delivered to him.

(2) Unless, before the end of the period of ten days beginning with the date of cancellation, the part-exchange goods are returned to the consumer in a condition substantially as good as when they were delivered to the trader, the consumer shall be entitled to recover from the trader a sum equal to the part-exchange allowance.

(3) During the period of ten days beginning with the date of cancellation, the consumer, if he is in possession of goods to which the cancelled contract relates, shall have a lien on them for–

(a) delivery of the part-exchange goods in a condition substantially as good as when they were delivered to the trader; or

(b) a sum equal to the part-exchange allowance;

and if the lien continues to the end of that period it shall thereafter subsist only as a lien for a sum equal to the part-exchange allowance.

(4) In this regulation the part-exchange allowance means the sum agreed as such in the cancelled contract, or if no such sum was agreed, such sum as it would have been reasonable to allow in respect of the part-exchange goods if no notice of cancellation had been served.

Amendment of the Consumer Credit Act 1974

9 After section 74(2) there shall be added the following subsection–
'(2A) In the case of an agreement to which the Consumer Protection (Cancellation of Contracts Concluded away from Business Premises) Regulations 1987 apply the reference in subsection (2) to a small agreement shall be construed as if in section 17(1) (a) and (b) '£35' were substituted for '£50'.'

No contracting-out

10–(1) A term contained in a contract to which these Regulations apply is void if, and to the extent that, it is inconsistent with a provision for the protection of the consumer contained in these Regulations.

(2) Where the provision of these Regulations specifies the duty or liability of the consumer in certain circumstances a term contained in a contract to which these Regulations apply is inconsistent with that provision if it purports to impose, directly or indirectly, an additional duty or liability on him in those circumstances.

Service of documents

11–(1) A document to be served under these Regulations on a person may be so served–

(a) by delivering it to him, or by sending it by post to him, or by leaving it with him, at his proper address addressed to him by name;

(b) if the person is a body corporate, by serving it in accordance with paragraph (a) above on the secretary or clerk of that body; or

(c) If the person is a partnership, by serving it in accordance with paragraph (a) above on a partner or on a person having the control or management of the partnership business.

(2) For the purposes of these Regulations, a document sent by post to, or left at, the address last known to the server of the document as the address of a person shall be treated as sent by post to, or left at, his proper address.

Francis Maude
Parliamentary Under-Secretary of State,
7th December 1987 Department of Trade and Industry

SCHEDULE

Regulation 4(i)

PART I

1 The name of the trader.

2 The trader's reference number, code or other details to enable the contract or offer to be identified.

3 A statement that the consumer has a right to cancel the contract if he wishes and that this right can be exercised by sending or taking a written notice of cancellation to the person mentioned in paragraph 4 within the period of 7 days following the making of the contract.

4 The name and address of a person to whom notice of cancellation may be given.

5 A statement that the consumer can use the cancellation form provided if he wishes.

PART II

CANCELLATION FORM TO BE INCLUDED IN NOTICE OF CANCELLATION RIGHTS

(Complete, detach and return this form ONLY IF YOU WISH TO CANCEL THE CONTRACT.)

To: 1

I/We* hereby give notice that I/we* wish to cancel my/our* contract
          2

Signed

Date

*Delete as appropriate

Notes:

1 Trader to insert name and address of person to whom notice may be given.

2 Trader to insert reference number, code or other details to enable the contract or offer to be identified. He may also insert the name and address of the consumer.

EXPLANATORY NOTE

(This note is not part of the Regulations)

These Regulations implement Council Directive 85/577/EEC (OJ No. L372, 20.12.85, p.31) to protect the consumer in respect of contracts made at the doorstep or otherwise concluded away from business premises. They apply to contracts under which a trader supplies goods or services to a consumer and which are concluded during an unsolicited visit by a trader.

(i) to the consumer's home or to the home of another person; or

(ii) to the consumer's place of work.

The Regulations also apply to contracts concluded during a visit made at the express request of the consumer which are for the supply of goods and services other than those concerning which the consumer requested the trader's visit. In these circumstances the Regulations apply only if the consumer did not know, or could not reasonably have known, when he requested the visit, that the supply of those other goods or services formed part of the trader's business activities.

The Regulations apply to contracts in respect of which an offer was made by the consumer under conditions similar to those described above.

The Regulations also apply to contracts concluded during an excursion organised by a trader away from premises on which he is carrying on any business.

Where the Regulations apply, they provide a cooling off period of 7 days enabling a consumer within that period to cancel the contract by giving a notice of cancellation. The Regulations provide that if the consumer does not receive a written notice informing him of this right of cancellation and of this period for reflection the contract will not be enforceable against him. Where the Consumer Credit Act 1974 applies, the question of unenforceability of contracts is governed by that Act.

Certain types of contracts are exempted from the application of the Regulations. These are:–

(a) contracts relating to land, but not contracts for the supply of goods and their incorporation into land or contracts for repairing or improving buildings on land;

(b) contracts for the supply of food, drink and other goods intended for current consumption in the household and supplied by regular roundsmen;

(c) certain contracts concluded on the basis of a trader's catalogue;

(d) insurance contracts;

(e) investment agreements;
(f) contracts not falling within sub-paragraph (g) which do not require the consumer to make total payments exceeding £35; and
(g) any contract under which credit is provided not exceeding £35.

The Regulations also deal with the consequences of cancellation of contracts such as the repayment of payments for goods or services and of credit provided and the return of goods received.

The Regulations apply to cash transactions and to credit transactions not already cancellable under the Consumer Credit Act 1974. Where the Act applies cancellation of contracts and the consequences of cancellation are governed by the provisions of the Act, and Regulations made under it, as amended by these Regulations.

Appendix 2

The Trading Schemes Act 1996 and Trading Schemes Regulations 1997*

Part XI, Fair Trading Act 1973 (c41) (as amended by the Trading Schemes Act 1996 (c32)

118–(1) This Part of this Act applies to any trading scheme if–

    (a) the prospect is held out to participants of receiving payments or other benefits in respect of any of the matters specified in subsection (2) of this section; and

    (b) (subject to subsection (7) of this section) either or both of the conditions in subsections (3) and (4) of this section are fulfilled in relation to the scheme.

  (2) The matters referred to in paragraph (a) of subsection (1) of this section are–

    (a) the introduction by any person of other persons who become participants in a trading scheme;

    (b) the continued participation of participants in a trading scheme;

    (c) the promotion, transfer or other change of status of participants within a trading scheme;

    (d) the supply of goods or services by any person to or for other persons;

    (e) the acquisition of goods or services by any person.

  (3) The condition in this subsection is that–

    (a) goods or services, or both, are to be provided by the person promoting the scheme (in this Part of this Act referred to as 'the promoter') or, in the case of a scheme promoted by two or more persons acting in concert (in this Part of this Act referred to as 'the promoters'), by one or more of those persons; and

   (b) the goods or services so provided–
      (i) are to be supplied to or for other persons under transactions effected by participants (whether in the capacity of agents of the promoter or of one of the promoters or in any other capacity), or
      (ii) are to be used for the purposes of the supply of goods or services to or for other persons under such transactions.

(4) The condition in this subsection is that goods or services, or both, are to be supplied by the promoter or any of the promoters to or for persons introduced to him or any of the other promoters (or an employee or agent of his or theirs) by participants.

(5) For the purposes of this Part of this Act a prospect of a kind mentioned in paragraph (a) of subsection (1) of this section shall be treated as being held out to a participant whether it is held out so as to confer on him legally enforceable right or not.

(6) This Part of this Act does not apply to any trading scheme–
   (a) under which the promoter or any of the promoters or participants is to carry on, or to purport to carry on, investment business in the United Kingdom (within the meaning of section 1 of the Financial Services Act 1986); or
   (b) which otherwise falls within a description prescribed by regulations made by the Secretary of State by statutory instrument.

(7) The Secretary of State may by order made by statutory instrument–
   (a) disapply paragraph (b) of subsection (1) of this section in relation to a trading scheme of a kind specified in the order; or
   (b) amend or repeal paragraph (a) of subsection (6) of this section;
and so such order, and no order varying or revoking any such order, shall be made under this subsection unless a draft of the order has been laid before Parliament and approved by a resolution of each House of Parliament.

(8) In this Part of this Act–
'goods' includes property of any description and a right to, or interest in, property;
'participant' means, in relation to a trading scheme, a person (other than the promoter or any of the promoters) participating in the scheme:
'trading scheme' includes any arrangements made in connection with the carrying on of a business, whether those arrangements are made or recorded wholly or partly in writing or not;

and any reference to the provision or supply of goods shall be construed as including a reference to the grant or transfer of a right or interest.

(9) In this section any reference to the provision or supply of goods or services by a person shall be construed as including a reference to the provision or supply of goods or services under arrangements to which that person is a party.][1]

119–(1) Regulations made by the Secretary of State by statutory instrument may make provision with respect to the issue, circulation or distribution of [any form of advertisement, prospectus, circular or notice which contains any information][2] calculated to lead directly or indirectly to persons becoming participants in such a trading scheme, and may prohibit any such [advertisement, prospectus, circular or notice][3] from being issued, circulated or distributed unless it complies with such requirements as to the matters to be included or not included in it as may be prescribed by the regulations.

(2) Regulations made by the Secretary of State by statutory instrument may prohibit the promoter or any of the promoters of, or any participant in, a trading scheme to which this Part of this Act applies from–

(a) supplying any goods to a participant in the trading scheme, or

(b) supplying any training facilities or other services for such a participant, or

(c) providing any goods or services under a transaction effected by such a participant, or

(d) being a party to any arrangements under which goods or services are supplied or provided as mentioned in any of the preceding paragraphs, or

(e) accepting from any such participant any payment, or any undertaking to make a payment, in respect of any goods or services supplied or provided as mentioned in any of the paragraphs (a) to (d) of this subsection or in respect of any goods or services to be so supplied or provided,

---

[1] Section 118 was substituted by section 1 of the Trading Schemes Act 1996 which will come into force on a day to be appointed.
[2] Words in square brackets were substituted by section 2(1)(a) of the Trading Schemes Act 1996
[3] Words in square brackets were substituted by section 2(1)(b) of the Trading Schemes Act 1996

unless (in any such case) such requirements as are prescribed by the regulations are complied with.

(3) Any requirements prescribed by regulations under subsection (2) of this section shall be such as the Secretary of State considers necessary or expedient for the purpose of preventing participants in trading schemes to which this Part of this Act applies from being unfairly treated; and, without prejudice to the generality of this subsection, any such requirements may include provisions–

(a) requiring the rights and obligations of every participant under such a trading scheme to be set out in full in an agreement in writing made between the participant and the promoter or (if more than one) each of the promoters;

(b) specifying rights required to be conferred on every such participant, and obligations required to be assumed by the promoter or promoters, under any such trading scheme; or

(c) imposing restrictions on the liabilities to be incurred by such a participant in respect of any of the matters mentioned in paragraphs (a) to (e) of subsection (2) of this section.

(4) Regulations made under subsection (2) of this section–

(a) may include provision for enabling a person who has made a payment as a participant in a trading scheme to which this Part of this Act applies, in circumstances where any of the requirements prescribed by the regulations were not complied with, to recover the whole or part of that payment from any person to whom or for whose benefit it was paid, and

(b) subject to any provision made in accordance with the preceding paragraph, may prescribe the degree to which anything done in contravention of the regulations is to be treated as valid or invalid for the purposes of any civil proceedings.

(5) The power to make regulations under this section may be exercised so as to make different provision–

(a) in relation to different descriptions of trading schemes to which this Part of this Act applies, or

(b) in relation to trading schemes which are or were in operation on a date specified in the regulations and trading schemes which are or were not in operation on that date,

or in relation to different descriptions of participants in such trading schemes.

120–(1) Subject to the next following section, any person who issues, circulates or distributes, or causes another person to issue, circulate or distribute, a [advertisement, prospectus, circular or notice]⁴ in contravention of any regulations made under subsection (1) of section 119 of this Act shall be guilty of an offence.

(2) Any person who contravenes any regulations made under subsection (2) of that section shall be guilty of an offence.

(3) If any person who is a participant in a trading scheme to which this Part of this Act applies, or has applied or been invited to become a participant in such a trading scheme,–

    (a) makes any payment to or for the benefit of the promoter or (if there is more than one) any of the promoters, or to or for the benefit of a participant in the trading scheme, and

    (b) is induced to make that payment by reason that the prospect is held out to him of receiving payments or other benefits in respect of the introduction of other persons who become participants in the trading scheme,

any person to whom or for whose benefit that payment is made shall be guilty of an offence.

(4) If the promoter or any of the promoters of a trading scheme to which this Part of this Act applies, or any other person acting in accordance with such a trading scheme, by holding out to any person such a prospect as is mentioned in subsection (3)(b) of this section, attempts to induce him–

    (a) if he is already a participant in the trading scheme, to make any payment to or for the benefit of the promoter or any of the promoters or to or for the benfit of a participant in the trading scheme, or

    (b) if he is not already a participant in the trading scheme, to become such a participant and to make any such payment as is mentioned in the preceding paragraph,

the person attempting to induce him to make that payment shall be guilty of an offence.

(5) In determining, for the purposes of subsection (3) or subsection (4) of this section, whether an inducement or attempt to induce is made by holding out such a prospect as is therein mentioned, it shall be sufficient if such a prospect constitutes or would constitute a substantial part of the inducement.

---

⁴ Words in square brackets were substituted by section 2(2) of the Trading Schemes Act 1996

(6) Where the person by whom an offence is committed under subsection (3) or subsection (4) of this section is not the sole promoter of the trading scheme in question, any other person who is the promoter or (as the case may be) one of the promoters of the trading scheme shall, subject to the next following section, also be guilty of that offence.

(7) Nothing in subsections (3) to (6) of this section shall be construed as limiting the circumstances in which the commission of any act may constitute an offence under subsection (1) or subsection (2) of this section.

(8) In this section any reference to the making of a payment to or for the benefit of a person shall be construed as including the making of a payment partly to or for the benefit of that person and partly to or for the benefit of one or more other persons.

121–(1) Where a person is charged with an offence under subsection (1) of section 120 of this Act in respect of an advertisement, it shall be a defence for him to prove that he is a person whose business it is to publish or arrange for the publication of advertisements, and that he received the advertisement for publication in the ordinary course of business and did not know, and had no reason to suspect, that its publication would amount to an offence under that subsection.

(2) Where a person is charged with an offence by virtue of subsection (6) of section 120 of this Act, it shall be a defence for him to prove–
(a) that the trading scheme to which the charge relates was in operation before the commencement of this Act, and
(b) that the act constituting the offence was committed without his consent or connivance.

122– A person guilty of an offence under this Part of this Act shall be liable–
(a) on summary conviction, to a fine not exceeding [the prescribed sum] or to imprisonment for a term not exceeding three months or both;
(b) on conviction on indictment, to a fine or to imprisonment for a term not exceeding two years or to both.

123–(1) The provisions of sections 29 to 32 of this Act shall have effect for the purposes of this Part of this Act as if in those provisions–
  (a) references to a weights and measures authority or a duly authorized officer of such an authority were omitted, and
  (b) any reference to an offence under section 23 of this Act were a reference to an offence under this Part of this Act.
(2) For the purposes of the application to Northern Ireland of those provisions as applied by the preceding subsection–
  (a) any reference to the Secretary of State shall be construed as a reference to the Ministry of Commerce for Northern Ireland, and
  (b) paragraphs (c) and (d) of section 33(2) of this Act shall have effect for the purposes of the application of Part II of this Act to Northern Ireland.

The Trading Schemes (Exclusion) Regulations 1997

Made	*13th January 1997*
Laid before Parliament	*14th January 1997*
Coming into force	*6th February 1997*

The Secretary of State in exercise of his powers under section 118(6)(b) of the Fair Trading Act 1973**(a)** hereby makes the following Regulations:

Citation and Commencement

1 These Regulations may be cited as the Trading Schemes (Exclusion) Regulations 1997 and shall come into force on 6th February 1997.

Interpretation

2 In these Regulations–

'the Act' means the Fair Trading Act 1973**(a)**

'annual profit of the trading scheme' means for each financial year the net profit of the promoter or promoters of the trading scheme as shown in the accounts of the trading scheme.

'chain letter' means any trading scheme under which a letter is sent to participants or prospective participants directly or indirectly instructing or requesting them to–

(a) send monies or other benefits to at least one of the individuals on a list of individuals, shown with their mailing addresses, which is contained in or accompanying that letter; and

(b) carry on the chain by sending copies of the letter to other individuals not on the list and removing from the list any one name and address and adding their own to it.

'participant' has the same meaning as in section 118(8) of the Act.

'single tier trading scheme' means a trading scheme the only members of which are the promoter or promoters and one or more participants and under which, in the United Kingdom, either a single promoter or a single participant operates at one level and any other participant or

---

(a) 1973 c.41; a new section 118 was substituted by section 1 of the Trading Schemes Act 1996 (c.32).

participants of the trading scheme operate at the same level below such promoter or participant aforesaid.

'trading scheme' has the same meaning as in section 118(8) of the Act.

Disapplication of Part XI of the Act

3 For the purpose of section 118(6)(b) of the Act the Secretary of State hereby prescribes trading schemes of the following description, that is to say–

(a) any trading scheme which is a single tier trading scheme under which a participant introducing another participant to the scheme does not receive any payment or benefit, or can only receive a single benefit or payment, in respect of the introduction of that participant, such payment or benefit not exceeding £50 and can receive no other benefit or payment in respect of or flowing directly or indirectly from the membership or activities of that participant in that or any other trading scheme, unless such other benefit or payment results from–

　　(i) a sharing of expenses of the operation of the trading scheme;

　　(ii) a share in the annual profit of the trading scheme; or

　　(iii) the sale of the participant's business, being a business in respect of which a registration under the Value Added Taxes Act 1994 was in force at the date of sale.

(b) any trading scheme the promoter or all of the promoters of which and all of the participants in which are registered for Value Added Tax; or

(c) any trading scheme which is a chain letter provided there is no requirement on the participant to send monies or other benefits

　　(i) to a central address or the promoter of the trading scheme for onward distribution; or

　　(ii) to any person or organisation other than or additional to the person whose name and address is to be deleted from the list when the participant sends the letter to others; or

　　(iii) to an organisation or person for onward transmission to a participant (whether or not that participant is identified on the list); and

where the promoter does not benefit from the provision of any other service or facilities offered or provided either by him or any other person or organisation to participants.

John M. Taylor
Parliamentary Under-Secretary of State
for Corporate and Consumer Affairs,
13th January 1997　　　　Department of Trade and Industry

EXPLANATORY NOTE

(This note is not part of the Regulations)

These Regulations disapply the provisions of Part XI of the Fair Trading Act 1973 in respect of certain single tier trading schemes, trading schemes in which the promoter or all the promoters and all participants are registered for Value Added Tax, and chain letters.

Part XI of the Fair Trading Act controls pyramid selling and similar trading schemes by creating offences relating to recruitment where the promise of rewards from others joining the scheme is used to persuade a participant or potential participant to make a payment, and by providing a power to make Regulations with which trading schemes must comply.

Part XI is disapplied in respect of single tier trading schemes under which all participants in the United Kingdom operate at the same level under a single promoter or a single participant and where the participants receive no benefit from recruiting new members to the scheme or only a single payment or benefit of small value and where they can receive no other benefit or payment in respect of or as a result of the membership or the activities of other participants except from the sharing of expenses or a share in the annual profit of the trading scheme or the sale of a participant's business provided such business was registered for VAT at the date of sale (regulation 3(a)). This provision will for the future exempt single tier trading schemes such as most franchises, agencies and distributorships that do not have the recruitment of new members as their main purpose from the controls of Part XI of the Fair Trading Act.

Part XI is disapplied in respect of trading schemes where the promoter or promoters and all participants are registered for VAT (regulation 3(b)).

Part XI is disapplied in respect of chain letters without a central organiser or beneficiary (regulation 3(c)).

The Trading Schemes Regulations 1997

Made	*13th January 1997*
Laid before Parliament	*14th January 1997*
Coming into force	*6th February 1997*

The Secretary of State in exercise of his powers under section 119 of the Fair Trading Act 1973**(a)** hereby makes the following Regulations:

Citation, commencement and application

1–(1) These Regulations may be cited as the Trading Schemes Regulations 1997 and shall come into force on 6th February 1997.

(2) Subject to paragraph (3) below, these Regulations shall apply:

(a) from the date of their coming into force to any trading scheme to which Part XI of the Fair Trading Act 1973 applies and which came into existence on or after the date of coming into force of these Regulations, and to any agreement made under such a trading scheme;

(b) after a period of six months from the date of their coming into force to any trading scheme in existence prior to the coming into force of the Act and to which Part XI of the Fair Trading Act 1973 did not apply prior to that date.

(3) Where an agreement is made after the date of coming into force of these Regulations but prior to the expiry of a six months period after that date under a trading scheme to which Part XI of the Fair Trading Act 1973 applied prior to the coming into force of the Act such agreement shall comply either with the 1989 Regulations or these Regulations.

(4) Subject to paragraph (3) above the 1989 Regulations shall not apply to any trading scheme coming into operation after the date of the coming into force of these Regulations or to any agreement made after that date under any trading scheme to which Part XI of the Fair Trading Act 1973 applies.

Interpretation

1 In these Regulations:

'the Act' means the Trading Schemes Act 1996**((b)**;

(a) 1973 c.41; Part XI was amended by the Trading Schemes Act 1996 c.32.
(b) 1996 c.32.

'advertisement' means any advertisement, document, prospectus, circular or notice, whether transmitted in electronic or any other form, which promotes a trading scheme;

'the 1989 Regulations' means the Pyramid Selling Schemes Regulations 1989**(a)**;

'the 1990 Regulations' means the Pyramid Selling Schemes (Amendment) Regulations 1990**(b)**;

'participant' has the same meaning as in Part XI of the Fair Trading Act 1973**(c)**;

'security' means a mortgage, charge, pledge, bond, debenture, indemnity, guarantee, bill, note or other right provided by the participant, or at his request (expressed or implied), to secure the carrying out of the obligations of the participant under an agreement referred to in regulation 4.

'trading scheme' has the same meaning as in Part XI of the Fair Trading Act 1973.

Contents of advertisements

3–(1) Subject to paragraph (2) of this regulation, a promoter of, or a participant in, a trading scheme shall not issue, circulate or distribute any advertisement which contains information likely to lead directly or indirectly to persons becoming participants in a trading scheme by any means unless such advertisement
   (a) states the name and address of the promoter, or in the case of a scheme promoted by more than one person, the names and addresses of all of the promoters;
   (b) describes the goods or services acquired or supplied under the trading scheme; and
   (c) contains the words set out in Schedule 1 to these Regulations which must
      (i) not appear at the beginning or the end of the advertisement;
      (ii) insofar as the advertisement contains any information as to the sources of income for participants from participation in the trading scheme, appear together with such information and be given no less prominence than such information;
      (iii) be easily legible or audible; and

(a) S.I. 1989/2195, amended by S.I. 1990/150.
(b) S.I. 1990/150.
(c) 1973 c.41; Part XI was amended by the Trading Schemes Act 1996 c.32.

(iv) be afforded no less prominence than that given to any other information in the advertisement apart from the heading of the advertisement.

(2) This regulation does not apply to any advertisement which–

(a) forms part of a newspaper or magazine; or

(b) is transmitted by way of a radio or television broadcast.

Pre-performance requirements

4–(1) Save where the requirements set out in paragraph (2) below are satisfied, no promoter of, nor participant in, a trading scheme shall–

(a) supply goods or services to a participant in the trading scheme;

(b) provide any goods or services under a transaction effected by such a participant;

(c) be a party to any arrangement under which goods or services are supplied or provided as aforesaid; or

(d) accept from any such participant any payment or undertaking to make a payment in respect of any goods or services supplied or provided as mentioned in any of the preceding paragraphs (a) to (c) above or in respect of any goods or services to be so supplied or provided.

(2) The requirements referred to in paragraph (1) above are that–

(a) the arrangements with a participant do not include a statement or promise that the participant will receive a payment or benefit in respect of the continued participation of another person in the trading scheme to which such arrangements relate or in any other trading scheme;

(b) the promoter or a participant and the participant joining the trading scheme shall have signed a written agreement which contains all the terms under which the participant joining the trading scheme is participating in the trading scheme and which complies with regulation 5;

(c) a copy of that agreement shall have been furnished to the participant joining the trading scheme.

Contents of contracts

5 The agreement referred to in regulation 4 shall include:

(a) the name and address of the promoter or, in the case of a scheme promoted by more than one person, the names and addresses of all the promoters;

(b) a description of the goods or services to be acquired by or supplied to the participant by the promoter or promoters, other participants or suppliers nominated by the promoter or promoters or any other person under the trading scheme;

(c) a statement describing the capacity in which the participant shall act for the purposes of any transaction which he may effect under the trading scheme;

(d) a statement describing the financial obligation of the participant during the period of twelve months from the commencement date of the agreement. The promoter shall give to the participant at least 60 days advance written notice of any subsequent changes in such financial obligation.

(e) a statement describing the right of the participant to cancel the agreement:

    (i) within 14 days of entering into the agreement without penalty and with the right to recover any monies which he had paid to or for the benefit of the promoter or any of the promoters or any other participant in connection with his participation in the trading scheme or paid to any other participant in accordance with the provisions of the trading scheme and the manner in which that cancellation and recovery shall be effected;

    (ii) within 14 days of entering into the agreement the right to return to an address specified in the agreement which must be an address in the United Kingdom, any goods the participant has purchased within that period under the trading scheme and which remain unsold provided that such unsold goods remain in the condition in which they were in at the time of purchase, whether or not their external wrappings have been broken and to recover any monies paid in respect of such goods;

    (iii) within 14 days of entering into the agreement the right to cancel any services ordered within that period under the trading scheme and to recover any monies paid in respect of such services not yet supplied to the participant;

and that the promoter or any other person who has supplied goods to the participant under the trading scheme shall not be entitled to make a handling charge in respect of goods returned under sub-paragraph (ii) above or services cancelled under sub-paragraph (iii) above;

(f) a statement describing the rights of the participant to terminate the agreement at any time without penalty by giving 14 days written notice to the promoter or any of the promoters at an address which is specified in the agreement;

(g) a statement describing the rights of the participant following termination of the agreement by the promoter or the participant as set out in these Regulations;

(h) the written warnings in the form set out in Part I and Part II of Schedule 2 hereto which comply with the following:
  (i) the words are easily legible; and
  (ii) the words in Part II are printed immediately above the space for the participant's signature.

(i) a statement setting out the conditions under which the participant shall be entitled to return goods to the promoter or any promoters or any other participant which shall include at least the rights conferred on the participant by regulation 6 below and which must include an address in the United Kingdom to which such goods can be returned.

(j) a statement setting out the conditions when commission already paid by the promoter or another participant will be recoverable from the participant which shall include at least the rights conferred on the participant by regulation 9.

(k) where the agreement comprises more than one document, a statement setting out all documents which form part of the contract between the parties and that those documents form the entire agreement between the parties.

Right to return goods to promoter on termination

6–(1) The rights referred to in regulation 5(i) are, that if a participant or the promoter or any of the promoters terminates an agreement referred to in regulation 4 or any agreement entered into in consequence of such an agreement with a participant, the participant shall, subject to subsection (2) below, have the right to be released from all future contractual obligations and to return to the promoter or any of the promoters or any other participant any goods the participant has purchased within a period of 90 days prior to such termination under the scheme and which remain unsold and to recover from the promoter or such other participant who supplied the goods–

(a) where the participant has terminated the agreement, the price (inclusive of Value Added Tax) which the participant paid for them less:
  (i) in the case of any goods the condition of which has deteriorated due to an act or default on the part of the

participant, an amount equal to the diminution in their value resulting from such deterioration; and

(ii) a reasonable handling charge;

(b) where the promoter or any of the promoters or any other participant has terminated the agreement the price (inclusive of Value Added Tax) which the participant paid for them together with any costs incurred by the participant for returning the goods to the promoter or any other participant;

(c) on terms whereby the purchase price is payable upon delivery of the goods or, if the goods are already held by the promoter or any of the promoters, forthwith, and

(d) on terms whereby the goods not already held by the promoter or any of the promoters will be delivered within 21 days of such termination at the promoter's expense to the address stated in the agreement.

(2) Where an agreement referred to in regulation 4 contains an obligation on the participant not to compete with the business of the promoter after termination of such agreement, such non-competition provision shall continue in force after the date of termination.

Securities and guarantees

7 A promoter of, or a participant in, a trading scheme shall not accept from a participant any guarantee or security in whatever form in respect of goods or services supplied or to be supplied or in respect of the payment of the price for goods or services supplied or to be supplied or an undertaking to provide such a guarantee or such security unless the creditor or a promoter or other supplier who is not a creditor has agreed in writing to refund the amount of that payment to the debtor upon his returning the relevant goods in an undamaged condition to the creditor or to any promoter or supplier.

Supply of goods and services

8 A promoter of, or a participant in, a trading scheme shall not make a supply of goods or services to the participant unless, in respect of every supply of goods or services under a trading scheme, such promoter or participant has provided the participant to whom the goods are supplied or to be supplied with an adequate record of the transaction in respect of which payment is due from that participant. For the purposes of this regulation an itemised order form, invoice or receipt shall constitute an adequate record.

Recovery of commission

9 The rights referred to in regulation 5(j) are the right to retain, after termination of an agreement referred to in regulation 4 or any agreement made thereunder, any commission paid to the participant under a trading scheme unless–
  (a) the commission was paid in respect of goods returned to the promoter or another participant who paid the commission;
  (b) the promoter has refunded all monies due to the participant under the agreement referred to in regulation 4 in respect of goods returned to him by the participant;
  (c) the commission payment is claimed within 120 days of the date of having been made; and
  (d) the promoter has entered into an agreement with the participant that complies with the requirements in regulation 5 and that agreement and any subsequent agreement contains a statement describing when commission becomes repayable to the promoter and the terms upon which recovery of that payment may be made; and
  (e) the promoter recovers the commission payment in accordance with the terms referred to in paragraph (d) above.

£200 liability limit

10 A promoter of, or a participant in, a trading scheme shall not accept from a participant joining the trading scheme any payment or an undertaking to make a payment of any sum exceeding £200 unless 7 days have expired from the making of the agreement relating to goods or services supplied or to be supplied under that agreement to the participant by the promoter or any other participant under the trading scheme.

Civil consequences of contraventions

11–(1) Where a participant makes a payment to or for the benefit of a promoter of, or to a participant in, a trading scheme and the acceptance of that payment involves a contravention of these Regulations, that contravention shall be actionable at the suit of the participant who suffers loss as a result of the contravention subject to the defences and other incidents applying to actions for breach of statutory duty.
  (2) No undertaking to make any payment given by a participant in a trading scheme involving a contravention of sub-paragraph (d) of paragraph (1) of regulation 4 or regulation 10 shall be enforceable

against him in any civil proceedings or recoverable in any other way.

(3) A participant in a trading scheme shall be under no liability to pay for any goods or services as the case may be–

(a) supplied to him in circumstances involving a contravention of regulations 4 to 10; or

(b) unless it was clearly explained to him by a promoter or a participant supplying or seeking to supply goods or services under the trading scheme, before he purchased the goods or services, that he had a free choice whether or not to purchase those goods or services and the purchase price for those goods or services and his annual financial obligation under the agreement was clearly stated.

John M. Taylor
Parliamentary Under-Secretary of State
for Corporate and Consumer Affairs,
13th January 1997   Department of Trade and Industry

SCHEDULE 1   Regulation 3(1)(c)

Warning for use in advertisements–

1 It is illegal for a promoter or a participant in a trading scheme to persuade anyone to make a payment by promising benefits from getting others to join a scheme.

2 Do not be misled by claims that high earnings are easily achieved.

SCHEDULE 2   Regulation 5

Warning for use in contracts–

Part I

1 It is illegal for a promoter or a participant in a trading scheme to persuade anyone to make a payment by promising benefits from getting others to join a scheme.

2 Do not be misled by claims that high earnings are easily achieved.

Part II

3 If you sign this contract, you have 14 days in which to cancel and get your money back.

EXPLANATORY NOTE

(This note is not part of the Regulations)

These Regulations apply to any pyramid selling or similar trading scheme to which Part XI of the Fair Trading Act 1973 as amended by the Trading Schemes Act 1996 applies and which came into existence after the date of coming into force of these Regulations, and to any agreement made under such a trading scheme. The Pyramid Selling Schemes Regulations 1989 as amended by the Pyramid Selling Schemes (Amendment) Regulations 1990 are disapplied in respect of these trading schemes and agreements.

There is a six months transitional provision for trading schemes which were in existence prior to the date of coming into force of the Trading Schemes Act 1996 and which were until then not within Part XI of the Fair Trading Act 1973.

Where a trading scheme was subject to Part XI or the Fair Trading Act 1973 prior to the coming into force of the Trading Schemes Act 1996 then any agreement made under such a trading scheme within six months from the date of the coming into force of these Regulations can be made either under the 1989 Regulations or these Regulations. Any agreements made after the six months period will need to be made under these Regulations.

The Regulations follow the framework of the 1989 Regulations.

The control of the content of advertisements (regulation 3) has been updated since the 1989 Regulations. The controls no longer apply to any person but only to a promoter or a participant. Advertisements in all forms including electronic form are now covered unless they form part of a newspaper or magazine or are transmitted by radio or television broadcast. The date of actual or proposed first operation of the scheme in the UK and the status of the participant need no longer be included in the advertisement.

The statutory warning has been simplified.

The exemption for papers handed out in public places and for advertisements not indicating financial benefits has been removed.

There is no longer a requirement to substantiate financial benefits.

Promoters and participants have to meet certain pre-contractual requirements (regulation 4). Statements or promises of benefits for continued participation of others in a trading scheme are prohibited. Participants must be supplied with a written contract.

The provisions as to the content of the contract have been extended since the 1989 Regulations (regulation 5). The requirements now cover statements on rights such as cancellation, termination, return of goods and recovery of sums paid, financial obligations and commission.

Participants have the right to return goods to the promoter subject to certain basic conditions (regulation 6). Goods can be returned if purchased within 90 days prior to termination.

The taking of securities and guarantees is prohibited (regulation 7).

A participant must be given an itemised record of goods he purchased (regulation 8).

The promoter's right to recover commission on termination of a contract is limited and subject to conditions (regulation 9). No commission can be recovered after a period of 120 days has elapsed since its payment.

A promoter or a participant is prohibited from accepting any sum exceeding £200 from a new participant until 7 days have expired from the making of the contract (regulation 10). The previous limit was £75.

Civil rights and remedies for breach of the Regulations are provided for (regulation 11).

Appendix 3

The DSA Code of Practice

Methods of selling

1 Members shall satisfy the Association:

(a) that adequate initial training and information is given to all direct sellers with particular regard to their responsibilities to the public; and that continuing training is made available throughout a direct seller's contract;

(b) that they have adequate cover against all claims for death, personal injury and damage to property arising out of the demonstration of goods or their use after sale; this cover may either be an insurance policy with a company approved by the association or by the member carrying the risk itself, subject to the approval of that arrangement by the Association;

(c) that direct sellers are encouraged to take out adequate public liability cover where appropriate.

Notes

'Adequate initial training and information' mean training and informing all newly recruited direct sellers where appropriate so that they understand:

(a) what it means to be self-employed;

(b) that they make provision for income tax and VAT;

(c) that they must have proper insurance cover for:
  (i) the use of motor vehicles for business purposes;
  (ii) personal liability for damage etc;

(d) that, as sellers of goods to the public, they have legal responsibility under the Sale of Goods Act 1979 for the quality and fitness of what they sell.

'Insurance' by members raises several issues. As direct sellers are self-employed they may not be included in the block insurance policies which members have to cover themselves and their employees.

For example, a direct seller demonstrating a product which is spilled into a television set which catches fire and damages furnishings may believe that the member's insurer will deal with the situation. Unless the member has made previous arrangements with its insurance company this may not be the case; direct sellers will be personally liable unless they have taken out business liability cover.

Some members provide direct sellers with insurance cover against loss of or damage to stock as well as for damage caused to the public or their property. Such extended cover is often provided at a very competitive rate likely to be attractive to direct sellers.

Likewise with motor insurance. All direct sellers driving cars for any reason connected with direct selling are using them for 'business purposes'. Many direct sellers may deliver goods while picking children up from school or on a domestic shopping trip and not realize that they are actually 'on business'. Unless they have extended the normal 'social, domestic and pleasure' cover, they will be driving uninsured. This is an added worry when they are driving someone else's car (such as their spouse's or a firm's car).

'Personal injury or damage to property' extends to:

(a) problems caused by a product being defective –
    e.g. a foreign body in a cosmetic

(b) damage caused by a product –
    e.g. staining a carpet

(c) damage caused by the direct seller –
    e.g. knocking over a breakable ornament

(d) consequential loss –
    e.g. loss of wages, rebuilding or repair costs.

Finally, direct sellers are retailers as far as the customer is concerned. This means that they have legal duties under the Sale of Goods Act 1979 and are directly liable to the customer if goods fail to correspond with any description, are not of satisfactory quality or fit for their intended use, or do not correspond with any sample.

Although direct sellers have legal remedies along the chain of distribution against the supplier (normally the Member) if all those behind them have gone out of business, the liability remains with the direct seller. Many direct sellers do not realize that.

2 **Members whose sales and/or recruiting methods include inviting would-be direct sellers and consumers to meetings shall ensure that all invitations:**

  (a) **Specify the purpose of the meeting**
  (b) **Explain that those invited are under no obligation to purchase anything.**

  Invitees shall be given details of a named contact person and telephone/fax number or address.

Notes

'Invitation' must contain the name of the member company and the name of any local organizer and a contact telephone number and/or address.

'Specify the purpose of the meeting' – some participants may gather would-be customers to an informal meeting (such as a dinner party) during which they may be intending to sell goods. It is a basic tenet of the Association's ethical position that all customers should know in advance why they are being asked to attend the meeting. It would therefore be a breach for anyone to use an otherwise innocuous gathering for a sales pitch unless the true purpose was made clear beforehand.

3 **Members shall satisfy the Association by production of written guidance that they have taken all reasonable steps to see that direct sellers act with integrity; and in particular:**

  (a) **Do not use misleading, deceptive or unfair sales practices**
  (b) **Respect the customers' right to privacy and their right to bring any contact to an end**
  (c) **Describe the goods or products truthfully and accurately**
  (d) **Answer customers' questions honestly and clearly**
  (e) **Give clear and legally accurate information about price and all aspects of after-sales service**
  (f) **Abide by all current guidelines covering the promoting and selling of goods**
  (g) **Refrain from exploiting the customer in any way.**

Notes

'Misleading or deceptive practices' would also cover making claims about goods which are not authorized by the member or which the direct seller knows are inaccurate and which he only makes to induce a customer to sign an order.

'The right to privacy' means that a person being approached has a complete right at any time, whether he is being reasonable or not, to ask a direct seller to bring any sales pitch to an end and to leave his property. Equally he has the right not to be telephoned persistently. The Association and Code Administrator will regard complaints about any persistent conduct as a breach of the right to privacy.

Although an Englishman's home is his castle, and it is actionable trespass to enter his land without express permission, the law takes a more realistic approach. It was held by the High Court in 1967 that when a householder lives in a dwelling house to which there is a garden in front and does not lock the garden gate, there is an implied licence to any member of the public (including a policeman) who has a lawful reason for doing so to proceed from the gate to the front or back door and to enquire whether he may be admitted and to conduct his lawful business.

Thus, any direct seller may go to a would-be customer's house and leave a catalogue or other material or knock and ask whether he may approach the customer. The householder may ask him to leave; or not to leave catalogues etc. in future. The direct seller must go there and then. If he returns he will be a trespasser – because the implied licence was withdrawn by the householder.

If a person contacts a member to say that direct sellers must not come to his house for any reason, the member must acknowledge that request in writing and do everything possible to notify all their direct sellers in the area to avoid the person's house. The person may argue that by giving notice in writing to the member he has withdrawn his licence and that anyone who then enters does so without consent and is a trespasser. The court might take the view that it is impossible for a large organization to control the actions of every single person connected with it and that if the member could show that it had circulated everyone with the person's address and told them not to go there on pain of sanctions, it had done its best.

The direct seller would still be at risk of a claim for damages for trespass, but the member would almost certainly be discharged from liability.

These two matters may be summarized that a direct seller should go when asked and not carry on trying to sell a product.

To be able to 'describe goods truthfully and accurately' members must give direct sellers the most up-to-date information about all aspects of goods bearing in mind that s.14 of the Sale of Goods Act 1979 (as amended in 1994) says that goods must be of 'satisfactory quality' and 'fit for their intended use'.

Because direct sellers are self-employed, they will be sellers of goods and, as such, will have all the legal liabilities of a seller under the Sale of Goods Act 1979 and will be assumed to have specialized product knowledge.

'Current guidelines' include the OFT rules on telephone sales; for example, not telephoning after 9 pm or at a person's place of work.

'Exploitation' includes not only taking advantage of customers who are socially or intellectually unsophisticated. It extends to applying pressure during sales pitches, coercing customers to sign orders or continuing to try to sell when a customer has made it clear that he does not want to buy.

4 Members shall satisfy the Association that:

(a) **They are familiar with current legislation on trade and consumer protection**
(b) **Where appropriate they inform direct sellers of their relevant legal obligations and keep them up to date with all changes as and when appropriate.**

Notes

Because the ultimate responsibility lies with members, because direct sellers will have legal remedies back along the chain of distribution, it is imperative that members ensure that, where appropriate, all direct sellers receive continuously updated information about all aspects of consumer law.

There are civil responsibilities under:

Misrepresentation Act 1967
Unfair Contract Terms Act 1977
Sale of Goods Act 1979
Supply of Goods and Services Act 1982
Consumer Protection Act 1987 (Part I – product liability)
Sale and Supply of Goods Act 1994
Control of Misleading Advertisements Regulations 1988
Consumer Protection (Cancellation of Contracts concluded away from Business Premises) Regulations 1987 (amended in 1988)
Unfair Terms in Consumer Contracts Regulations 1994

There are criminal liabilities arising under:

Trade Descriptions Act 1968
Administration of Justice Act 1970
Fair Trading Act 1973
Prices Act 1974
Business Names Act 1985
Consumer Protection Act 1987 (Parts II, III, IV and V)
[Trading Schemes Act 1996]
Pyramid Selling Schemes Regulations 1973
Consumer Transactions (Restrictions on Statements) Order 1976 (as amended in 1978)
Pyramid Selling Schemes Regulations 1989
General Product Safety Regulations 1994
[Trading Schemes Regulations 1997]

There are also many regulations made under the Consumer Protection Acts 1971 and 1987 dealing with specific product types.

Advertisements

5 (a) **Members' advertisements shall be truthful and accurate and, as a general rule, shall incorporate a reference to their membership of the Association. Members' sales and promotional literature shall also be truthful and accurate and shall always contain a reference to their membership of the Association.**
   (b) **Members must be able to satisfy the Association that they comply with the British Codes of Advertising Practice and Sales Promotion where relevant.**
   (c) **Where members use direct mail or telephone selling they will make use of the Mailing Preference Service and Telephone Preference Service.**

Notes

Members should make it a term of the contract with direct sellers that all advertising copy referring to the member and using its name or logo must either follow what the member prepares or must be submitted to the member for vetting.

The requirement to use the Telephone Preference Service only applies to members who themselves use telephone marketing.

Identification

6 All direct sellers should immediately:

    (a) Identify themselves to prospective customers
    (b) Explain the purpose of their approach
    (c) Identify the member and the goods.

7 Members will supply copies of this Code of Practice to all direct sellers. It must be available for any customer to look at.

Notes

Customers need to have confidence in direct sellers and in the companies whose products they supply. It is therefore a basic courtesy that catalogues and other material which may be given to a customer or left at his house should contain the name and address of the member and of the direct seller.

'Purpose of the approach' – in order that a customer is not misled, members must explain to direct sellers that an open, honest initial contact is more likely to result in a satisfied customer placing an order.

'Copies of the Code' means either the code as published by the Association or its text reprinted in easily legible type by a member as part of its training or business packs.

Order forms

8 Customers' order forms must be approved by the Association and Code Administrator before they are used. They must:

    (a) Contain the member's full name and address
    (b) Set out any guarantee referred to Rule 9
    (c) Show that the member belongs to the Association and contain the Association's logo
    (d) Give contact details of the direct seller.

A copy of an order must be given to the customer when it is placed.

Notes

It is essential that the name and address of the member appears on the customer's order form, and that the customer has a copy to retain at all times. This enables him to know where the goods he is ordering will be coming from which is particularly important as Members have such different systems for processing orders and delivering the goods.

It is also important that members remember the requirements of the Business Names Act 1985 which contains two separate disclosure requirements. The corporate name and an address in the United Kingdom at which documents may be served must be shown on all:

- Business letters
- Written orders for goods and services
- Invoices and receipts
- Written demands for the payment of business debts.

The customer's order form clearly comes within the third group.

Membership of the Association must be shown in order to reinforce the confidence which the customer should expect. This can be done by using the DSA logo or by stating 'Member of the Direct Selling Association' or preferably both.

As direct sellers are retailers, as far as the customer is concerned, their names and addresses are essential so that customers know with whom they are dealing.

Guarantees

9 **Any guarantee of goods shall be clear and easy to understand. It must exceed the customer's existing legal rights, and not affect his statutory rights.**

The terms of all guarantees must be approved by the Association and the Code Administrator before they are used.

Notes

There is a wide range of guarantees offered by members and, bearing in mind the provisions of the Consumer Transactions (Restrictions on Statements) Order 1976 members must ensure that care is taken not to limit or exclude the customer's inalienable rights under the Sale of Goods Act.

Should there be any wording which might be interpreted as restricting the rights under sections 13 to 15 Sale of Goods Act 1979, members must make sure that the words 'This does not affect your statutory rights' appear.

The Association regards guarantees as an added sales benefit.

After-sales service

**10 When an after-sales service is offered, details and limitations must
be clearly stated in writing. Where a customer would normally
expect an after-sales service but none is offered, this must be stated
in writing and given to the customer.**

Notes

It is in the interest of members to provide after-sales service. It enhances
the value of the goods and gives customers confidence that they are
dealing with a reputable manufacturer.

Rights of cancellation

**11 Members must ensure that customers are allowed to cancel any
order within fourteen days from the date of an order and are
informed of that right in writing. A full refund of the price or any
deposit shall be made forthwith. If, within that period, the goods
have deteriorated or been misused, the member may make an
appropriate adjustment.**

Notes

This paragraph confers a considerable benefit on customers. It gives them
the right to cancel a contract *for any reason* within fourteen days of the
date of placing an order. They may have decided they cannot afford it,
seen it cheaper elsewhere, do not like the goods when they arrive or
simply changed their mind. It is important to understand that the reason
is immaterial. So long as the customer gives notice within fourteen days,
the contract must be cancelled and a full refund made.

Some members give a far longer period. This right is absolute so long
as the goods are not damaged or have not deteriorated in some way. This
'cooling-off' right is in addition to any other legal rights which the
customer has.

It would be sensible that this important additional right is put in the
order form which is retained by the customer.

The benefit in this paragraph must be distinguished from the general
law about the way contracts are made and specific areas where there are
particular rules.

(A) Most credit agreements, although signed by the customer, are
merely 'offers' to enter into a contract and do not have any legal effect

until the applications have been vetted by the member or the creditor and have been 'accepted' by being signed on their behalf. In these cases, the customer has complete freedom to withdraw his offer at any time up to the moment when the member/creditor 'accepts'.

Thereafter, the usual cooling-off rules under the Consumer Credit Act come into force.

In either case, all money paid in advance must be refunded (and any goods actually supplied handed back).

(B) Secondly, after the fourteen days has passed the customer is in the same position as anyone else who buys unseen and has to rely on the rights (and obligations) in the Sale of Goods Act (as substantially amended in 1994).

Section 34 of the Act says:

> that unless otherwise agreed, when the seller tenders delivery of goods to a buyer, he is bound on request to afford the buyer a reasonable opportunity of examining the goods for the purpose of ascertaining whether they are in conformity to the contract (or any sample).

Thus, any goods bought by mail or through direct selling will not have been seen and examined by the buyer at the time of the sale; or he may have been shown a sample and have been told that what is supplied with be the same.

The buyer must be given a 'reasonable opportunity' to examine for conformity. This means that he can check whether it meets the specification, corresponds with any sample and/or with any description and whether it is of 'satisfactory quality' within section 14 of the Act (as inserted in 1994).

What amounts to 'examination' depends on the goods. An ornament delivered in a box, is 'examined' by looking carefully at it to see whether there are any blemishes. A washing machine, on the other hand, can only be 'examined' for conformity with the contract by being plumbed in, filled with clothes and switched on. Only then will the buyer be able to see that it works properly.

Under the Sale of Goods Act 1979 a buyer may reject goods and treat the contract as cancelled if – *and only if* – there is something wrong with the goods.

If the goods do NOT conform, the buyer may reject them and recover the price.

However, so long as the goods do not breach any of the conditions in the Act, the buyer has no right to reject. He certainly is not allowed to reject simply because he has changed his mind or regrets his buying decision.

The only proviso to this statement is where the seller has given a wider right to a refund (e.g. Marks & Spencer and many DSA members).

As before, goods will be of a 'satisfactory quality' if they meet the standard expected by a reasonable person to be 'satisfactory' taking account of any description, price and other relevant circumstances.

However, there is a new, non-exhaustive list of factors to be taken into consideration when measuring how satisfactory goods are, which include: their state or condition, fitness for purpose, appearance and finish, freedom from minor defects, safety and durability.

A trader who fails to indicate that the goods are not fit for all their common purposes may be in breach if he sells something commonly supplied for two purposes but which is in fact only fit for one.

So long as DSA members are aware of the new definition of quality, and familiarize themselves with the legal position, they have nothing to worry about if they deliver goods after fourteen days from the contract.

(C) The Consumer Protection (Cancellation of Contracts concluded away from Trade Premises) Regulations 1988 ('the Doorstep Selling Regulations') apply to all contracts (among others) made during an unsolicited visit by a trader to a consumer at his home or someone else's home or his place of work.

'Unsolicited visit' means not only a 'cold call' (a visit which is completely unexpected by the consumer) but one where the trader first telephones to say that he is willing to visit a consumer. It is probable that 'unsolicited' does not cover a call made after a phone call from a consumer, or when a consumer returns a card requesting a call.

Excepted from the Doorstep Selling Regulations are contracts which meet three tests summarized as follows:

(a) The terms are set out in a catalogue which the consumer may read in private before a contract is made
(b) The trader and consumer intend an on-going relationship
(c) The catalogue and subsequent contract contain a notice that the consumer has at least seven days to cancel the contract without any cost. In addition, the Regulations do not apply where the total price payable is under £35.

In direct selling, a very large proportion of business is carried out by individual self-employed salespeople calling at houses and leaving catalogues or cards inviting consumers to think about buying goods or attending a group or party where goods may be on offer.

A great deal of direct selling is between traders and long-standing customers, who are used to seeing regular new catalogues or attending parties, and the relationship meets all three elements of the exception outlined above.

However, there is a continual turnover of customers and traders who have a regular round will always try to interest new people. Even though they leave a catalogue which complies, or fix a party which the consumer may cancel, it is always arguable that the second element is not met, because the consumer did not intend there to be any continuity of relationship. Then, even though the catalogue and contract contain the information required by the Doorstep Selling Regulations, the contract will not be exempt.

The Regulations require a cooling-off period of 'at least seven days' and the statutory form of words contained in the Schedule stipulates this length of time.

Members should understand that if a direct seller makes a 'cold call', sells goods there and then and receives payment, and the customer then uses the goods – he still has an absolute right to cancel the goods and recover the money paid so long as notice is given within seven days. If the contract does not contain the statutory notice of rights, the customer can claim the money back outside the seven days.

The Association advises all members to print the statutory form of words on the order form which the customer retains.

(D) Finally, the ingredients of a valid contract are an 'offer' and an 'acceptance' which meet the expectations of both parties. The vast majority of offers are offers to buy made by consumers. It is important to realize that the person making an offer has an absolute right to withdraw it *at any time* before acceptance by the trader.

Self regulation

12 Members must:

   (a) **Make regular audits of systems, procedures and documentation to prove compliance with this code of practice**
   (b) **Keep records of customers' complaints and of the action taken in response.**

Notes

The object of this rule is to ensure that members understand that belonging to the Association means adherence to this Code in spirit as well as its letter.

Code administration

13.1 DSA Codes are supervised and administered by an independent, legally qualified Administrator appointed by the Council on behalf of the Association.

13.2 The Code Administrator shall:

(a) Satisfy himself that members' trading practices and documentation comply with the Codes

(b) Report any breach of the Codes to the member's Chief Executive and recommend appropriate remedial action

(c) Investigate any failure by a member to act upon any recommendation

(d) Report any failure by a member to remedy any breach to the Council of the Association

(e) Publish an annual report.

Breaches of the Consumer Code

14 Any complaint about a breach of the Consumer Code shall be treated in the following way:

(a) The complainant may refer it:

(i) To the Chief Executive of the member; or

(ii) The Director of the Association.

(b) If the complainant is dissatisfied with any solution proposed by the member, or it is referred initially to the Director, the following procedure will be used:

(i) The complainant will be asked to set out details of the complaint in writing.

(ii) The Director will send a copy of the written complaint to the member requesting prompt remedial action; the complainant will be kept informed at all times.

(iii) If the Director is not notified within twenty-one days that the matter has been resolved, he shall refer it to the Code Administrator and may notify the Council of the Association.

(c) If the complainant is dissatisfied with the recommended action, or if the member fails to act as required by the Director, the Director shall refer the complaint to the Code Administrator.

Investigations by the code administrator

15.1 The Code Administrator will investigate any complaint referred to him, obtain evidence from the complainant, from the member and any other relevant person and make a written adjudication as quickly as possible.

15.2 The adjudication is binding on the member and any direct seller; the complainant is not bound by the adjudication.

Sanctions

16.1 Where a member is found to be in breach of the Consumer Code or in breach of contract, the Code Administrator may:

(a) Require the member to repay all money paid by the complainant

(b) Require the member to replace or repair any product without charge

(c) Require the member to pay any costs incurred by the Code Administrator for technical advice or testing

(d) Require the member to give a written undertaking to observe the Code and to take all reasonable steps to prevent a recurrence of the breach

(e) Direct the member to pay compensation to the complainant.

16.2 The Code Administrator will report to the Council of the Association any failure by a member to comply with any of his directions.

16.3 The Association may expel any member who fails to comply with adjudications or directions from the Code Administrator.

16.4 Any recommendation, by the Code Administrator, that a member be expelled shall be considered by a Disciplinary Committee comprised of two Council Members and three independent members nominated by the Council. The member and the Council of the Association are bound by the adjudication of the Disciplinary Committee.

Definitions

'The Association' and 'DSA' means the Direct Selling Association.

'Direct seller' means any person involved in direct selling in any capacity.

'Direct selling' means the direct selling of consumer products either in the home or away from normal retail premises by which a salesperson either: demonstrates the product or presents a product catalogue; or, collects an order; or arranges for the delivery of the products; or collects payment for the product or arranges for credit.

'Member' means a member of the Association and includes its employees.

'Product' means any goods or services.

Appendix 4

The DSA Code of Business Conduct

1. Scope
This Code concerns a Member Company's dealings with:
- (a) Its employed and self-employed people, and
- (b) Other Member Companies.

2. Recruitment
2.1 Advertisements placed by either a Member Company or its independent salespersons shall not make extravagant earnings claims.

2.2 Advertisements shall not, for any reason, refer by name to any other direct selling company.

2.3 A Member Company shall neither promote nor endorse any direct or indirect recruitment activity offering employment or self-employment to persons known to be working with another Member Company and shall actively dissuade its salespeople from making such approaches.

2.4 Any personal invitation, either verbal or written, to a presentation of a business opportunity shall:
- (a) State the name of the company supplying the products and/or service and in any reference to the DSA shall state class of membership.
- (b) Not give the impression that it relates to an offer of employment or describe the event as anything other than an occasion to learn about a business opportunity.

2.5 All circulars, advertisements or other forms of communication whether written, audio, visual or otherwise, used for the purpose of recruitment or which teach methods of recruitment must be approved in advance by the Member Company.

3. Presenting business opportunities

3.1 All face-to-face presentations of business opportunities in direct sales whether written, verbal or visual shall refer to the name of the company supplying the product or services and, in any reference to the DSA, state the class of membership. (Only members of the DSA are permitted to use the DSA logo and to state that they are members of the DSA.)

3.2 At all times during the presentation and events leading to a presentation of a business opportunity all Member Companies and its independent salespersons shall promote the opportunity as a business relationship with the Member Company and not with a person. Nor shall they suggest, directly or indirectly, that the business opportunity, its products and/or services are part of any business other than the business of the Member Company.

3.3 During the presentation of a business opportunity no Member Company, or its salespersons shall represent that benefits can be gained solely by introducing others and/or obtaining products for personal use or for demonstration purposes and must promote the business as an opportunity for every participant to retail products to end users at a realistic profit.

3.4 Personal testimonials of salespersons, shall reflect actual earnings attributed to such individuals' activities, and shall not include commissions or earnings of other related salespersons.

3.5 Neither a Member Company, nor their self-employed salespersons, shall cause to denigrate nor to disseminate information about another direct selling company which may be harmful to that company.

4. Investments in business opportunities

4.1 Member Companies and independent salespersons working with members shall not, at any time, permit an independent salesperson to purchase any more goods for resale than are needed to enable that independent salesperson to make demonstrations and personal sales on their own account and to meet customer orders that have been previously obtained.

4.2 Member Companies shall permit all independent salespersons to return goods for resale in merchantable condition for their net purchase price less a reasonable handling charge.

4.3 Members shall not permit any participant to qualify for a higher level of appointment in the distributorship structure unless a participant is able to provide proof that at least 50 per cent of qualifying purchases are accounted for by sales of product to end users.

5. Training

5.1 All Member Companies shall provide or arrange for the provision of a reasonable standard of training in product and business development.

5.2 All Member Companies who permit their independent sales-people to create, arrange and provide training in their company's product and business development shall ensure that:

(a) All reproduceable materials as it relates to the company shall be approved by the Member Company prior to its use.

(b) Participants are made aware that the purchase of training material is not a condition for gaining help and advice from a sponsor and that such purchases are optional.

5.3 All Member Companies and their independent distributors and salespeople who make charges for attendance by others at business meetings shall:

(a) Offer a full refund of the business element of the cost of meetings where a participant expresses dissatisfaction with the contents of the meeting. This refund shall be available for fourteen days after the date of the meeting and shall exclude any subsistence costs.

(b) Not offer training by way of regular prepayments.

5.4 All Member Companies and their independent distributors who supply business building aids and other training materials excluding sample products and product catalogues shall provide a full refund on any such aids which are subsequently returned within fourteen days of purchase with proof of purchase.

6. Code responsibilities

The chief executive of a Member Company shall be responsible for the observation of this Code by the Member Company, its employees and the independent salespersons working with it and for ensuring that a copy of this Code shall be supplied to all salespeople with the opportunity and/or responsibility for recruitment.

7. Code enforcement and administration

Breaches of this Code shall be dealt with in the first instance by the Director of the Association. If appropriate corrective action is not taken the matter shall be referred to the Association's independent Code Administrator who shall decide on the action to be taken by the Member Company concerned. This adjudication, if not complied with, could lead to expulsion from membership.

Appendix 5

The FEDSA Directory

Federation of European Direct Selling Associations (FEDSA)
Avenue de Tervuren, 14
B-1040 Brussels
Tel: 32-2/7361014
Fax: 32-2/7363497
Chairman: Erich Schott
Director: Marie-Andrée Vander Elst

Austria

Handelsverband
Arbeitsgruppe Direkvertrieb
Alser Strasse, 45
A – 1080 Wien
Tel: 43 – 1/4062236
Fax: 43 – 1/4086481
Vorsitzender: Ing. Erich Schott
Geschäftsführer: Dr Hildegard Fischer

Belgium

Association Professionnelle de la Vente
Directe (APVD)
Beroepsvereniging der Direkte Verkoop (BVD)
avenue de Tervueren, 14
B-1040 Brussels
Tel + Fax: 32-2/7326813
Président: Hugo Lemmens
Secrétaire Générale: Sophie Castelein

Croatia

Hrvatska Gospodarska Komora (HGK)
Grupacija direktne prodaje
Rooseveltov trg 2
CR-41000 Zagreb, Hrvatska
Tel: 385-1/461555
Fax: 385-1/448618
Chairman: Damir Strejcek

Czech Republic

Ceský národní svaz prímého prodeje (CNSPP)
c/o Amway
K Zizkova 4
CZ-190 00Prha 9
Tel 42-2/661 220464
Fax 42-2/684 63 85
Chairman: Jan Strarzky

Denmark

Direkte Salgs Föreningen (DSF)
c/o Tupperware Scandinavia A/S
Sejrogade 9
DK-2100 Copenhagen O
Tel: 45-39/272324
Fax: 45-39/272664
Chairman: Søren E. Sørensen

Finland

Finnish Direct Marketing Association (SSML)
Lönnrotinkatu 11A
SF-00120 Helsinki
Tel: 358-0/6121030
Fax: 358-0/6121039
Chairman: Antis Vainio
Executive Director: Sakari Virtanen

France

Syndicat de la Vente Directe (SVD)
8, Place d'Iéna
F-75783 Paris Cédex
Tel: 33-1/44346860
Fax: 33-1/47551783
Président: Jean-Pierre Gié
Délégué Général: Philippe Dailey

Germany

Arbeitskreis 'Gut beraten,zu Hause gekauft'
e.V.
Klugstrasse 53
D-80638 München
Tel: 49-89/154634
Fax: 49-89/1576684
Vorsitzender: Dr Hans Adelmann
Geschäftsführer: Wolfgang Bohle

Greece

Greek Association of Direct Selling Companies
(SEADIP)
Vas. Sofias Avenue, 67
GR-115 21 Athens
Tel: 30-1/7227534
Fax: 30-1/7249329
Chairman: Yannis Yannacopoulos
Secretary General: Stavros Efremidis

Hungary

Közvetlen Értekesítok Szövetsége (KESZ)
DSA Hungary
Szilaĝyi Deszö Ter 3
H-1011 Budapest
Tel 36-1 201 3655
Fax 36-1 212 2341
Chairman: Otto Demjen
Secretary General: Eva Rajki

Ireland

Direct Selling Association of Ireland (DSA)
Number One
Upper Grand Canal Street
IRL-Dublin 4
Tel: 352-1/6671146
Fax: 352-1/6671147
Chairman: James R. Threlfall
Secretary: Peter Grala

Italy

Associazione Nazionale Vendite Dirette
Servizio Consumatori (AVEDISCO)
Viale Andréa Doria, 8
1-20214 Milano
Tel: 39-2/6702744
Fax: 39-2/6705141
Presidente: Marisa Brambilla
Segretario Generale: Giorgio Giuliani

Netherlands

Vereniging Direkte Verkoop (VDV)
Postbus 90154
NL-5000 LG Tilburg
Tel: 31-13/5944300
Fax: 31-13/4639677
Voorzitter: Hans van de Leur
Sekretaris: Godewinus (Gody) van den Hurk

Norway

Direktesalgsforbundet (DF)
c/o Oriflame Norge AS
Ulvenveien 92A – Postboks 95 (Okern)
N-0509 Oslo
Tel: 47-22/643550
Fax: 47-22/649433
Chairman: Nils J. Moen

Poland

Polskie Stowarzyszenie Sprzedazy
Bezposredneij (PSBB)
c/o AMC Polska
Polna 50
PL-00644 Warszawa
Tel: 48-22/259783
Fax: 48-22/255450
Chairman: Kurt Bressler

Portugal

Associaçao de Empresas de Venda Directa (AVD)
Rua Tomás Ribeiro 45,7°
P-1000 Lisboa
Tel: 351-1/548821
Fax: 351-1/548540
Chairman: Rui Rodrigues
Secretary General: Luis Afonseca

Russia

Russian Association of Direct Selling Companies
c/o Mary Kay Cosmetics
3rd Samotycchniy Pereulck
Dom 3
Moscow 103473
Tel: 7-095/974 1000
Fax: 7-502/221 3436
Chairperson: Julie Rasmussen

Slovakia

ZPP Slovakia
Mliekárenská 10
SK-824 92 Bratislava
Tel: 42-7/5212538
Fax: 42-7/5212506
Chairman: Sylvester Bucek

Slovenia

Sekcija Podjetij Direktne
Prodaje Slovenije (SPDPS)
Slovenian Direct Selling Association
Chamber of Economy Slovenska c. 54/VIII
SLO-61000 Ljubljana
Tel: 386-61/316048
Fax: 386-61/317443
Chairman: Bostjan Erzen

Spain

Asociación de Empresas de Venta Directa (AVD)
Calle Aragón, 210 – 7th Floor
E-08011 Barcelona
Tel: 34-3/4515617
Fax: 34-3/4515942
Presidente: Adrián Orgaz
Executive Director: Juan Turró

Sweden

Direkthandelsföretagens Förening (DF)
Box 180
S-56123 Huskvarna 1
Tel: 46-36/145250
Fax: 46-36/145259
Chairman: Lars Qvarnström

Switzerland

Schweizerischer Verband der Direktverkaufsfirmen
(VDF)
Association Suisse pour la Vente Directe
Elisabethenanlage 7
PO Box 3257
CH-4002 Basel
Tel: 41-61/2711919
Fax: 41-61/2718502
Vorsitzender: Heinz Studer
Geschäftsführer: Dr Hans Georg Hinderling

Turkey

Dogrudan Satis Dernegi (DSD)
Bogaz Sokak 17/4
TR-06700 Gaziosmanpasa Ankara
Tel: 90-312/4679227
Fax: 90-312/4278207
Chairman: Tom Schafer

United Kingdom

Direct Selling Association Ltd (DSA)
29 Floral Street
London WC 2E 9DP
Tel: 44-171/4971234
Fax: 44-171/4973144
Chairman: Ric Hobby
Director: Richard Berry

Appendix 6

Prominent direct selling businesses operating in the UK in 1997

Trading name	UK office	Status	Principal product	Selling method	Structure
Amway	Amway (UK) Ltd Ambassador House Queensway Bletchley Milton Keynes MK2 2EH tel. 01908 363000	US private corporation Multinational	Household and personal	Person to person	NM
Ann Summers	Ann Summers Ltd Gadoline House 2 Godstone Road Whyteleafe Surrey CR3 0EA tel. 0181 660 0102	UK private company Multinational	Lingerie	Party plan	Single-level
Avon	Avon Cosmetics Ltd Nunn Mills Road Northampton NN1 5PA tel. 01604 232425	US public corporation Multinational	Cosmetics	Person to person	Single-level

Company	Address	Type	Product	Selling method	Level
Betterware	Betterware PLC, Stanley House, Park Lane, Castle Vale, Birmingham, B35 6LJ, tel. 0121 693 1000	UK plc Multinational	Household	Person to person	Single-level
Cabouchon	Cabouchon Ltd, West Cross House, 2 West Cross Way, Brentford, Middlesex, TW8 9DG, tel. 0181 213 7100	UK private company Multinational	Jewellery	Person to person and party plan	NM
Cambridge	Cambridge Health Plan Ltd, Deben House, Old King's Head Yard, Magdalen Street, Norwich, NR3 1JF, tel. 01603 760777	UK private company	Diet plans	Person to person	Single-level
Children's Warehouse	Children's Warehouse Ltd, Unit 4, 44 Colville Road, London, W3 8BL, tel. 0181 752 1166	UK private company	Children's clothes	Person to person	NM

Trading name	UK office	Status	Principal product	Selling method	Structure
Colour Library Direct	Quadrillion Publishing Ltd Godalming Business Centre Woolsack Way Godalming Surrey GU7 1XW tel. 01483 426266	UK private company	Books	Person to person	Single-level
Creative Memories	The Antioch Company 9 Pipers Lane Estate Thatcham Berkshire RG19 4NA tel. 01635 294709	US private company Multinational	Photo-safe albums	Party plan	NM
Cutco	Cutco Club Culinaire Springlands Crazies Hill Wargrave Berks RG10 8LT tel. 01189 401929	UK private company	Cutlery	Party plan	Single-level
Deesse	Deesse UK Ltd 31 Melford Court Hardwick Grange Woolston Warrington WA1 4RZ tel. 01925 811120	Swiss private company Multinational	Skincare	Person to person and party plan	NM

DKFL	Dorling Kindersley Family Library Ltd 1 Horsham Gate North Street Horsham West Sussex RH13 5PJ tel. 01403 270274	UK subsidiary plc Multinational	Books and CD ROMs	Person to person and party plan	NM
DNI	NSA NSA House 39 Queen Street Maidenhead Berks SL6 1NB tel. 01628 776044	UK private company US licensee	Nutrition	Person to person	NM
Eismann	Eismann International Ltd Margarethe House Eismann Way Phoenix Park Industrial Estate Corby Northants NN17 1YN tel. 01536 407010	UK/German joint operation Private company Multinational	Frozen foods	Person to person	Single-level
Encylopaedia Britannica	Encylopaedia Britannica Ltd Chancery House Nicholas Way Sutton Surrey SM1 1JB tel. 0181 770 7766	US private corporation Multinational	Books	Person to person	Single-level

Trading name	UK office	Status	Principal product	Selling method	Structure
Enrich	Enrich UK 26 Vincent Avenue Crownhill Milton Keynes Bucks MK8 0AB tel. 01908 565 331	US private corporation Multinational	Nutrition	Person to person	NM
Farepak	Farepak plc Farepak House Westmead Drive Westlea Swindon SN5 7YZ tel. 01793 486441	UK plc	Food hampers	Person to person	Single-level
Forever Living	Forever Living Products Longbridge Manor Longbridge Warwick CV34 6RB tel. 01926 408800	US private corporation Multinational	Nutrition	Person to person	NM
Golden Neo-life	Golden Neo-Life Diamite Int. Parc d'activités de Limonest 1 rue des Vergers F-69760 Lyon France tel. 0033 0800 125732	French licensee US private corporation Multinational	Nutrition	Person to person	NM

Company	Address	Structure	Product	Selling method	Type
Goldshield	Goldshield Healthcare NLA Tower 12–16 Addiscombe Rd Croydon Surrey CR9 6BP tel. 0181 649 0807	UK subsidiary private company	Nutrition	Person to person and party plan	NM
Herbalife	Herbalife (UK) Ltd Senator Court 4 Belmont Road Uxbridge Middx UB8 1SA tel. 01895 819000	US public corporation Multinational	Nutrition	Person to person	NM
Home Farm & Studio	Fine Art Developments plc Dawson Lane Bradford W. Yorks BD4 6HW tel. 01274 651188	UK subsidiary of plc	Food hampers	Person to person	Single-level
Kirby	Kirby European Div. 10 Colemeadow Rd North Moons Moat Redditch Worcs B98 9PB tel. 01527 61034	US subsidiary Public corporation Multinational	Vacuum cleaners	Person to person	Single-level

Trading name	UK office	Status	Principal product	Selling method	Structure
Kleeneze	Kleeneze Ltd Martins Road Hanham Bristol BS15 3DY tel. 01179 750350	UK subsidiary plc	Household	Person to person	NM
Lady Remington	Lady Remington International 1 Crystal Business Centre Ramsgate Road Sandwich Kent CT13 9OX tel. 01304 612907	US private corporation Multinational	Jewellery	Party plan	NM
Langtrees	Langtrees Ltd Langtrees House Northampton NN1 5PA tel. 0990 143082	US subsidiary Public corporation	Jewellery	Person to person	NM
Mary Kay	Mary Kay Cosmetics (UK) Ltd 39 Park Street London W1Y 3HG tel. 0171 495 4142	US subsidiary Private corporation Multinational	Cosmetics	Party plan NM	

Nature's Sunshine	Nature's Sunshine Products Hortonwood 32 Telford, Shropshire TF1 4EU tel. 01952 670151	US public corporation Multinational	Nutrition	Person to person	NM
Nikken	Nikken UK Ltd Matrix House 2 North Fourth St Milton Keynes Bucks MK9 1NJ tel. 0990 225525	US subsidiary Private corporation Multinational	Magnetic health products	Person to person	NM
Nu-Skin	Nu-Skin UK Ltd Windsor Court Kingsmead London Road High Wycombe Bucks HP11 1JU tel. 01494 443484	US private corporation Multinational	Skincare	Person to person	NM
NutraProducts	NutraProducts Ltd (as for Cambridge Health Plan Ltd)	UK subsidiary Private company	Nutrition	Person to person	NM
Nutri-Metics	Nutri-Metics International Ltd 3 Garamonde Drive Wymbush Milton Keynes Bucks MK8 8DF tel. 01908 262020	Australian private corporation Multinational	Skincare	Person to person	NM

Trading name	UK office	Status	Principal product	Selling method	Structure
Oriflame	Oriflame UK Ltd Tilers Road Kiln Farm Milton Keynes Bucks MK11 3EH tel. 01908 261126	Belgian UK reg. plc Multinational	Skincare	Person to person and party plan	NM
Partylite	Partylite UK Ltd Monument House 215 Marsh Road Pinner Middlesex HA5 5NE tel. 0181 426 1822	US private corporation Multinational	Candles	Party plan	NM
Pierre Lang	Pierre Lang UK Ltd Highway House Norreys Drive Maidenhead Berks SL6 4BN tel. 01628 23476	Austrian private company Multinational	Jewellery	Party plan	Single-level
Pippa Dee & Dee Minor	The Dee Group plc Anglesey House Anglesey Road Burton-on-Trent Staffs DE14 3QS tel. 01283 566344	UK subsidiary plc	Ladies' and children's fashion wear	Party plan	Single-level

Princess House	Princess House Ltd West Point West Rd. Hexham Northumberland NE46 3RR tel. 01434 606741	UK private company	Home decorative	Party plan	NM
Pro-Ma	Pro-Ma Systems UK Osprey House Haddenham Aerodrome Haddenham Bucks HP17 2JD tel. 01844 292852	UK Australian licensee Private company	Nutrition	Person to person	NM
Reliv	Reliv UK Ltd The Gatehouse Fryers Works Abercromby Av. High Wycombe Bucks HP12 3BW tel. 01494 539733	UK US licensee Multinational	Nutrition	Person to person	NM
Quorum	Quorum Int. UK Ltd 3–5 Newmarket Court Kingston Milton Keynes Bucks MK10 0AG tel. 01908 285100	US subsidiary Hong Kong plc Multinational	Electronics and security	Person to person	NM

Trading name	UK office	Status	Principal product	Selling method	Structure
Southwestern	The Southwestern Company Goldsmiths House Broad Plain Bristol BS2 0JP tel. 01179 304274	US subsidiary Private corporation	Books	Person to person	Single-level
Sunrider	Sunrider Europe 1st Floor, South 195 Knightsbridge London SW7 1RE tel. 0171 838 0900	US division Private corporation Multinational	Nutrition	Person to person	NM
Tupperware	The Tupperware Company Chaplin House Widewater Business Centre Moorhall Road Harefield Uxbridge UB9 6NS tel. 01895 826400	US public corporation Multinational	Kitchenwares	Party plan	Single-level
Usborne	Usborne Books at Home Unit 8 Oasis Park Eynsham Witney Oxon OX8 1TU tel. 01865 883731	UK subsidiary Private company	Books	Party plan	Single-level

Vorwerk	Vorwerk UK Ltd Ashville Way Wokingham Berks RG41 2PL tel. 01189 794 753	German private company Multinational	Vacuum cleaners	Person to person	Single-level
Weekenders	Weekenders Ladieswear Ltd 1 Vincent Avenue Crownhill Milton Keynes Bucks MK8 0AQ tel. 01908 262101	Canadian private corporation Multinational	Fashion wear	Person to person and party plan	NM
World Book	World Book Childcraft International World Book House Mount Ephraim Tunbridge Wells Kent TN4 8AZ tel. 01892 547811	US subsidiary Public corporation Multinational	Books	Person to person	Single-level

Appendix 7

Advice for party plan demonstrators

1 A party line-up

The first point to remember is that party plan bookings are the lifeblood for every demonstrator. Without bookings, no sales are made and no commission is earned. It is usually a requirement of most DSOs that before a kit is issued, a demonstrator must have arranged a line-up of six parties. After your first party, remember to continue to maintain a line-up of six parties – as a minimum target.

2 Booking parties at parties

Booking parties is as important as selling. In fact it is even more important, because if there are no more bookings for future parties, then the selling process stops. Remember the following:

- Enjoyable parties are usually successful parties and make future bookings easier.
- Start thinking of future bookings when planning a party with the hostess. Give a blank guest list to your hostess and offer to help her complete it. While doing so, encourage the hostess to give at least two names of possible future hostesses. Later, when you arrive at the party, ask the hostess to point out the friends she has noted as possible future hostesses. Make a point of speaking to them as soon as they arrive. With practice, you will be able to make one or two bookings to start off the evening, leaving you more time to spend with other guests not mentioned by your hostess.
- During your demonstration be sure to talk about the current and future hostess promotions.

- Try not to book parties more than six weeks ahead, as these parties can be lost if the hostess forgets, goes on holiday or starts a new job.
- After your demonstration invite the guests to come up to the display and try out or examine the products. Move away from the product display, as this encourages more people to come up. You can stand behind them, listen to their comments and pick up clues for likely dating prospects. For example, you might hear 'I'd love to have this, but I can't afford it.' With hostess incentives you can always show the guest that the item that they would like can be obtained at little or no cost.
- When you write out each guest's order, ask for her full name, address and telephone number. Fill in her order and say: ' I saw that you liked . . . you know that you could have that with our hostess commission. When would you be able to hold a party, daytime or evening?'
- When you are taking orders, make sure that guests, as well as the hostess, know just what item is available as a hostess reward based on the total party sales. This will often secure another party booking.
- Finally, always have your diary ready. Do not be afraid to ask for dates. The most important thing to remember is that dating never stops. With practice you will find more opportunities for booking than you expect. Date as many as possible whenever you can. Remember, you are now running you own business, so it is up to you to make a success of it and remember also – the best place to book a party is at a party!

3 Planning your diary

First, decide how many times per week you are prepared to work. Fill in each available date in one week, before moving on to the next. When asking for bookings, do not say 'Would you like to hold a party for me?' Instead say: 'When would YOU like to hold a . . . party?' Follow up this question immediately by offering two or three optional dates and/or times. These will be the ones you wish to fill first. By working in this way, you not only build your own confidence, but will very quickly build up a bank of parties in your diary. Always try to overbook, i.e. book three or four parties in each week instead of two. This will compensate for possible postponements or cancellations.

4 Creative party bookings

Apart from booking dates at parties, always be on the lookout for any opportunities to make a booking. Always take your diary with you – everywhere. Whenever you meet old friends in the street, or other parents collecting their children from school, tell them about your new job and how they can help you by booking a party.

5 Preparing for a party

After booking a party, keep in contact with the hostess. This reduces the chance of the party being cancelled or postponed. The best timetable is as follows:

- When you book the party give the hostess a card with the date and time of her party clearly marked, and with your name and telephone number.
- At least ten days before the party, contact the hostess, preferably by visiting, to give her a sufficient supply of invitation cards. Remind her again of the benefits of the party, i.e. hostess gifts and special offers.
- If the party was booked less than ten days in advance, then the invitation cards should be given to the hostess there and then.
- On the day of the party, telephone the hostess to ensure that there are no last-minute problems. Offer to pick up any guests who may live near you.
- Remind the hostess to keep refreshments to a minimum. Tea and coffee and biscuits is all that is required. Too much catering can put off possible future hostesses.

6 The party presentation

It is a good idea to make the presentation in the following way:

- Start off the event by greeting everybody, introducing yourself and thanking the hostess for holding the party.
- Explain that you are working for a company called ... which specializes in ...
- Explain how many people today welcome the opportunity of choosing and selecting products in the comfort of someone's home.
- If the company you are working for is a member of the Direct Selling Association, explain that the business operates under the DSA Code of Practice, which offers safeguards and a standard of fair trading that are as good as, if not better than, those offered by leading high street stores.
- Remind those present of how they must have looked at similar items in large stores or in catalogues, and wished to try them out, or see them shown off in a home environment.
- Explain that the range is comprehensive to suit everybody's taste and pocket, and that it starts at the very reasonable price of ... Go through as many items as possible for as long as you can hold their attention.
- Select an item from each range, point out its special features and how to care for it.

- Point out to the guests that if there is anything that any one of them would like to own, but which they feel they cannot afford, then by having a party themselves, then they could buy it at a discount.
- Explain that for having a party, the company gives an allowance of . . . per cent off the total value of the party sales.
- Ask the guests to come up and look at the product and ask any questions that they may have.
- Explain the payment procedure.
- Collect the orders.

7 How to announce hostess commission and special offers

Remember the following:

- Hostess gifts should be explained during the demonstration.
- Special hostess promotions should be publicized well before a party is held. For example, if the company is offering extra commissions for those hostesses who have parties with more than, say, ten buying guests, it is no good announcing this at the end of the party.
- Let the guests know what the hostess has chosen for her gift. This helps encourage other bookings.
- Explain hostess dating gifts by giving the product a thorough demonstration and telling the guests that they can all have one of these items, completely free, if they book a party of their own.
- Pass the dating gift around the guests, noting those who seem really interested. Book parties with these guests first, then ask everyone else for a party date.

8 How to finish a party

- Always work to a timetable and aim to start putting your demonstration kit away before 10 pm. Do not outstay your welcome, even if the guests are showing no signs of leaving.
- Check that you have handed out guest lists to those who have booked parties. Explain how to use them. Point out that it is important to invite each guest personally, rather than pushing cards through letter boxes.
- Ask each future hostess which particular item she would like to have as a reward for having a party. When you contact her later, remind her of the gift she has selected.
- Finally, thank the guests and hostess for an enjoyable evening and make a point of rebooking the hostess for another party later in the year.

Bibliography and suggested further reading

Bartlett, R.C. (1994), *The Direct Option*, Texas A & M University Press, College Station, TX

Biggert, N.W. (1989), *Charismatic Capitalism*, University of Chicago Press, Chicago

Brodie, A.S. (1995), *Sales Force Turnover in Direct Selling Organizations in the United Kingdom and France*, University of Keele (MA Dissertation)

Clothier, P.J. (1992), *Multi-Level Marketing – A Practical Guide to Successful Network Selling*, Kogan Page, London

Crawford, J.C. and Garland, B.C. (1988), ' A Profile of a Party Plan Sales Force', *Akron Business & Economic Review*, **81**, No. 12

Croft, R. and Woodruffe, H. (1996), Network Marketing; The Ultimate in International Distribution? *Journal of Marketing Management*, **12**, 201–214

Dewandre, P. and Mahieu, C. (1995), *The Future of Multi Level Marketing in Europe*, Les Editions du Saint-Bernard, Brussels

Direct Selling Association (1987–1996) *Direct Selling of Consumer Goods: Annual Survey*, London

Federation of European Direct Selling Associations (1996), A Profile of Direct Selling; Submission to European Commission; (1996) Annual Report 1995; (1996) Direct Selling in Central & Eastern Europe, Report on Academic Symposium in Prague 1995, FEDSA, Brussels

Fontaine, L. (1996), *History of Pedlars in Europe*, Polity Press, Cambridge

Futrell, C. (1994), *Sales Management*, The Dryden Press, Fort Worth, TX

Granfield, M. and Nicols, A. (1975) 'Economic and Marketing Aspects of the Direct Selling Industry', *Journal of Retailing*, **51**, No.1

Grayson, K. (1996), 'Commercial Activity at Home: The Private Service-scape', Centre for Marketing Working Paper (96–501). London Business School, London; 'Examining the Embedded Markets of Network Marketing Organizations' in Iacobucci, D. (ed.), Networks in Marketing, Sage, Thousand Oaks, CA

Harris, L. and Associates (1977), *A Comprehensive Survey of the Direct Selling Industry; A study for the Direct Selling Association, Washington, DC*

Jolson, M.A. (1970), *Consumer Attitudes toward Direct-to-Home Marketing Systems*, Dunellen Publishing, New York; (1972) 'Direct Selling: Consumer v Salesmen: Is Conflict Inevitable?' *Business Horizons*, **15**, October

Nathan Associates (1992), *A Profile of Direct Salespeople: Survey for the Direct Selling Association*, Direct Selling Educational Foundation, Washington, DC

Nowland Organization (1982), *Consumer Experiences and Attitudes with Respect to Direct Selling*, Direct Selling Educational Foundation, Washington, DC

Ogilvy, D. (1983), *Ogilvy on Advertising*, Random House, New York

Peterson, R.A., Albaum, G. and Ridgway, N.M. (1989), 'Consumers Who Buy from Direct Sales Companies', *Journal of Retailing*, **65**, No.2

Rosenbloom, B. (1992), *Direct Selling Channels*, The Haworth Press, Birmingham, NY

Tyagi, P.T. (1991), 'Job Security in Direct Selling', *American Journal of Marketing*, **3**, No.1

Wirthlin Worldwide (1996), *Survey of Attitudes towards Direct Selling*, Commissioned by US Direct Selling Association, Washington, DC

Wotruba, T.R. (1989), 'The Effect of Goal-Setting on the Performance of Independent Sales Agents in Direct Selling', *Journal of Personal Selling and Sales Management*, **IX**; (1990), 'The Relationship of Job Image, Performance and Job Satisfaction to Interactivity-Proneness of Direct Salespeople', *Journal of the Acadamy of Marketing Science*, **18**, No.2; (1990), 'Full-Time vs. Part-Time Salespeople: A Comparison of Job Satisfaction, Performance and Turnover in Direct Selling', *International Journal of Research in Marketing*, **7**, No.2; (1992) 'Direct Selling in the Year 2000', in Peterson, R.A. (ed.), *The Future of US Retailing: An Agenda for the 21st Century*, Quorum Books, New York

Wotruba, T.R., Sciglimpaglia, D. and Tyagi, P.K. (1987), 'Toward a Model of Turnover in Direct Selling Organizations', in Belck, R.W. and Zaltman, G. (eds), *American Marketing Association Winter Conference Proceedings*, Chicago

Wotruba, T.R. and Tyagi, P.K. (1991), 'Met Expectations and Turnover in Direct Selling', *Journal of Marketing*, **55**, No.3; (1992), *Motivation to Become a Direct Salesperson and Its Relationship with Work Outcome*, The Haworth Press, Birmingham, NY; (1993), 'An Exploratory Study of Reverse Causality Relationships amongst Sales Force Turnover Variables', *Journal of the Academy of Marketing Science*, **21**, No.21

Xardel, D. (1993), *The Direct Selling Revolution*, Blackwell, Oxford

Index